P9-DNS-568

Modern Language Association of America

Options for Teaching

Joseph Gibaldi, Series Editor

Teaching Children's Literature: Issues, Pedagogy, Resources

Edited by

Glenn Edward Sadler

Consultant Editor
U. C. Knoepflmacher

The Modern Language Association of America
New York   1992

OUACHITA TECHNICAL COLLEGE

© 1992 by The Modern Language Association of America

Library of Congress Cataloging-in-Publication Data

Teaching children's literature : issues, pedagogy, resources / edited
    by Glenn Edward Sadler : consultant editor, U. C. Knoepflmacher.
        p.   cm.—(Options for teaching : 11)
    Includes bibliographical references and index.
    ISBN 0-87352-366-0   ISBN 0-87352-367-9 (pbk.)
    1. Children's literature—Study and teaching (Higher)   I. Sadler,
Glenn Edward.   II. Series.
PN1009.A1T44   1992
809'.89282'0711—dc20   92–3112

Glenn Edward Sadler, "A Conversation with Maurice Sendak and Dr. Seuss,"
originally published in the *Horn Book Magazine* (Sept.-Oct. 1989, 582–88) and
reprinted in *Carver: An Interdisciplinary Journal* (Bloomsburg, PA: Bloomsburg U,
1990, 25–34) is reprinted here, with revisions, by permission of the Horn
Book, Inc., 14 Beacon Street, Boston, MA 02108.

Published by The Modern Language Association of America
10 Astor Place, New York, New York 10003-6981

PN
1009
.A1
T44
1992

To the Memory of

Ronald E. Freeman
(1926–85)

Come, dear children, let us away;
Down and away below!
Now my brothers call from the bay,
Now the great winds shoreward blow,
Now the salt tides seaward flow;
Champ and chafe and toss in the spray,
Children dear, let us away!
This way, this way!

> *—Matthew Arnold,*
> *"The Forsaken Merman"*

Contents

PART IV: TWO CHILDREN'S LITERATURE COLLECTIONS

PART V: READINGS AND RESOURCES
Rachel Fordyce and Mary Beth Dunhouse

Preface

The aim of the book is to present a comprehensive report on the present state of teaching children's literature in undergraduate and graduate institutions. Toward this goal, a national survey was conducted over a four-year period and representative selections were made from respondents. The essays selected for part 1, "Critical Issues and Approaches," were submitted by invitation. The course descriptions in parts 2 and 3 represent every section of the United States (and select sections of Canada), and every size and type of institution. Contributors of the course descriptions replied to the initial survey and submitted a distinctive course option. Duplications were by necessity eliminated.

Teaching Children's Literature is a volume in the Options for Teaching series, sponsored by the Modern Language Association and its Publications Committee. It is meant to serve as an informative guide for those interested in current trends in the teaching of children's literature, as well as for those interested in constructing courses in the field. The five divisions of the book—"Critical Issues and Approaches," "Course Descriptions," "Research Programs," "Selected Collections of Children's Literatures," and "Readings and Resources"—reflect its scope.

To the contributors and members of the Children's Literature Division of the Modern Language Association and the Children's Literature Association who have talked with me at length about this volume for the past ten years, I should like to offer thanks. I should especially like to thank Francelia Butler, University of Connecticut, for assisting with the original survey and for encouragement along the way. To U. C. Knoepflmacher, Princeton University, I owe special thanks for editorial assistance with the volume in its latter stages.

I should like to express appreciation to Virginia Duck, Professor Emeritus of English, Bloomsburg University, for reading the first draft, and Fern Agresta, of the Word Processing Center at Bloomsburg University, for professionally preparing the manuscript for publication.

Finally, I wish to thank Joseph Gibaldi, Director of Acquisitions and Development, Division of Publications, Modern Language Association, for seeing the project to fruition.

GES

Introduction

The appearance of this volume in a respected series of publications devoted to the teaching of literature and language only helps to confirm the serious place that the study of children's literature now holds in college courses across the United States and Canada. In 1980 the Modern Language Association recognized the burgeoning interest in this field by granting it the status of an MLA division. Yet since then, the yearly proliferation of undergraduate courses devoted to texts written for children and juveniles, as well as the increasing volume and sophistication of scholarly discussion, makes a collection such as this more urgent than those devoted to the teaching of well-established texts such as *The Canterbury Tales* or *The Scarlet Letter*. As the descriptions of courses, seminars, and special programs gathered by Glenn Edward Sadler in parts 2 and 3 suggest, children's literature is being studied from multiple perspectives that may actually be wider in range than the approaches we take toward texts firmly ensconced in a traditional "adult" canon. This diversity undoubtedly reflects an excitement similar to that which marked the efforts by major feminist critics of the 1970s in mining the untapped wealth of a rich "literature of their own": as the first three essays in part 1 of this collection show, questions of canonicity remain of preeminent interest to those eager to define the field and to validate its importance.

Yet the strides made by children's literature as a subject of instruction also have much to do with a process of defamiliarization and refamiliarization that accounts for its unique appeal to college students hovering between maturity and adolescence. Whereas a typical undergraduate faces *The Divine Comedy* or *Middlemarch* for the first time, the encounter with *Alice in Wonderland* or *The Secret Garden* all too often involves a reencounter with a text already familiar since childhood. The new reading amends, complicates, and even disturbs the memory of earlier perceptions. Because those earlier child perceptions are powerfully reanimated, however, the student is forced to recognize a conflict in reader positions that need to be accommodated. Teacher and student thus find themselves participating in a creative tension that reproduces an adult author's own activation of a latent child self in fashioning a text simultaneously addressed to child and grown-up (or, as the Victorians liked to call this dual audience, "children young and old"). Wishfulness and enchantment now coexist with an acceptance of adult realities. The ensuing dynamic of response thus involves something like the interpenetration of the two "contrary states" that William Blake labeled Innocence and Experience. For the conflicting criteria of what constitutes "reality" require a balancing act that combines the emotional gratification furnished by wish fulfillment and make-believe with the more skeptical pleasures of intellectual or analytical discovery. The combination inevitably stimulates acuity. Students are as ready to spot sentimental falsifications as to denounce the betrayal of make-believe.

The essays Sadler has gathered in part 1 of this collection eloquently demonstrate how the interdisciplinary nature of children's literature contributes to the versatility and vitality of the field. The time may not be far away when universities and colleges institute cross-curricular programs devoted to studies in childhood. Such programs would enlist the expertise of child psychologists, anthropologists, folklorists, sociologists, social historians, art historians, theologians, film and theater experts, as well as teachers of literature who might be called on to play a central role by offering their well-established courses as core studies. The realization that "childhood" is a rather recent social artifact, a post-Enlightenment fabrication that arose concurrently with new notions of selfhood, "naturalness," and civilization, lends a special cultural poignancy to children's literature as well as to those many adult texts, from Blake and Wordsworth to J. D. Salinger and William Golding, that are centered on the child or adolescent. Social critics like Neil Postman keep warning us that the division between childhood and adulthood, first propagated through the disseminating power of books, may collapse in an electronic age that once again prefers to blur "the two stages of life" by appealing to a hybrid "adult-child" (99).

The systematic and syncretic investigation that a program in studies in childhood would help to promote in colleges and universities cannot, however, be put into place until children's literature receives the same serious attention academia expends on so-called adult texts. Even though a child reader's perspective remains embedded in the responses of every mature reader, the ideal reader posited by critics such as Wayne Booth, Wolfgang Iser, and Stanley Fish remains a single entity. The child selves and adolescent selves who compete with each other and with that "mature" reader in the full experience of a text are seldom given a sympathetic hearing. When Booth dismisses as "immature readers" (284) those who overly identify with the narcissistic energies of Jane Austen's Emma Woodhouse, he fails to acknowledge that an innocent or immature reader's response cannot simply be set aside—that identification inevitably vies with irony and distancing in texts written by authors who exploit the tension between contrary states. Indeed, texts that are taught as masterpieces of "adult" irony—*Gulliver's Travels*, for instance—are notable for the same tension between childlike innocence and adult disenchantment that is exploited in many children's classics. It is no coincidence, therefore, that the first two books of *Gulliv-*

er's Travels should have been quickly converted into a much-reprinted children's book and have acted as the forerunner of many a Lilliputian or Brobdingnagian fantasy for children. Dr. Johnson's famous remark about the presumed simplicity of Swift's formula of dividing people into little and large folk thus carries an unintended poignancy for the student of children's literature who knows how the oppositions of child and adult, and of the child-in-the-adult and the adult-in-the-child, can lead to extraordinarily sophisticated permutations and reversals.

As Felicity A. Hughes shrewdly noted some time ago, the lack of interest shown by literary theorists in the role played by the "immature" reader has a venerable ancestry. This disregard goes back to aesthetic theorists of the novel, like George Moore and Henry James, whose eagerness to vindicate the "craft" of fiction led them to single out the efforts of late-Victorian women writers such as Frances Hodgson Burnett and Maria Louisa Molesworth, both of whom had been highly successful in capturing a market for children's books as well as for adult romances. In 1885 Moore proclaimed that it was simply impossible "to reconcile these two irreconcilable things—art and young girls." For his part, James inveighed, a little later but even more misogynistically, against a market dominated by "the presence of ladies and children—by whom I mean, in other words, the reader irreflective and uncritical" (qtd. by Hughes 547, 546).

Although the dismissal of "kiddie lit" has certainly abated in academic circles in recent years, the segregation of children's literature seems to persist as much as before, even though attention to its texts should be of enormous concern to the student of "adult" classics. At a time when criticism has stressed the authority of language over that of a mimetic representation of "reality," texts that are marked by self-consciousness, that habitually invoke the coordinates of the fairy tale and rely on the untrue truths of fantasy or the incongruous yokings of parody, that rhetorically or semantically subvert our assent to verisimilitude, ought, one would assume, be of profound interest to all students of literature. It is reassuring to find that a text such as Lewis Carroll's "Gardener's Song," from *Sylvie and Bruno*, receives serious consideration in the taxonomy Clayton Koelb works out in his provocative *The Incredulous Reader*. Even more encouraging is Juliet Dusinberre's argument that not only Carroll but also E. Nesbit, Rudyard Kipling, and Burnett had a share in fashioning Virginia Woolf's "radical experiments in art" (*Alice to the Lighthouse*). Nevertheless, contemporary theoreticians and formalist critics have tended to ignore the rich materials furnished by major children's texts.

Literary historians, too, might benefit from a closer look at the relation between child texts and adult texts. A recent edition of *On Heroes, Hero-Worship, and the Heroic in History*, for instance, makes much of the ideological impact on later writers of Thomas Carlyle's lectures on eminent historical figures such as Mohammed, Cromwell, and Napoleon. Yet the implications of Carlyle's deliberately ahistorical incursion into Norse mythology in his opening lecture, "The Hero as Divinity," are slighted. As his invocation of the brothers Grimm suggests, Carlyle here joins all those nineteenth-century fabulists who, following the example of the German Romantics, recognized in the fairy tale and folk tale a symbolic outlet for an imagination eager to free itself from the trammels and constraints of their civilization. The northern fairy tales (collected by folklorists like Thomas Keightley and Archibald Campbell) offered creative freedom not just for writers such as Alfred, Lord Tennyson, Matthew Arnold, William Morris, and George Eliot but also for children's authors from George MacDonald and Jean Ingelow to Kipling and Nesbit. As Alan Richardson implies in his essay in this volume, "Childhood and Romanticism," the fine discussions of Romantic texts that we now possess thanks to critics like Geoffrey Hartman and Harold Bloom are sadly remiss in their disregard of the major children's books Romanticism helped to spawn. The "dream children" that appear in Charles Lamb, Thomas De Quincey, William Wordsworth, and Emily Brontë remain unrelated to their kin in numerous fantasies written for children. And as Mitzi Myers, in her essay in this volume, wisely reminds us, we need a fuller investigation of pre-Romantic texts if we are to historicize the changes in the representation of child-adult relations and to understand better the impact of female folk tales and fairy tales on the varieties of eighteenth-century fiction.

Although feminist criticism has produced first-rate readings of influential texts such as Louisa May Alcott's *Little Women*, the important role played by women in shaping the two major traditions of Anglo-American children's literature has yet to be comprehensively documented. From the eighteenth century onward, these two traditions become increasingly intertwined: the didactic mode of Sarah Fielding, adapted by Mme Beaumont, Trimmer, and Sherwood, and perfected by figures such as Mary Wollstonecraft and Maria Edgeworth (whose imaginative achievement Myers has established so well) gradually blends with the much older folkloric tradition that goes back to anonymous storytellers. As Ruth Bottigheimer and Maria Tatar show here and elsewhere, male appropriators of the *contes de vieilles* or *Frauenmärchen* (female folk narratives) steadfastly defeminized their sources. The reclamation of this female material therefore became a major agenda for women authors. Poems such as *Aurora Leigh* or *Goblin Market* or novels such as *Jane Eyre*, *Silas Marner*, or *To the Lighthouse* (with its inserted tale of unbridled female ambition, "The Fisherman's Wife") go to the fairy tale as much as the revisionist fables produced by children's authors like Juliana Horatia Ewing (in *Amelia and the Dwarfs*), Ingelow (in *Mopsa the Fairy*), Nesbit (in *The Story of the Amulet* and in *Nine Unlikely Tales*), or, in our times, Mary Norton, Joan Aiken, or Ursula Le Guin. At the same time, however, male writers for children continued to rely on female or androgynous protagonists as well as on magical godmothers and mother surrogates (from MacDonald's mighty North Wind to E. B. White's fragile but infinitely resourceful Charlotte, a male pig's best friend). By identifying with female sources, these male fabulists thus managed to retain an unbroken access to powers once invested in the Fates, those antique weavers and spinners who became transformed into fays and fairies in the popular imagination.

The segregation of "adult" and "child" texts is evident in other areas as well. Americanists who regularly teach *The Scarlet Letter* and *Huckleberry Finn* seem uninterested in linking these works to antecedent texts such as *A Wonderbook for Boys and Girls* and *The Prince and the Pauper*, despite the illuminations that such pairings might produce. Those who know *Riddley Walker* as a futuristic version of *Huckleberry Finn* are perhaps unaware of the existence of *The Mouse and His Child*, the story of the quest for a "territory" that, according to Russell Hoban, could just as easily have been classified as a book for grownups. Though much energy has been spent, in American studies, in establishing an autonomous native literary tradition, the difficulties encountered by American writers in creating children's books that might be independent of cross-Atlantic precedents apparently hold little interest for those professedly concerned with the definition of American culture. Bruce A. Ronda's attempt in this volume to establish an American canon of children's literature is therefore a much-valued and badly needed effort.

If the teaching of children's literature is to become fully integrated into our current undergraduate and graduate programs of instruction, we will have to go beyond the parochial (or territorial) attitudes responsible for its segregation. That parochialism, however, cannot be attributed exclusively to the smugness of those who would persuade themselves that child texts are lacking in the Arnoldian "high seriousness" or the Jamesian craftsmanship of the adult classics they prefer to teach. The blame falls just as squarely on those who still welcome the isolation of a field once confined to schools of education, who continue to regard the study of child texts as a less demanding and less rigorous enterprise. It is their own devaluation of their field that has contributed to its belittlement. As the submissions of essays to journals such as *Children's Literature* (the Yale University Press annual), the *Children's Literature Association Quarterly*, and the *Lion and the Unicorn* show, a large number of professionals still believe that a spirited "appreciation" of this or that children's book suffices to merit publication. At the same time, however, as more and more serious articles on children's literature appear in these journals, as well as in *PMLA*, *ELH*, *Nineteenth-Century Literature* and *Critical Inquiry*, the standards (and stakes) are steadily raised.

Asked by Mr. Brooke, in *Middlemarch*, how he files the materials he expects to integrate into his syncretic "Key to All Mythologies," Mr. Casaubon explains, "in pigeon-holes, partly" (14). Notoriously prone to what might be called "Casaubonism," literature departments need to go beyond the pigeonholing of "adult" and "children's" texts. The inter-mingling of such texts may not produce the "Key to All Literature," but it could well result in much richer dividends. Some such intermingling is already taking place. Those who teach courses in fantasy seem just as ready to include works by MacDonald or Madeleine L'Engle as texts by Poe or Lautréamont. And even in more traditional survey courses in nineteenth-century British fiction, the insertion of Carroll's Alice books can facilitate what a reading of *Wuthering Heights* or *Great Expectations* of-ten still fails to achieve, by curing students of the notion that they are reading nothing more than a mimetic replication of experiences identi-cal to their very own.

I am not suggesting that *Middlemarch* be taught in apposition to *Charlotte's Web*. But I am suggesting that a greater attention to the inter-action of child and adult readers might allow us to reassess texts as well as methods of interpretation. Children's literature reminds us that an implied reader is made up of a multitude of selves. These selves can be

Yet the intermingling I have in mind would involve a more thor-ough testing than we so far have of the multileveled responses evoked by adult and child texts alike. Does *Middlemarch*, that novel for grown-ups, as Virginia Woolf called it, not also encode the childlike responses it discourages? The novel that begins with a child pilgrimage may cor-rect the childish notions about grownup reality held by Dorothea Brooke; and yet, at the same time, it presents the fruition eventually al-lowed to Dorothea as well as to Mary Garth through images of child-hood that had become Victorian icons of pastoralism. Does not that acknowledged "adult" masterpiece of illusionless realism, then, also encourage the erasure of the too rigid polarities of child and adult? George Eliot, after all, already had more openly promoted such a blur-ring in the fluid fairy tale *Silas Marner*. Conversely, many a deceptively "simple" book for children encodes adult modes of signification. Stu-dents are startled to discover that the text of *Charlotte's Web* is not as "humble" as it seemed when the book was first read to them or when they saw the horrible film in which songs and gosling antics were en-listed to offset the impact of Charlotte's death. They discover, among other things, that this fantasy is also an antifantasy ("people believe al-most anything they see in print," observes Charlotte [89]) directed at the credulity of those who believe in modern advertising, that it in-volves a tribute to the good writing instilled by a fatherly Professor Strunk (and by the shrewd editing of a maternal Katharine White), and, finally, that it offers a theological fable about "natural supernaturalism" in which immortality and resurrection can become naturalized and in which Garth Williams's drawings gently parody the icons of sacred art.

I am not suggesting that *Middlemarch* be taught in apposition to *Charlotte's Web*. But I am suggesting that a greater attention to the inter-action of child and adult readers might allow us to reassess texts as well as methods of interpretation. Children's literature reminds us that an implied reader is made up of a multitude of selves. These selves can be identified with different age groups to which the text may simultaneously appeal. Librarians, publishers, and educators exert considerable effort to determine the exact age level (down to decimal points) for the children's books they then promote. Yet if, say Kipling's *Just So Stories for Little Children* is indeed, as its title suggests, intended for very young listeners, the pleasures of that text are just as exquisite, albeit on different levels, for older children, adolescents, and adults. It is not necessary to relegate the book into the pigeonhole marked "preschool" and to reserve the *Jungle Books* for older boys, *Kim* for adolescents, and stories such as "Baa Baa, Black Sheep" and "They" for adult readers. The small child who finds pictures more interesting than words, the older child interested in verbal mastery, the preadolescent who is privy to Kipling's subversion of accepted meanings, the adolescent and adult who return to the book, can all overlap, as Kipling intended them to do. Kipling's stories for little Effie are, for all their regressiveness, steadily told from the vantage point of the adult. The case of that "Wild Thing out of the Woods," the Cat who walked by himself, thus contains the ever-active coordinates of Innocence and Experience. Like Maurice Sendak's story of Max's return to domesticity, this is a fable for children small and old.

Once we admit the possibility of the coincidence of such multiple perspectives, texts now confined to either "adult" or "children's" literature can be reexamined in ways that might illuminate either category. Are texts designed for children necessarily more "reality-ordering" in their closures than romances or fantasies designed for adult readers? In "Magic Abjured: Closure in Children's Fantasy Fiction," Sarah Gilead finds the "return" endings of books such as *The Wizard of Oz* and *In the Night Kitchen* to offer concessions to what is familiar and ordinary, yet notes the instability of a hierarchy of realities in which what remains most vivid is the sojourn in a fantasy realm. A course devoted exclusively to the narrative frames and closures of romances and fantasies written for adult as well as for child audiences might well come up with valuable discriminations. Is Jane Eyre's "return" to Rochester after she hears his eerie call the exact reverse of the waking Alice's repression of the jarring Wonderland voices her nondreaming older sister must now process? Or is the ending of *Wuthering Heights*, with Lockwood's questioning, similar to Alice's own questioning whether she has dreamed or been dreamed up by the Red King?

An entire course could examine, for instance, the fleshing out of the differences between three kinds of narratives involving a presentation of childhood innocence: (1) first-person narratives shaped by the innocent point of view of a child or childlike narrator (Huck Finn, Holden Caulfield, Gulliver, Riddley Walker); (2) first-person narratives in which a remembering adult reconstructs her or his own childhood (Jane Eyre, David Copperfield, Ewing's Margaret in *From Six to Sixteen*);

(3) those third-person narratives in which childhood innocence is persistently qualified by the omnipresence of an adult commentator (MacDonald, Carroll, Nesbit, the Twain of *The Prince and the Pauper*, A. A. Milne, E. B. White) or by a surrogate narrator (Hawthorne's young Eustace Bright or Norton's aged Mrs. May). This admittedly incomplete list raises some immediate questions. Why do so few authors writing for a primary audience of children resort to an "I" narrator? (The one exception above seems to be Ewing.) Does the adult "I" who reverts to the state of childhood or adolescence by impersonating Huck or Caulden actually resist growth and socialization more strenuously than the narrator who "empowers" the child to grow up either through retrospection or through the counterbalancing insertion of an adult narrator's point of view?

Given that figures such as Hawthorne, Twain, Alcott, Burnett, Kipling, Molesworth, and MacDonald alternated between publishing books for children and books for adults and that Thomas Hardy, Gertrude Stein, Virginia Woolf, James Thurber, Randall Jarrell, and others wrote at least one work for children, it seems surprising that, to my knowledge, no one has thought of devising a course in which adult and child texts would be paired in a systematic fashion. Again, the interaction between certain writers—a Tennyson assumed to write "adult" poetry and a Lewis Carroll or Edward Lear associated with nonsense poetry for children—could be fruitfully taken up. And what about the status of texts that stubbornly defy categorization into "adult" or "child" pigeonholes? Is Christina Rossetti's *Goblin Market* a children's fairy tale in verse, a decidedly adult poem, or both? Is the appeal of *Jane Eyre* and *Little Women* to girl readers separable from their appeal for grownup women? Is Dickens, the novelist of childhood, ever a children's author?

As Harry Stone's *Dickens and the Invisible World: Fairy Tales, Fantasy, and Novel-Making* so persuasively established, we should pay more attention to the childhood readings of the writers we have canonized. *Sanford and Merton* may no longer have the appeal it held for earlier generations, but we need to know the texts that shaped later imaginations. If we truly intend to study the constructions of culture and nationality in adult texts, our students must look not only at the books but also at the juvenile magazines and encyclopedias that, in England and North America, were a prime means of instruction for the young. We ought to look at the retellings of classical mythology by the many authors who have followed Hawthorne's example. And, lastly, we need more courses in which students can trace the impact of traditional fairy tales or of *The Arabian Nights* on an enormous variety of texts, including poetry, fiction, and nonfictional prose, such as Carlyle's "The Hero as Divinity" as well as much of John Ruskin's richly allusive writings.

Would such a collaborative effort erase the uniqueness of the child texts that courses in children's literature have been insisting on? I think not. Indeed, as George R. Bodmer's contribution to this volume suggests and as the work of Perry Nodelman and, more recently, of Margaret Higonnet has incontestably shown, the discussion of picture books and illustrated texts carries theoretical implications that are unique to the genre—implications that might never have been tapped, given the isolated attention to but a few figures acceptable to "high culture" such as Hogarth, Blake, or Daumier. When studied more fully, the relation of text and image in children's books is bound to yield productive results. We will not only gain a better understanding of the interactions created by writer-artists such as Thackeray, Beatrix Potter, Kipling, Sendak, Mitsumasa Anno, and others but also extend to the visual realm many of our too exclusively literary or thematic concerns with framing, marginality, repetition, and the transgression of boundaries. By studying graphics much more inclusively than heretofore, paying attention to the role played by earlier cartoonists and illustrators, we will once again be able to stress the interconnectedness that defies the pigeonholings of academic Casaubonism.

U. C. Knoepflmacher
Princeton University

Works Cited

Booth, Wayne. *The Rhetoric of Fiction*. Chicago: U of Chicago P, 1961.

Dusinberre, Juliet. *Alice to the Lighthouse: Children's Books and Radical Experiments in Art*. New York: St. Martin's, 1987.

Eliot, George. *Middlemarch: A Study of Provincial Life*. Boston: Houghton, 1956.

Gilead, Sarah. "Magic Abjured: Closure in Children's Fantasy Fiction." *PMLA* 106 (1991): 277–93.

Hughes, Felicity. "Children's Literature: Theory and Practice." *ELH* 45 (1978): 542–61.

Koelb, Clayton. *The Incredulous Reader: Literature and the Function of Disbelief*. Ithaca: Cornell UP, 1984.

Postman, Neil. *The Disappearance of Childhood*. New York: Delacorte, 1982.

Stone, Harry. *Dickens and the Invisible World: Fairy Tales, Fantasy, and Novel-Making*. Bloomington: Indiana UP, 1979.

White, E. B. *Charlotte's Web*. New York: Harper, 1952.

Part I:
Critical Issues
and Approaches

CANONICAL ISSUES

Canon Formation: A Historical and Psychological Perspective

John Daniel Stahl

Even if we leave aside temporarily the knotty issues of canon formation, teaching children's literature requires us to make the practical choices of selecting texts that become, de facto, a personal, if provisional, canon. Such a canon is an expression of the philosophy and methodology of our teaching. I wish to argue in favor of an approach to the teaching of children's literature that unites a historical survey with the examination of the psychological and social contradictions—or, at the least, tensions—inherent in literature written by adults for children. My observations are based partly on several years' experience in teaching courses in children's literature, partly on theoretical reflections on the historically evolving nature of the relations of child and adult in that literature.

Children's literature, as Roger Sale has pointed out, is "the only literary category that defines an audience rather than a subject or an author" or, one might add, a form (78). Yet even the definition of its audience is problematic, and it can be (and has been) argued that the best children's literature is not exclusively for children. Certainly, as Sale and C. S. Lewis have argued, nothing is so fatal in the writing of children's literature as contriving an image of the typical child reader and aiming to please that fictional being. The authors whose works deserve a place in the canon have written, at their best, out of a passionate integrity.

The task of establishing a canon is analogous to determining the nature of childhood. It would be as vain to expect general agreement on the nature of either as it would be naive to think that there is no cultural consensus in the West on the character of both. Malte Dahrendorf points to the obviously ideological nature of the statement "the natural make-up of the child is immutable" ("Unwandelbar ist die natürliche Beschaffenheit des Kindes" 21), a conviction characteristic of an earlier era. Though some now fear the disappearance of childhood, literature for children paradoxically is entering into its own as a field of study. Recognizing the historical and ideological (cultural, political, sexual, racial) relativity of the definition of "the canon" as well as of childhood is a necessary first step toward understanding the problematic hermeneutics of both.

One of the most valuable and difficult tasks of teaching children's literature is to convey a historical sense of how authors of works for the young have constructed their images of their readers in accordance with the conception of childhood (or immaturity) in various eras. As any teacher of undergraduates knows, it is an imposing challenge to create or evoke a historical perspective in students.[1] Seldom is the historical approach to the interpretation of literature so necessary and appropriate as in the teaching of works such as Aelfric's *Colloquy* (c. 1000), *The Babees Book* (c. 1475), or the hornbook. Excerpts from the *Colloquy* illustrate the inspired didactic method of the Benedictine scholar but also the harsh methods of discipline common to the age and the circumscribed occupational roles of medieval society. In a later period, Johan Amos Comenius, the innovative Czech educator, is notable for the aboriginal brilliance of coupling text with image to stimulate the youthful imagination and memory in *Orbis Sensualium Pictus* (1659).

The thesis of the discovery of childhood in the Renaissance, advanced by Philippe Ariès, is a stimulant to the historical imagination and can be pursued into the Puritan era, bridging the transition from Europe to the New World.[2] Among the Puritans, the fusion of religion with all forms of instruction is as evident as in medieval material. In a similar vein, the scriptural fanaticism of James Janeway's *A Token for Children* (1672) is linked to the egalitarian view of the value of all souls that helped initiate universal literacy as an ideal in our society. A century later, the refinement of the woodcuts that illustrate *The New England Primer* from the edition of 1727 to the version of 1777 and the shift in political point of view shown by the substitution of overtly or covertly antiroyalist and anti-British items such as "Proud Korah's troop / was swallowed up" (1777) for "Our KING the good / no man of blood"(1723) demonstrate the movement of American society from colony to nation.

Evidence that the child is an imperfectly but always potentially rational being appears in Maria Edgeworth's writing. Her skill at characterization is revealed in "The Purple Jar" (1796), which displays the utilitarian orientation of the new rationalism. The influence of John Locke and Jean-Jacques Rousseau on educational theories as well as on the concept of the child in the eighteenth century is reflected in the reading material of the time, particularly in the endorsement of the child's right to experiment and in the idea of the kindly tutor augmenting and directing the child's experience. John Newbery's groundbreaking *Little Pretty Pocketbook* (1744) is of interest for, among other things, its sidelight on social history and the emergence of a rationale of instruction and amusement in literature for the young. Despite their sometimes mercenary, bourgeois emphasis, the naive and often disingenuous morals have a droll, entertaining quality. The ironic undercurrent of Newbery's instruction introduces a theme pertinent to all children's literature: the mastery of rules of behavior as a means to social empowerment, yet with those rules not necessarily being considered as absolute.

The seeming simplicity of a children's literature text frequently reveals, on closer examination, a subtext of rebellion, repression, or, even more fundamentally, alternative perception. The difference between the dominant mode of consciousness and the child's alternate vision may express itself through broad or subtle comedy, satire, parody, or irony. Since, as many adults are subliminally aware, adult and child perspectives are always potentially antagonistic, and every adult has once been a child, it is a temptation most adults cannot resist to define maturity as the opposite of childhood consciousness. Thus, to many adults, the perspective of childhood poses a threat in the same way that the comic impulse undermines the sobrieties of institutions that are not willing to acknowledge the relativity of their rules and verities. Since children do not institutionalize canons, the concept of a canon of children's literature is naturally fraught with ironies, particularly since writing for children was long used to suppress what we today tend to think of as the child's natural urges.

However, as many useful selections in the anthology *From Instruction to Delight* show, the repressive function of instructional writing for children can sometimes have a liberating or subversive tendency. For instance, the severity of didactic intent is lightened in some of the medieval and Renaissance works, as in the cycle plays, by an undercurrent of humor (e.g., Aelfric's pupils' declaration "Carius est nobis flagellari pro doctrina quam nescire"—"It is dearer to us to be beaten for the sake of learning than not to know"; or the comedy in Erasmus's *Colloquies*; see also Gilkey). It is worth noting Comenius's touches of humor (as when he perhaps self-deprecatingly mocks his own scholarly bald pate as the culminating entry under the illustrative farrago of "Deformed and Monstrous People").

Moving beyond the scope of Patricia Demers and Gordon Moyles's anthology of children's literature to 1850, the revolution in the adult writer's attitude toward the child reader in the nineteenth century can be summed up by discussion of two paradigmatic works: *The Adventures of Huckleberry Finn* in America and *Alice in Wonderland* in Britain. By legitimizing the perspective of Huck Finn, ragamuffin, outcast, and goodhearted bad boy whose authentic perceptions implicitly criticize the status quo, Mark Twain struck a resounding blow for the endorsement of childhood consciousness. No less subversive is Lewis Carroll's use of parody to undermine the dominant moralism of juvenile literature. Carroll demonstrated the vigor of the antimoralistic stance by writing poems such as "Father William," a parody that is a far better poem than Robert Southey's platitudinous original. The ironic attack on traditional children's literature is unmistakable:

> [S]he had read several nice little stories about children who had got burnt, and eaten up by wild beasts, and other unpleasant things, all because they *would* not remember the simple rules their friends had taught them: such as, that a red-hot poker will burn you if you hold it too long; and that, if you cut your finger *very* deeply with a knife, it usually bleeds; and she had never forgotten that, if you drink much from a bottle marked "poison," it is almost certain to disagree with you, sooner or later. (10–11)

The anarchy of Wonderland is antiauthoritarian, even though "poor Alice," like Huck Finn, does not have the perspective to recognize her autonomy fully. In *Through the Looking Glass* to a fuller extent than in *Wonderland*, Carroll assumes, with tortured ambivalence, the perspective of the child Alice.

But it is important to acknowledge that Twain and Carroll (both writing under pseudonyms) were not unequivocal innovators. Dodgson's deference to the Romantic mystification of childhood is evident in his opening poem, "All in the Golden Afternoon," and in the sentimental conclusion that misrepresents Alice's adventures as "happy summer days." Clemens thought more highly of his genteel Tudor romance *The Prince and the Pauper* than of his rough frontier book. "He thought of the carefully constructed book [*The Prince and the Pauper*] as art and of his improvisatory river volumes [*Life on the Mississippi* and *Huckleberry Finn*] as business" (Andrews 195). Though we tend to value the naturalism of Twain's work at the expense of his more conventional writings, we should not lose sight of the genteel educational ideals that Twain, Harriet Beecher Stowe, and Mary Mapes Dodge, among others, placed such firm faith in.

It has been a common twentieth-century error, in reaction to the nineteenth century, to underrate the force and value of the genteel tradition. Recent attention to *St. Nicholas* magazine and other influential periodicals has discovered the extent and sophistication of polite concern with literature as well as with science, ecology, and urbanization (Erisman; Kelly; Keyser). The formulas of periodical fiction permitted, even if they did not guarantee, literary excellence, and they attracted writers such as Frances Hodgson Burnett, Louisa May Alcott, Rudyard Kipling, and Jack London. *The Prince and the Pauper* and *The Adventures of Tom Sawyer*, in different ways, represent an important counterpoint to the world of *Huck Finn* by portraying the ideals, achievements, and limitations of the genteel tradition.

In the twentieth century, a major shift to emphasize is the change from the essentially idyllic representation of the child's world that lasted through the 1950s, to the problematic, naturalistic vision of writers since the early 1960s. The extraordinary popularity of Judy Blume's works is a symptom of a trend among better writers: the growing refusal to shelter young readers from the realities of life. In fact, the new realism is characterized by concentration on social and personal problems and the denial of conclusive solutions. Louise Fitzhugh's work, with its increasingly radical criticism of adult domination of children and its satiric naturalism, can be seen as a watershed in the development of the new children's literature (Wolf), corresponding to, if considerably trailing behind, a similar change in American literature generally.

A significant part of Fitzhugh's achievement is her perceptive delineation of social class differences. Her subversion of the Horatio Alger myth, particularly in the form of Mr. Waldenstein's willed descent from wealth and social position to delivery man, and her presentation of the regressive effects of money, represent a critique of dominant values that is accessible to children. The depiction of social class and its effects on character and values is a dimension of children's literature too often neglected in American literary criticism. The capacity of children to assimilate and respond to subtle as well as obvious signs of social rank should not be underestimated. Consequently, the study of social differentiation is a central and legitimate purpose of children's literature criticism and teaching.

The infantilizing influence of wealth and power, for example, is a theme that unites *Harriet the Spy*, *The Wind in the Willows*, and *Alice in Wonderland*. The Robinsons' moronic preoccupation with absurd icons of aesthetics and money corresponds to the ephemeral self-indulgences of Toad's dilettante passions. The Duchess (who may be interpreted as a parody of a governess) and the Queen act threateningly to their subordinates, while the White Rabbit, a caricature of an aristocrat, is dictatorial with his inferiors and sycophantic with his superiors—a pattern of behavior children will readily recognize. "Poor Bill," the lizard/gardener's boy, is sent down the chimney, having been assigned the dirty work without hesitation, and Alice, in one of her compassionless moods, is not reluctant to kick him. The low comedy of servant life appears here in a new guise.

In American children's literature, the predominantly white perspective on race relations in the South, extending from *Uncle Tom's Cabin* to *Sounder*, can be complemented and in part counterbalanced by a work such as Mildred Taylor's *Roll of Thunder, Hear My Cry*. Themes familiar from literature of the frontier experience such as *Little House on the Prairie*—family solidarity, hard work, love of the land, pride, and strength—appear here, with the difference that the family suffers oppression because of their race. Taylor succeeds in her aim of showing "a family united in love and self-respect, and parents, strong and sensitive, attempting to guide their children successfully, without harming their spirits, through the hazardous maze of living in a discriminatory society" ("Sidelights"). The complexities and hazards that make black-white friendship difficult if not impossible in a racist society are treated realistically, supplying an essential dimension lacking in Twain's portrait of black-white friendship, the more idyllic portrait achieved by temporarily isolating Jim and Huck from the constraints of the society around them.

Among contemporary novels, *Bridge to Terabithia* is notable, among other things, for its carefully shaded and accurate depiction of cultural and regional differences in a rural Virginia community. Katherine Paterson captures, with the familiarity of an insider and the keenness of an outsider, the conflict between believable urban, liberal, upper-middle-class attitudes and rural, religious, conservative, working-class values as children experience them. Paterson's novel is rewarding to teach partly because the characters experience genuine growth. Early, easy judgments and antagonisms are questioned and altered through confrontations with complex realities. Paterson is particularly good at showing how social conditioning merges into psychological formation. Jess craves attention and physical affection from his father, but while his sisters receive it, he discovers that he was considered too old for that sort of thing from the moment he was born, which plainly indicates that the reason for his treatment is that he is a boy. He learns quickly not to admit to his love of drawing for fear of ridicule, and to feign an interest in football instead.

In general, the psychological dimension of children's literature is far richer than concentration on developmental stages, though Piaget, Freud, and others can be highly illuminating, particularly in relation to the conceptual world of the young child who lives imaginatively through the fairy tale realm (Piaget; Fraiberg). Reading the original Grimm and Perrault versions of the fairy tales is instructive (and sometimes startling) to students who know only the bowdlerized Disney versions, and can serve as a valuable introduction to the oral tradition, partially preserved in the early written forms of these tales. The primitive imaginative centeredness of the child has its corollary in children's literature in the search for—and at times the realization of —a primordially unified realm of experience, whether it be the unity of nature, family, friendship, or self. Thus one of the fundamental themes of children's literature is growth, both away from and toward that primal unity. The mythic yearning for oneness, at times intensified to mysticism, finds its expression in works such as *The Secret Garden* (in the incompletely realized longing for the reconstruction of the family and in the mythic locus of Nature, the secret garden), *The Wind in the Willows* (in the mystical attraction of home and in Pan, the "piper at the gates of dawn"), and *Charlotte's Web*.[3] In E. B. White's novel, the cyclical patterns of nature enclose the life and death of Charlotte in an all-encompassing unity, which it is Wilbur's task to find his place in. Though Fern's estrangement from Wilbur and her premature interest in Henry Fussy may not be developmentally accurate, the alteration in her is psychologically true. Other works that are more chronologically realistic about children's development do not achieve the trenchant wisdom of White's work.[4]

One method to select suitable texts is to choose works that exemplify central thematic concerns such as those delineated above. Another approach is to examine works that, in their stylistic technique and through their narrative strategies, illustrate central tensions, even paradoxes of children's literature. Perhaps the most important example of such a paradox is the fundamental opposition between the child's untamed, anarchic energies and the organizing, subordinating consciousness and activity of the adult author. One expression of this opposition is the child's simplifying, ironic awareness of the adult world. Thus what might appear to the adult reader as a form of distortion or naïveté in children's literature may in fact be an effective representation of a child's vision. As can readily be seen, the tension described here can become a dynamic, compelling theme in teaching children's literature.

An awareness of the child's subversive consciousness in the adult writer's text illuminates the reading of children's literature. The method of description employed by the narrator in *Harriet the Spy* approximates the blunt perceptions of Harriet herself. In a further example, the representation of adults in *Charlotte's Web* is a sophisticated choice of childlike perspective on adult attitudes. Only Mrs. Zuckerman recognizes that it is not Wilbur but the spider who writes in webs who is out of the ordinary. All other adults pay simple-minded homage to the pig, the minister even "explaining the miracle." "If I can fool a bug," Charlotte thinks, "I can surely fool a man." Further, in one of White's ironic half-truths, she claims that "people believe almost anything they see in print" (89). Another is Charlotte's claim that, though human beings weave webs such as the Queensborough Bridge, they don't know the proper use of a web: "If they'd hang head-down at the top of the thing and wait quietly, maybe something good would come along. But no—with men it's rush, rush, rush, every minute" (60).

Similarly, the narrator in *Little House on the Prairie*, a Laura who is a composite of the adult and the child, describes her conflicts with the process of genteel socialization, especially by her Ma, in ways that allow us to understand both her accommodations to adult expectations and her revolt against them. It would be a mistake to interpret her narrative technique either as an endorsement of the sometimes repressive parental ethos or as unqualified advocacy of the child's mutinous impulses. Yet the love of primordial nature is on a continuum with Laura's love of wildness—her desire to ride a pony, bare naked—and the lucidity of Wilder's language is a corresponding aesthetic match for the beauty of the unspoiled prairie, comparable to Willa Cather's luminous prose.

As Kenneth Koch has persuasively demonstrated, the canon of poetry for children should not be limited to poetry written specifically for children. Koch argues that much of the poetry conventionally thought of as being appropriate for children is condescending, sentimental, and not about anything that matters very much to anyone—one of the reasons children are often alienated from the enjoyment of poetry through their experiences in school. Koch presents a convincing alternative: teaching poems by writers such as William Carlos Williams, Wallace Stevens, and Federico García Lorca, with the aid of what he calls a "poetry idea," which in essence is a strategy of approaching the poem that gives children the power of encoding and decoding messages, often in dramatic dialogues. Koch has a shrewd grasp of children's psychology of communication, but it is not his personal skill as a teacher alone that motivates pupils to respond to great poetry and occasionally to write excellent poetry themselves, as he proves in *Rose, Where Did You Get That Red*?

Internationalism is an important dimension of children's literature too often neglected in the United States. Whereas in most countries of the world a high proportion of children's literature consists of works from other cultures and nations, in the United States the proportion of works translated from other languages is negligible. British and American authors dominate the curricula; even Canadian authors are underrepresented. That this is due to educators', editors', and publishers' attitudes as well as public demand may be suggested by the fact that in 1984–85, there were no American editions of Erich Kästner's *Emil and the Detectives* in print, while there were five editions available in Britain. Kästner's 1928 novel, which pioneered a new realism in German children's literature, presents a socially and psychologically interesting portrait of children's street life in pre–World War II Berlin. While Myron Levoy's *Der Gelbe Vogel* (originally *Alan and Naomi*) received the highest award for children's literature in German including translations, in 1982 (Deutscher Jugendliteraturpreis), the Mildred Batchelder Award, which honors translated works in the United States, is relatively unknown and no recently translated work has had a comparable impact here. As Barbara Herrnstein Smith points out, "the value of a literary work is continuously produced and re-produced by the very acts of implicit and explicit evaluation that are frequently invoked as 'reflecting' its value and therefore as being evidence of it" (34). The exclusion of works translated from other languages from the canon of children's literature as it is being defined in the United States is a form of cultural poverty and testifies to a lack of imagination in an information-rich world.

As should be obvious, the intersection of the concept of a canon of children's literature and the selection of suitable texts for teaching ought not to be a matter of retreating to the supposed safety of carefully circumscribed classics, but rather a process of discovery and analysis concerning which works serve best to exemplify and illustrate the cruxes of children's literature. Malte Dahrendorf points out that the ideological character of classic texts lies not only in what they convey but in the process of interpretation that, in its historical development, has become ideological also (29). If the texts we select to teach and our methods of interpretation succeed in relativizing and expanding our understanding of the rich and complicated nature of children's literature, we will have taken some modest steps toward understanding our culture and ourselves.

Virginia Polytechnic Institute and State University

Notes

[1] All the works cited in the following section on early children's literature are to be found, in excerpts, in Demers and Moyles and are cited from that source. Since children's literature before the mid-nineteenth century has traditionally been slighted and texts have been relatively inaccessible, this task has been greatly facilitated by the publication of this collection, with its concise, erudite introductory discussions.

[2] An image such as Brueghel's painting *The Peasant Dance* (c. 1568) illustrates vividly the absence of the modern concept of childhood in the Middle Ages. The clothing of the children left foreground and the proportions of their bodies are miniature replicas of those of adults.

[3] As Christopher Clausen has argued, the desire to return home is one expression of that central longing. For an informative discussion linking *Watership Down* and other children's books with the "anti-modern stance" of a rural tradition reaching back to Isaac Walton, see Sell 29–33.

[4] Examples would include Elizabeth Enright's delightfully written children's novels such as *Gone-Away Lake*, which portray realistic and finely detailed characters and experiences, described with humor and insight.

Works Cited

Andrews, Kenneth R. *Nook Farm: Mark Twain's Hartford Circle*. Seattle: U of Washington P, 1950.

Ariès, Philippe. *Centuries of Childhood: A Social History of Family Life*. Trans. Robert Baldick. London: Cape, 1962.

Carroll, Lewis. *Alice in Wonderland*. Ed. Donald J. Gray. New York: Norton, 1971.

Clausen, Christopher. "Home and Away in Children's Fiction." *Children's Literature* 10 (1982): 141–52.

Dahrendorf, Malte. "Der Ideologietransport in der klassischen Kinderliteratur." *Kinder- und Jugendliteratur*. Ed. Margareta Gorschenek and Annamaria Rucktäschel. München: Fink, 1979. 20–48.

Demers, Patricia, and Gordon Moyles, eds. *From Instruction to Delight: An Anthology of Children's Literature to 1850.* Toronto: Oxford UP, 1982.

Enright, Elizabeth. *Gone-Away Lake.* New York: Harcourt, 1957.

Erisman, Fred. "St. Nicholas." *Children's Periodicals of the United States.* Ed. R. Gordon Kelly. Westport: Greenwood, 1984. 377–88.

Fitzhugh, Louise. *Harriet the Spy.* New York: Dell, 1964.

——— . *Nobody's Family Is Going to Change.* New York: Dell, 1974.

Fraiberg, Selma. *The Magic Years.* New York: Scribner's, 1959.

Gilkey, Dennis M. "Erasmus's "First Reader": The *Colloquies* in Early English Pedagogy." *Children's Literature Association Quarterly* 10 (1985): 24–26.

Grahame, Kenneth. *The Wind in the Willows.* New York: Scribner's, 1908.

Kästner, Erich. *Emil und die Detektive.* Berlin: Williams, 1928.

Kelly, R. Gordon. *Mother Was a Lady.* Westport: Greenwood, 1974.

Keyser, Elizabeth. Rev. of *Children's Periodicals of the United States,* ed. R. Gordon Kelly. *Resources for American Literary Study* 13 (Spring 1983): 79–84.

Koch, Kenneth. *Rose, Where Did You Get That Red? Teaching Great Poetry to Children.* New York: Random, 1973.

Levoy, Myron. *Der Gelbe Vogel.* Trans. Fred Schmitz. München: Deutscher Taschenbuch, 1977.

Lewis, C. S. "On Three Ways of Writing for Children." *Of Other Worlds.* Ed. Walter Hooper. New York: Harcourt, 1966. 22–34.

Paterson, Katherine. *Bridge to Terabithia.* New York: Harper, 1977.

Piaget, Jean. *The Growth of Logical Thinking from Childhood to Adolescence.* Trans. A. Parsons and S. Seagrin. New York: Basic, 1958.

Sale, Roger. "The Audience in Children's Literature." *Bridges to Fantasy.* Ed. George E. Slusser, Eric S. Rabkin, and Robert Scholes. Carbondale: Southern Illinois UP, 1982. 78 79.

Sell, Roger D. "*Watership Down* and the Rehabilitation of Pleasure." *Neuphilologische Mitteilungen* 82 (1981): 28–35.

Smith, Barbara Herrnstein. "Contingencies of Value." *Canons.* Ed. Robert von Hallberg. Chicago: U of Chicago P, 1984. 5–39.

Taylor, Mildred D. *Roll of Thunder, Hear My Cry.* New York: Bantam, 1976.

——— . "Sidelights." *Something about the Author.* Ed. Anne Commire. Vol. 15. Detroit: Gale, 1979. 277.

White, E. B. *Charlotte's Web.* New York, Harper, 1952.

Wilder, Laura Ingalls. *Little House on the Prairie.* Rev. ed. New York: Harper, 1953.

Wolf, Virginia. "*Harriet the Spy*: Milestone, Masterpiece?" *Children's Literature* 4 (1975): 120–26.

——— . *Louise Fitzhugh.* New York: Twayne, 1991.

On Teaching the Canon of Children's Literature

John Griffith and Charles Frey

We might forgivably assume that one of our major functions as teachers of children's literature is to help students appreciate the best that has been read to and read by children in our tradition. And yet, simply to teach "literature" is to enter a complex web of assumptions about values of tradition, cultural integrity, and respect for classics and canons. "Literature" is what we and our forebears have been taught to revere, and teaching that literature should be, at least in part, a reverential act; but we are also the inheritors of change. Our respect for the altering shapes of time past implies our willingness to help mold a changing future.

"Children's" literature is what we did read or feel we should have read (or listened to) as children. It is also what our forebears read and heard as children. This much easily can be said; but who, really, are "we," and who, really, are our "forebears"? Is there, in fact, a readily identifiable body of children's literature? Or even a set of concentric circles whose inner rings would be considered by most teachers of children's literature to be the essential works, the classics—an anthology list, even, perhaps, a canon? To give an affirmative answer would be to point to such well-known works as *Alice's Adventures in Wonderland*, tales of Charles Perrault, the Grimms, Joseph Jacobs, and Andrew Lang, Mother Goose rhymes and the limericks of Edward Lear, *Treasure Island*, *The Adventures of Tom Sawyer*, *The Wind in the Willows*, *Charlotte's Web*, and so on, works whose collective absence from a reading list in college introductory courses would seem to deny cultural history and to blank out the origins and life of children's literature.[1] Within even so cautious an affirmative answer as this, however, there lie many assumptions and, possibly, contradictions that deserve exploration.

First, it is one thing to recognize *past* canons, but it is quite another thing to assert *present* canons: the very notion of canonicity implies authority, the kind of authority that sees itself empowered to exclude certain works from legitimacy, empowered to create margins. Many teachers may now prefer to include several recognized classics in their reading lists while explicitly denying, or at least questioning, their current canonicity. *Struwwelpeter*, for example, ranks as a classic in the tradition of children's literature, but few of its sentiments or techniques would be regarded as canonical now; it has lost much of its weight, its authority. Other works, particularly in the strenuously didactic or hugely sentimental modes (*The Little Lame Prince*, for instance) seem to be in the process of losing their canonical status more rapidly than their status as classics. Still other works (such as the *Oz* books) were initially denied endorsement or praise by many librarians, teachers, and critics but are now studied in part because they won a readership and have taken a place in the history of children. As we weaken in our grasp of (and perhaps belief in) canonical authority, canonicity itself comes to be examined more and more as a relic of past traditions.

Second, the kinds of canonicity accorded in the past to such works as the northern folktales, to "golden age" children's literature, to the Narnia books of C. S. Lewis, to Tolkien's *Hobbit* and *Fellowship of the Rings*, or to Rudyard Kipling's *Jungle Books* reflect quite directly just whose taste, whose values, and whose culture has been advanced as authoritative. Such works speak for the values and interests of relatively well-to-do well-educated whites, males, Christians, northern Europeans. Declaring such writing to be canonical and then teaching it to students who include women, members of the middle classes and "lower classes," nonwhites, non-Christians, and persons of non-European descent might amount to indoctrination by the few against the many, might it not? In the canon, as so defined, men tend to have most of the adventures and most of the power. For the most part, princes rescue princesses. Kings and fathers rule, while women's place is generally in the home. Everyone of any importance is white; most life patterns of home and society are northern European in origin and character. Poor people dream of and sometimes receive riches from on high, but they never organize to better themselves. When there is romance, heterosexuality is the assumed norm. In addition to its glories, this is a meat-eating, wine-drinking, wife- and children-beating, fight-enjoying, night-fearing, son-worshiping, undemocratic society. Desirable power is power over, domination, not power in reciprocity and sharing. Competition and rivalry lead to winners and losers, and we are to identify with and dream of becoming winners.

Such a skeptical reading of certain classics, classics that still seem canonical because they are anthologized and taught widely and often with reverence, deserves consideration if only to rouse students to a more balanced and sophisticated inspection of children's literature. It will do little good, moreover, for even the most radical teacher simply to attack works of our canonical past as reactionary monoliths: not only will the students resent the oversimplification, but the works "themselves" (that is, the texts together with the cultures in which they have been embedded then and now) are much too complex to avoid recognition of cross-qualifying and even deeply antagonistic and paradoxical stances within single stories, poems, plays, and novels. True, children's literature—of all the subdivisions of our literatures—seems most prone to canonical judgment, because the readers and hearers have "tender minds," and everything they do may receive the judgmental scrutiny of parents, teachers, psychologists, the clergy, politicians, and the other moral guardians of the day. It is our experience, however, that the ephemeral works of children's literature are likely to be the more ideologically stringent, or strident, whereas canonical authors tend to imagine their fictive situations with a depth and breadth that provide abundant space, and even inspiration, for critics of their worldviews to express their concerns. To see, and perhaps to suffer, with Alice in the "wonderland" of grownup tyranny, to meditate on the major defeats and minor victories of "little" women, to question even the happy fantasy of E. B. White's Charlotte, spider-writing her piggy friend into "radiant" independence and maturity—to do any of these things is to recognize problems within our shared social past as well as to follow the openings of childlike dreaming. Teachers of children's literature at the college level thus have a special duty and a special difficulty facing them: they must teach works that often have been predigested by their students and the media into cartoon simplicities and stubbornly defensive judgments. Such teachers must find ways to read afresh and explore for themselves, as well as to accept their students' fears and other slippery feelings about, the children's classics—a relatively few works that must seem to students like mingled yarns among the brighter wools of contemporary weave.

Kipling's Mowgli stories, from his *Jungle Books*, are a case in point. From the perspective of twentieth-century liberal ideology, there is much to criticize about them. Kipling himself, of course, is associated in many people's minds with a racist, sexist, imperialist value system. As the first Briton to win the Nobel Prize for literature, he is, in conventional terms at least, a presence to be reckoned with. A devout supporter of the British Empire and its mission of bringing moral and political enlightenment to the "dusky races" of the Third World, Kipling believed in traditional hierarchies and in the maintenance of law and order, through force of arms when necessary. He tended to think of humanity as a vast herd, unwashed and potentially unruly, to be controlled for the good of society by oligarchies of superior beings. In his life and in his fiction, he took a pronouncedly masculine point of view, conservative and militaristic.

This is the prevalent viewpoint in the saga of Mowgli. Social life in these stories is always on the edge of breaking down into squalid anarchy, mob rule of the least common denominator. "Pack behavior"—whether it be wolf pack, monkey pack, man pack, or dog pack—is always linked to unprincipled living, cowardice, weakness, irresolution, vulgarity, meanness, and shortsighted self-interest. Over against the sordid life of hoi polloi stands the law of the jungle, an elaborate code of rule and structure and right principle that the wise characters in Kipling's stories swear by. It is intensely traditional, staunchly authoritarian and hierarchical, and generally committed to restraint, responsibility, and the long view. And it provides a basis for heroism, a system under which a strong man can win eminence and respect.

The Mowgli saga is a rich example of the high heroic style in its late-Victorian/early-modern form. But it is also an implicit critique, the story of heroism developing out of the frustrated need for something better. It actually traces the pathology of Mowgli's emergence into a hero, which stems from the denial of love and acceptance. As an infant, Mowgli wanders into a family of wolves, looking for food and care and love. Naively, he supposes he has found what he sought and lives unselfconsciously among "his people" for several years. But as he comes to an age of awareness, he learns that he is wrong; the wolves resent him. Later, attempting to fit into human society, he is rejected again: the superstitious villagers drive him out.

As a direct result of this emotional trauma, Mowgli becomes preoccupied with honor and with revenge. He kills Shere Khan, the tiger who has goaded the wolves into driving him out; he marshals the animals in a stampede that levels the human village that has offended him; he destroys a huge pack of wild dogs that presumes to invade "his jungle." Mowgli rises to be master of the jungle, all because wolves and humans have refused him kinship. The subtext of his whole life is this: "You deny me love; very well, I cannot force you to give it. But I can make you see how wrong you were to deny me, by making you fear and respect me."

"The Spring Running," the last of the Mowgli stories, dramatizes the limitations of the proud and violent masculine code. Mowgli, now seventeen, feels the stirrings of sexual desire and is drawn toward the human village in search of a mate. He feels lonely and sorry for himself and starved for gentleness and love and warmth—emotions that are, by the heroic code, ignoble and unmanly. Yet they are nonetheless real and compelling. It is both necessary and right for Mowgli to leave his male gang behind and follow his tenderer impulses to the world that includes women.

It is undoubtedly a mark of Kipling's old-fashionedness that he emphasizes so dramatically an emotional conflict between "male" ideals of pride and honor, on the one hand, and "female" qualities like trust, acceptance, and domesticity, on the other. Contemporary readers and critics may challenge Kipling's assumption that such a conflict is necessary, or that the transition from headstrong, egotistic days of boyish adventure and the test of one's manhood in risk taking and fighting to the world of mature responsibility is such a sad thing, as "The Spring Running" clearly shows it to be. But the point is that Kipling himself provides room for these criticisms to be discussed; his stories themselves frame the issue, showing with considerable force and clarity the basic human needs that drive Mowgli.

In *The Wind in the Willows*, another example of canonical yet nonetheless self-imploding children's literature, the chummy, homosocial, escapist, nostalgic, "nature"-worshiping society of Mole, Rat, Badger, and the rest is of course rife with internal contradictions that students should be willing, even if at first grudgingly, to note. Why is Toad by far the most memorable, exciting, and even three-dimensionally "human" character in the book? Because he loves power? flaunts his riches? puffs with vanity and egotism? uses women? argues? rants? immerses himself in the material world? The creatures may rest at sublime moments in the embrace of Pan, at the still center of natural security, but the business of life is toad-spotted pride and war with weasels, is it not?

One could, and should, counterargue that there is much instinctive appreciation in *The Wind in the Willows* of nature's imperious call, not prompted by negative reactions to Toad or cars or courts or officious grownups. The love of nature is a positive stirring from within the hearts of the creatures and not just an escape from industrial blight. Still, when that "nature" is personified, it turns out to be the great god Pan, who is worshiped surely in part for a version of male power—"the rippling muscles," "the broad chest," "the splendid curve of the shaggy limbs disposed in majestic ease" (Griffith 908). Pan holds between his legs the little boy otter, Portly, who is imagined as having been deprived of feminine comfort, "as a child that has fallen happily asleep in its nurse's arms, and wakes to find itself alone and laid in a strange place" (909). The answer to the panic from the rejecting nurse is, apparently, the lap of Pan, the protection of a chumship or nearly all-male society. Of course, another high canonical work from the same era, *Peter Pan*, also shows the child separated from its nurse and taken that very night into the company of Pan, Pan seen specifically as leader of boys and rejecter of women.

That canonical entries such as *The Jungle Books*, *The Wind in the Willows*, and *Peter Pan* (as well as *Tom Sawyer*, *Treasure Island*, *The Hobbit*, and the like) should revolve so imperiously around questions of male self-sufficiency may help to account for their status, since the place and pressure of male domination is itself a canonical topic. Whether works so centrally devoted to the topic will deserve, in our eyes or the eyes of students, to remain canonical or will become fading classics depends on how the topic itself develops in our era. For the present, inner contradictions in the social ethos inscribed in such works appear lively enough to promote continued reading. And for the present, each teacher must confront each day anew just how to interpret and teach that liveliness.

Classics written by women and focused on heroines present their own critical issues. *Heidi*, for instance, is a classic girls' book, a senti-

mental fantasy of sweetness and light in which the heroine is the quint-
essential "good little girl"—innocent and cute and complaisant and
self-effacing. She lives only for her friends and her grandfather; her only
unalloyed pleasure, Johanna Spyri suggests, is in doing good for others.
Virtually everyone in the novel adores her and seeks to serve her and to
enjoy her company. Crusty old grandfather takes her into his hut and
his life, Peter becomes devoted to her, Clara and the servants fall in love
with her and do everything they can to help her, the doctor and Clara's
grandmother press on her affection and food and money. Peter's blind
grandmother speaks for them all when she laments, "Alas! all our happiness and pleasure have gone with the child, and now the days are so
long and dreary! Pray God, I see Heidi again once more before I die!"
(Spyri 63).[2] To the imagination devoted to an ideal of selflessness and
service to others, to be thus passionately appreciated is the highest reward, and Heidi receives it abundantly.

But *Heidi* also dramatizes the pain inherent in its own code of "feminine" selflessness. A most revealing episode occurs when Heidi moves
away from the mountains to Frankfurt, as a companion for the sickly
Clara. Spyri's Frankfurt is a kind of hell. Instead of love and appreciation, Heidi there encounters frozen rules of etiquette, a harsh pecking
order, and emotional tyranny. She wants terribly to leave; but, being as
complaisant as she is, she cannot ask it. Good little girls don't complain:

> She understood that Herr Sesemann [Clara's father] would think it un-
> grateful of her if she wished to leave, and she believed that the grand-
> mother and Clara would think the same. So there was nobody to whom
> she dared confide her longing to go home, for she would not for the world
> have given the grandmother, who was so kind to her, any reason for being
> as angry as Fräulein Rottenmeier [the despotic housekeeper, the only
> character impervious to Heidi's sweet nature] had been. (106)

Acting as she has been taught, Heidi only prays that God will help
her. Her distress is driven inward. She begins to walk in her sleep,
and when her white-clad figure moves through the darkened house
and the servants think she is a ghost, Herr Sesemann and the doctor
investigate and discover her plight. They immediately sympathize and
send her home.

To discuss with one's students the implications of this episode is to
look into the shadows of Spyri's vision of self-denial. Was it really good
for Heidi to keep her unhappiness a secret from the sympathetic grandmother, Herr Sesemann, and the doctor? Is it God, or Heidi's own subconscious, that sets her walking in her sleep? Is utter self-denial really a
virtuous state or one that will make you sick? Here and elsewhere in
this vivid fantasy of the code of the good little girl, the pitfalls are discernible to the reader who is willing to see them.

So far we have argued, mainly, that canonical and semicanonical classics can and should be taught more pluralistically than may be commonly tried. Increasing sensitivity to the best insights and points of view of feminist criticisms, in particular, may encourage in the classroom a reevaluation of children's literature that is more responsive to the evolving life of our culture.[3]

Some teachers of literature may be inclined to sidestep the more troublesome political, moral, or psychological implications of the works they take up in their classes, to pursue instead purely aesthetic or formal concerns. The sheer stylistic power of such canonical writers for children as Lewis Carroll, Mark Twain, Robert Louis Stevenson, Rudyard Kipling, Kenneth Grahame, Beatrix Potter, Laura Ingalls Wilder, and E. B. White might seem to encourage such an approach. There is much to admire and comment on in their creative virtuosity alone; they seem to open up an ahistorical, nonideological preserve for literary study. And there is truth to the argument that the formation of literary canons takes place among literary people. Authors make canons; they read each others' works; they admire prior works of the greatest stylistic richness; for they are, at bottom, writers, not ideologues. The languages of literature are themselves at least semiclosed systems in that they require certain kinds of expressive problem solving. We pun in English, for instance, in certain ways because of the phonic peculiarities of our language; many stylistic decisions seem internally dictated by just such purely linguistic factors, factors on which class time may suitably be spent. It seems especially tempting, furthermore, to connect stylistic power and an aesthetic approach to children's literature, because children often seem to live apolitically, to live life as an end in itself—aesthetically, as it were. Literature that claims to be created or read "just for literature's sake" may thus seem to suit the conditions of childhood. Much of the training, moreover, that literature teachers have received emphasizes formal and structural concerns of writing. English teachers are not, and are not supposed to be, political scientists, sociologists, psychologists, or philosophers. Their primary concern is the language, its use and abuse, its grand expressing song and play and story.

There is a good deal to be said for the approach to children's literature that treats it as if it were a sort of playful exercise in a vacuum, detached from the practical and moral concerns of life. Ultimately, though, this approach is a kind of evasion, one that handles problematic themes and value systems in the enshrined works of children's literature by ignoring them. Underneath it all, children's literature speaks to the needs of children, to the process of emotional and spiritual growth in each young person, and that growth can never be divorced for long from the issues of class, race, nation, religion, aging, and sex that make each society a part of history. We think the most fruitful way to teach the masterpieces of children's literature is, first, to treat them with the respect that their stylistic brilliance and historical status deserve and, second, to face head-on the problems of value and belief that they raise, to face those problems with all the intelligence and wisdom that students and teachers can devote to the enterprise.

It may be difficult enough for teachers to problematize canonical classics of children's literature, yet such teachers must also help their students evaluate with self-awareness the very processes of canon formation and deformation. *Children's literature* is itself a paradoxical concept, for the word *children* refers to the millions of human beings all over the earth who are young, but the word *literature* refers to the works introduced to children whose parents (or teachers) may "appreciate" a relatively narrow range of children's reading, a "finer," "higher" range than that embodied in the comics, joke books, mad magazines, perishable picture books, preteen romance series, and, indeed, the vast run of paperbacks for children sold each year by the millions but evanescent in the long run. In the term *children's literature*, the word *literature* cuts backward into the word *children*, identifying only certain children and only a relatively small portion of their reading experience. The question thus arises: What recognition may teachers take in the classroom of the huge and clamoring margins of children's "literature"?

In approaching this question, much depends on the context of the children's literature course, particularly whether it is in English, education, or library science. While primary and elementary teachers and children's librarians must evaluate numerous categories in the vast subcanonical reaches of works that children read and listen to, English teachers may not consider themselves obligated to survey the popular spectrum. But even those who recognize a need to teach complete individual works—rather than engage in a taxonomic scramble over histories and categories—may wonder if they are addressing in their students primarily former children (who may not have read many of the "better" books), current students of cultural traditions, future parents, possible teachers, or some generalizing mixture. For English teachers to spend much time, in one-quarter or one-semester courses (which most children's literature courses are), on the infant picture books, the Hollywood reproductions of classics, the syndicated series, the comics, the sports, science fiction, and animal stories, and the other seeming flotsam and jetsam of students' actual reading experience as children would appear perverse, unless the courses were conceived as broadly anthropological or sociological surveys. To spend at least some time, however, on the popular matrices of canon formation and on the intensely competitive arenas of semiclassical children's literature is, we think, indispensable.

Because children's literature in English has traditionally included folktales from many lands and standard stories from Germany, France, and a few other countries, because childhood embraces so many stages

OUACHITA TECHNICAL COLLEGE

in human growth, and because works of wildly competing appeal jostle and vie with one another for attention on library shelves, it is, perhaps luckily, almost impossible to define a teachable canon or body of classics for even a relatively conservative English course in children's literature. Yes, anthologies have offered and will continue to offer either popularistic samplings from dozens of works or even whole-work collections of twenty or more past high canonical classics; but, if an English course aims, as we think it should, to explore our culture's collective understanding and misunderstanding of childhood, then sustained attention probably should be divided among three endeavors: (1) close reading of classics by traditional authors such as the Grimms, Hans Christian Andersen, Carroll, Twain, and Potter; (2) comparisons involving couldbe canonicals or lesser classics by such writers as Antoine St.-Exupéry, Marjorie Rawlings, P. L. Travers, Roald Dahl, Jack London, Astrid Lindgren, Dr. Seuss, L. Frank Baum, and so on; and (3) discussion of children's development and culture generally and the place of literature within it.

Children's literature is, certainly, a separable subject in literary study. It is defined, initially, by the age range of its readers and hearers, but that very restriction of audience also means that the thematics of children's literature may constellate about issues of maturation, family life, play, and elemental feelings (of the body, of innocence, of nostalgia). What have we thought children can know, do, and be? These are critical issues indeed, and it behooves us to ask in our teaching how well our noble classics and their scruffier cousins may have explored them. To teach the canon more critically and the noncanon more seriously, to admit and explore the surprising darkness in children's literature, to find much to celebrate beneath our healthy skepticisms and debunkings—these practices can only help our students develop their own capacities to enjoy and evaluate classic and nonclassic alike.

University of Washington

Notes

[1] The children's classics are readily available in numerous separate editions. Nearly all the classics we discuss here may be found in Griffith and Frey, *Classics*.

[2] In discussing Kipling, Grahame, Spyri, and other children's authors, we have sometimes drawn on material in Frey and Griffith, *The Literary Heritage*.

[3] Lawrence Lipking comments on this notion:

> Some old masters even look silly. Under the gaze of women, strong writers turn pale. Hence the concern often voiced about theory in our time, that all its sophisticated speculations and deconstructions leave the canon firmly in place—"An agony of flame that cannot singe a sleeve"—falls away from a woman's poetics. Its

flames can scorch and burn, refining some authors and wasting others forever. Not even our secret places—our language, our habits of reading—can be immune from that fire. (79)

Works Cited

Frey, Charles, and John Griffith. *The Literary Heritage of Childhood: An Appraisal of Children's Classics in the Western Tradition*. New York: Greenwood, 1987.

Griffith, John W., and Charles H. Frey, eds. *Classics of Children's Literature*. 1980. 3rd ed. New York: Macmillan, 1992.

Lipking, Lawrence. "Aristotle's Sister: A Poetics of Abandonment." *Critical Inquiry* 10 (1983): 61–81.

Spyri, Johanna. *Heidi*. New York: Airmont, 1963.

An American Canon of Children's Literature

Bruce A. Ronda

The phrase *American canon* is a troubling one. By *canon* we typically mean those texts that are said to have an enduring quality by virtue of their universal themes, literary craft, or surplus of meaning. But to add *American* to *canon* suggests another set of determinants, some cultural or historical measure of literary value. It is precisely this confusion that I find provocative and rewarding, for the deliberate linking of *American* and *canon* promises to lift us beyond repetitious debates over strictly literary and intrinsic merit into a deeper consideration of cultural criticism, an area of interest to a growing number of interpreters.

But what do these terms—*American, canon, cultural criticism*—mean, and how do they relate to children's literature? To describe as *American* writing for children (here limited to prose fiction) composed in the United States is to plunge immediately into a consideration of ideology. Sacvan Bercovitch has noted that *America* has become completely synonymous with *United States*, yet this linkage ignores the fact that millions of other residents in the Western Hemisphere lay equal claim to being American. Linguistic appropriation, says Bercovitch, is a trope for a history of cultural, political, and economic domination. Using the term *American* is inescapably an ideological act, a means by which a certain version of reality validates a given power arrangement. Still, ideology need not mean systematic or deliberate distortion, as Max Weber and others have pointed out. It can be virtually equivalent to *culture*, describing the way humans construct and interpret social reality (Bercovitch and Jehlen 10–15). In understanding culture as ideological, we see that there may be nothing conspiratorial about the way a society organizes its dominant worldview, and yet we may also see that any social construction is partial, following the dominant lines of economic and political power, aiming to validate some people's experience, ending up excluding or distorting others'.

To speak of an American canon of children's literature, then, is to remind ourselves of the inextricably historical and cultural nature of all writing. Language is constitutive of culture, expressive of a society's version of the real. But, as many critics point out, culture is not univocal. In 1955, well before the current interests in hermeneutics and interpretation theory, R. W. B. Lewis described culture as a conversation over central issues and images. While Lewis limited his conversation to white males and his debated images to one—the American Adam—that was particularly relevant to male experience, still his notion of culture as dialogue and argument is a useful one. A decade later, Raymond Williams mapped out the class basis for participation in cultural dialogue, suggesting the kinds of discourse one might use according to social position.

So if *American* implies ideology, culture, and conversation, what do we make of *canon*? Canonical criticism is clearly one of the most hotly debated topics in literary circles these days, as once-sacred classics of Western literature are scrutinized for their political and social biases and as neglected texts are thrust forward for our consideration. What are the merits on which a text is recommended? Which communities of readers and critics are competent to judge works that appear to come from outside the canonical mainstream? These are extremely vexed and difficult questions. My sense is that understanding literature as culture and ideology—that is, as connected to the real world of experience and values beyond the printed page—helps us in assessing which works can be singled out as having long-term significance. This cultural bias is the reason I am attracted to David Tracy's understanding of canon as "classic." Tracy suggests that a classic is an exemplary text that has the appearance of permanence but in fact is radically unstable because it contains an excess of meaning. The classic attains its status in the rich and multiple ways it addresses the central issues around which a culture conducts its arguments or conversations. It combines and recombines the different ideological and linguistic possibilities in a given culture, moving beyond propaganda into the creation of something distinctively new and unexpected (99–154).

Of the several cultural conversations carried on in the United States and evident in writing composed for children, I emphasize three as central: family, self, and place. As in all societies, the most powerful social and economic groups in the United States used institutions and the media to promote their understanding of these three elements. Children's literature in particular appealed to social and economic elites as a means of stabilizing American society, which has always been marked by rapid change, pluralism, and racial and ethnic violence. Still, like the society from which it emerges, children's literature does not speak with a single voice. It reflects, and reflects on, the same passionate arguments that may be seen in adult society and in literature meant for adults.

The ideology of the nuclear family took shape in the early decades of the nineteenth century. As several historians have shown, the family was a far more varied and fluid institution than the emergent domestic ideology was prepared to sanction. Many middle-class (but not working-class or nonwhite) people viewed the family as a "haven in a heartless world," to use Christopher Lasch's term, imagining it as a source of emotional nurture and spiritual guidance in a world increasingly given over to the pursuit of wealth and subject to the manipulations of the marketplace.

The family, according to domestic ideologists like Francis Wayland and Catharine Beecher, was a little commonwealth where differences in power, preferences, and talent met and were reconciled, where power coexisted with rights. Far more than the English nuclear family, the mid-nineteenth-century American family existed in a tension between "natural" hierarchies like male dominance, on the one hand, and natural rights, on the other. Somehow, the familial discourse taught, children and adults would be contained within this institution yet also encouraged to be their own distinctive selves (an encouragement more ambiguously given to females).

The classic texts that have helped convey this vision of the family as tidy blend of domestic structure and natural rights included Louisa May Alcott's *Little Women*, Eleanor Estes's *Moffatts*, Dorothy Canfield Fisher's *Understood Betsy*, Irene Hunt's *Up a Road Slowly*, and, most of all, Laura Ingalls Wilder's *Little House* series. For over a hundred years, books like these helped project the dominant view of family as model community and moral center. While the March girls or the Trelling sisters quarrel, and while parents may be dead or absent, the family unit endures and is emotionally reliable. Wilder's series demonstrates simply but memorably the family as moral fulcrum, a still center in a turning world of dangerous nature and unpredictable humans.

It is no accident, given the centrality of family discourse in a culture that associates women with children and places women at the center of family, that these books feature girls both as main characters and as preferred readers. Unlike the texts already mentioned, Twain's *Adventures of Tom Sawyer* does not sketch out the means whereby a happy family might be constructed, but it does posit a stable home from which Tom forays, a "permanent truant," in Alfred Kazin's happy term. But in *The Adventures of Huckleberry Finn*, Twain responds to the prevailing literary values by deconstructing the family altogether. He exposes the limits of its ideology and pitches his hero against society, "the biggest family of all, the most tyrannical family," as Kazin says. Twain does so not only by having Huck expose adult hypocrisies and brutalities, but by invoking a language whose very barbarities are an affront (Kazin 180).

Chester Aaron's *American Ghost* is a direct descendant of *Huckleberry Finn*, both in its river setting and frontier violence and in its abrasive conversation/argument with the discourse of Alcott and Wilder. Here the family vanishes, the boy is swept away in a flood, befriends a mountain lion—an "American ghost"—and eventually returns home, only to find that the adults there had shot and skinned the lion. The novel's last lines measure the distance between this version of the family and that of the domestic ideology: "Albie turned to confront Alice Anne. And Elizabeth and his mother and father. And the Abernathys" (Aaron 189). A whole set of recent books takes Twain's and Aaron's perspective and pushes it toward active hostility to family and society, including Paul Zindel's several works, June Jordan's *His Own Where—*, Robert Cormier's *Chocolate War*. In Elaine Konigsburg's *From the Mixed-up Files of Mrs. Basil E. Frankweiler* the children easily and rapidly slip away from home and take up residence in the Metropolitan Museum of Art, while in Louise Fitzhugh's *Harriet the Spy* it is the nurse, Ole Golly, rather than Harriet's parents, who educates and guides the child.

Thus, in the century and a half since the domestic ideology emerged, the theme of secure home and confident adults has been challenged periodically. In the alternative discourse, the family is weak or nonexistent, or else an agent of adult violence. This version of the family is often one example of the American male's rebellion against confinement and high culture—Huck's heading out for the territories matches Whitman's desire to be on the open road or Ahab's obsession, in *Moby-Dick*, with striking through the mask.

A third voice in the conversation about families in children's literature has no comfortably domestic or boldly rebellious quality about it. It emerges in texts like Elizabeth Coatsworth's *Marra's World*, Eleanor Cameron's *Room Made of Windows* and *The Court of the Stone Children*, Cynthia Voigt's *Dicey's Song*, and Irene Hunt's *Across Five Aprils*. Here the family is neither all-powerful and all-sheltering nor a brutal agent of socialization; rather, it is made up of fallible, suffering, ambivalent people bound by biology, custom, and mutuality. In these texts, another "family way" is apparent, no less or more accurate than the other two, but an imaginative possibility that draws on the fluidity and complexity of our social experience.

A second major theme around which American children's writing orbits is the nature of the self. If Wilder, Twain, and Cameron write paradigmatic texts on the family, then Alcott's *Little Women* is surely a paradigm of the dominant version of the self. Blending John Calvin, John Locke, and (later) Charles Darwin, this version in countless pieces of self-help literature and works of fiction is strenuously autonomous. Vaguely discernible in infancy, becoming more focused as the child grows and engages the world, the nineteenth- and early-twentieth-century "inner-directed self" is the model pressed relentlessly on youthful readers. Alcott gives us such sharply delineated characters in *Little Women*, where life is growth from an inner core, an unfolding of unique identities. Retelling a Greek myth, Nathaniel Hawthorne (whose house The Wayside is next door to the Alcotts' Orchard House in Concord) employs the same discourse in "The Paradise of Children" in *A Wonder Book*. Here the children live in a timeless but boring world. With the release of Troubles (through Pandora's

female curiosity and ingenuity) also comes Hope and a deepening
of character. A similar outlook shapes some twentieth-century works,
like Katherine Paterson's exquisite *Jacob Have I Loved* and Hunt's *Up a
Road Slowly*.

It is not incompatible with the vision of self developing into an autonomous individual to observe that such selves bear striking resem-
blance to one another. Consider Thomas Bailey Aldrich's description of
the all-American boy: "an amiable, impulsive lad, blessed with fine di-
gestive powers, and no hypocrite . . . in short . . . a real human boy,
such as you may meet anywhere in New England, and no more like the
impossible boy in a storybook than a sound orange is like one that has
been sucked dry" (7–8). Despite its autobiographical flavor, Aldrich's
Story of a Bad Boy is a storybook, and that is precisely where we meet
his fictional self. Ironically, Aldrich's ruggedly autonomous male
individual—square-jawed, fun-loving, unimpeachably moral—appears
again and again in the works of Howard Pyle and the series featuring
the Rover Boys, the Merriwells, Tom Swift, Tom Swift, Jr., and the
Hardy Boys (Kazin 172). In their exploration of the territory between autonomous selfhood and adherence to social and gender roles, the American writers for children corroborate Tocqueville's original insight into
the paradox of American individualism and American conformity.

But autonomy is not the only discourse of selfhood. Current
feminist criticism, most notably in the genre of autobiography, reveals
that the notion of the autonomous self is largely a male creation, even
a male fantasy, one infrequently shared by women who feel very
much defined by and as the Other. In the past, some authors, beginning
with Charles Brockdon Brown and Edgar Allan Poe, have likewise
challenged the ideology of autonomous selfhood, preferring to explore
shifting boundaries, dreamlike situations, and dissolving selves. In
children's literature, we find this same direction in books like Paul
Zindel's *Pigman*, in which the child characters lack firm definition, responding sometimes warmly, sometimes cruelly and manipulatively to
those around them. Their fluidity illustrates Robert Jay Lifton's theory
of "protean man." Lifton argues that in the postmodern age, personality is a constantly shifting entity, a game of mirrors reflecting differently
in different situations (37–63). It is in animal tales, however, that we
find the greatest willingness to play with the definitions of self. From
the innumerable stories of Thornton Burgess to Robert O'Brien's *Mrs.
Frisby and the Rats of NIMH*, authors have gently expanded the boundaries of what is biologically and culturally possible, of what is "human"
and "humane."

Still, a large portion of American writing for children, even that
which posits a rebellious child against a hypocritical adult society, accepts the dominant discourse of autonomous selfhood. As a culture we
have insisted on development as the prime motif of identity—hence the

profound importance of Erik Erikson's stages of development as a cultural artifact. While Americans have preferred to think of theirs as a youthful society, we also tend to relegate childlikeness to children or to eccentrics. This gives rise both to intense nostalgia for childhood and an equal insistence on a rhetoric of growth. Few American books have explored the theme of arrested development that we find in English children's books like *Alice in Wonderland*, George MacDonald's *At the Back of the North Wind*, or *Peter Pan*.

The third issue that pervades American children's literature is that of place. The predominant view of the American landscape, according to many observers, has been one of conquest. Wendell Berry believes that the prevailing Western and especially American attitude and behavior have been antiplace, restless, nomadic, destructive, a pattern of uprooting and moving on (3–7). In writings for children, this stance is evident in the dime novels of the mid- and late-nineteenth century, in the many adventure tales of Joseph Altsheler and in the Stratemeyer series. In these books, nature is always "over there," passive and yielding, or else the enemy or a shelter for our enemies.

However, if much children's writing echoes the dominant view of selfhood, the same cannot be said of its relation to the generally accepted view of place. Indeed, much American children's literature celebrates place. In this regard, it reinforces the psychologist Edith Cobb's notion that the project of childhood is "to make a world in which to find a place to discover a self" (540). Perhaps writers sense that "place" provides shelter against the inconsistencies and irrational behavior of adults. Or perhaps it is in exploration of children's sense of place and in the employment of a counter discourse that writers best express the vulnerability and powerlessness that young people share with other marginalized communities.

This intense commitment to place runs like a leitmotif through a century and more of children's writing, from Jacob Abbott's *Franconia Stories*, Lucretia Hale's *Peterkin Papers*, and Horace Scudder's *Bodley Family* series to Wilder's *Little House Books* and a number of more recent texts. These later books include Virginia Hamilton's *M. C. Higgins the Great* and *Sweet Whispers, Brother Rush*, Scott O'Dell's *Island of the Blue Dolphins* and *Sing Down the Moon*, Katherine Paterson's *Bridge to Terebithia*, Gene Stratton Porter's *Girl of the Limberlost*, E. B. White's *Charlotte's Web*, and William Steig's *Amos and Boris*.

In illustrating my chief point—that the distinctive tone of a culture and its products comes from an argument over that culture's central issues—I seem to be suggesting that these literary texts divide up neatly, representing one voice or another. Perhaps categorizing books (or people) into opposing camps is useful for the purposes of analysis and fills our need for clarity, but it does injustice to the very canonical nature of the books I have mentioned. Nearly all these works, even the most overtly propagandistic, contain hints of an opposing discourse. Consider L. Frank Baum's *Wonderful Wizard of Oz*. Here several different perspectives on family, self, and place blend and fuse, making this indeed a classic of American children's literature.

Clearly Dorothy cares very much about her family, Uncle Henry and Aunt Em, and is single-minded about her desire to return to them. Despite their grayness and joylessness, they are Dorothy's primary social environment, the touchstone of her life. Nothing is complete until she can recover them. Still, if part of the pro-family discourse is deference to adults, Dorothy has not learned this lesson very well. She chides the Wizard, melts the Wicked Witch of the West, and generally holds her own in conversations with characters older than herself. Indeed, the whole notion of trust in adults as possessors of wisdom and skill is undermined in this book. After all, the Wizard, however lovable, is also deceitful to the core.

Baum's book seems likewise to be rooted in the dominant view of self. Dorothy is a strong character who knows what she wants. She employs a language of practicality quite in keeping with the Populist era in which Baum wrote. Indeed, Baum as narrator often undercuts the lofty rhetoric and formulaic language of the traditional fairy tale with shockingly down-to-earth passages. When the Scarecrow meets Oz for the first time, the latter appears as a beautiful lady who tells the stuffed man he must kill the Wicked Witch: " 'I thought you asked Dorothy to kill the Witch,' said the Scarecrow, in surprise. 'So I did. I don't care who kills her' " is the lady's rather inelegant reply. But this mundane approach, which seems to comport so well with the American notion of individualism, is itself undermined by the book's suspension of common-sense reality; here scarecrows and tin men speak, monkeys fly, and witches have supernatural powers. Ultimately it is fantasy, not practicality or even self-reliance, that gets Dorothy back to Kansas, although they help.

Finally, home is fundamental and celebrated. Home is a place, Kansas, as well as a set of people, and Dorothy's home is the moral center, to which she must return after her adventures. As in so many children's books, environment takes on moral character—the tended fields of the Munchkins and Quadlings, the inhospitable land of the Winkies under the Witch's power. Yet the equation of beauty with morality is unstable; the Emerald City is only apparently green, the field of poppies brings eternal sleep, and even Kansas is relentlessly gray.

I have offered by no means a complete list of classical works, works that illustrate and advance the cultural dialogue. Nor would I necessarily adhere to my choices over others. I would insist, however, on the validity of the approach that links American children's writing to the culture in which it is embedded. Simply focusing on the author's background or intentions, while useful in literary biography, is insufficient for criticism. Claims for intrinsic merit risk the tides of fashion, while reading texts simply as historical documents makes them equivalent to the *Congressional Record*. Identifying the deep discourses that run beneath the works and demonstrating the ways texts can fuse these themes help us link children's literature to the cultural project of American society.

Colorado State University

Works Cited

Aaron, Chester. *An American Ghost*. New York: Harcourt, 1973.

Abbott, Jacob. *Franconia Stories*. 10 vols. New York: Harper, 1850–81.

Alcott, Louisa May. *Little Women*. Boston: Roberts, 1868.

Aldrich, Thomas Bailey. *Story of a Bad Boy*. Boston: Houghton, 1869.

Baum, L. Frank. *The Wonderful Wizard of Oz*. New York: Bantam, 1900.

Bercovitch, Sacvan. "America as Canon and Context: Literary History in a Time of Descensus." *American Literature* 58 (1986): 99–108.

Bercovitch, Sacvan, and Myra Jehlen, eds. *Ideology and Classic American Literature*. Cambridge: Cambridge, 1986.

Berry, Wendell. *The Unsettling of America*. New York: Avon, 1977.

Cameron, Eleanor. *The Court of the Stone Children*. New York: Dutton, 1973.

———. *A Room Made of Windows*. Boston: Little, 1971.

Coatsworth, Elizabeth. *Marra's World*. New York: Greenwillow, 1975.

Cobb, Edith. "The Ecology of Imagination in Childhood." *Daedalus* 8 (1959): 537–48.

Cormier, Robert. *The Chocolate War*. New York: Pantheon, 1974.

Estes, Eleanor. *The Moffatts*. New York: Harcourt, 1941.

Fisher, Dorothy Canfield. *Understood Betsy*. New York: Holt, 1917.

Fitzhugh, Louise. *Harriet the Spy*. New York: Harper, 1964.

Hale, Lucretia. *The Peterkin Papers*. Boston: Osgood, 1880.

Hamilton, Virginia. *M. C. Higgins the Great*. New York: MacMillan, 1974.

———. *Sweet Whispers, Brother Rush*. New York: Philomel, 1982.

Hawthorne, Nathaniel. *A Wonder Book*. Boston: Ticknor, 1852.

Hunt, Irene. *Across Five Aprils*. Chicago: Follett, 1964.

———. *Up a Road Slowly*. Chicago: Follett, 1966.

Jordan, June. *His Own Where—*. New York: Crowell, 1971.

Kazin, Alfred. "The Scholar Cornered: A Procession of Children." *American Scholar* 33 (1964): 171–83.

Konigsburg, Elaine. *From the Mixed-up Files of Mrs. Basil E. Frankweiler*. New York: Atheneum, 1967.

Lewis, R. W. B. *The American Adam*. Chicago: U of Chicago P, 1955.

Lifton, Robert Jay. *Boundaries: Psychological Man in Revolution*. New York: Vintage–Random, 1967.

O'Brien, Robert C. *Mrs. Frisby and the Rats of NIMH*. New York: Atheneum, 1971.

O'Dell, Scott. *Island of the Blue Dolphins*. Boston: Houghton, 1960.

———— . *Sing down the Moon*. Boston: Houghton, 1970.

Paterson, Katherine. *Bridge to Terebithia*. New York: Thomas Crowell, 1977.

———— . *Jacob Have I Loved*. New York: Crowell, 1980.

Porter, Gene Stratton. *A Girl of the Limberlost*. New York: Doubleday, 1904.

Scudder, Horace. *The Bodley Family*. 6 vols. Boston: Houghton, 1878–84.

Steig, William. *Amos and Boris*. New York: Farrar, 1971.

Tracy, David. *The Analogical Imagination*. New York: Crossroad, 1981.

Twain, Mark. *The Adventures of Huckleberry Finn*. New York: Webster, 1885.

———— . *The Adventures of Tom Sawyer*. Hartford: American, 1876.

Voigt, Cynthia. *Dicey's Song*. New York: Atheneum, 1983.

White, E. B. *Charlotte's Web*. New York: Harper, 1952.

Wilder, Laura Ingalls. *Little House Books*. 9 vols. New York: Harper, 1932–64.

Williams, Raymond. *The Long Revolution*. Harmondsworth, Eng.: Penguin, 1965.

Zindel, Paul. *Pigman*. New York: Harper, 1968.

Native American Narratives and the Children's Literature Curriculum

Jon C. Stott

Although the current interest in multiculturalism has done much to overcome the European ethnocentrism that has long dominated most children's literature in English, much remains to be done. Stereotypes are now being rigorously avoided, and narratives are generally accurate factually. However, most of the picture books, folktale adaptations, and novels are still being written by members of the majority culture, who, despite the good intentions of the authors, are essentially outsiders. As such, they cannot reproduce fully the aesthetic and cultural foundations of the stories and the ways characters would respond intellectually, spiritually, and emotionally to their worlds. This is particularly true of stories written about Native American peoples, whose traditional worldviews (many of which are still current) differ widely from those of the Western world.

Instructors of university-level introductory courses in children's literature seldom have the time, experience, or resources to assess the accuracy of available texts relating to traditional life. Nor are they usually able to find stories written by native authors. The most practical solution for instructors is to examine those works they have access to, using the following guidelines. Stories by nonnative writers should first be considered as they reflect the attitudes the authors hold toward the cultures from which the stories derive and the prevailing attitudes toward native peoples during the time of the writing. In this way, students will come to recognize when ethnocentrism, with its danger of stereotyping, is present. Some works will be found to be more accurate in their presentations than others. The more accurate ones should then be examined carefully so that readers become aware of how authors and artists communicate, in words and pictures, the cultural elements in the narratives. Instructors should avoid two extremes: totally integrating native materials with treatment of European narratives, and treating them as completely foreign stories. The former approach fosters the notion that all people are the same or, as Joseph Campbell has written, that there is only one basic hero and that, beneath the surface, there "will always be the one, shape-shifting yet marvelously constant story" (1). Such an attitude was ultimately responsible for the assimilation movements of the nineteenth century, which assumed that native peoples could be happy (and safe) only when they had lost all cultural distinctiveness, all sense of their heritage, and been made as much like Europeans as possible. However, to emphasize only the differences is to make historical and contemporary Indians into curios or alien beings. In the history of race relations, such approaches have often bred fear or contempt and encouraged attempts at extermination. Native narratives are stories, and, as such, they share characteristics of theme and technique with stories around the world. But the native worldview and aesthetic were and are different, and the difference must be accepted and understood if readers are to appreciate the native stories they encounter. Campbell may be right when he says that, finally, there is only one hero but that figure wears a thousand faces, and we must respect the face the hero wears in a specific culture. As Weston La Barre wrote in *The Peyote Cult,* "to know only one's own tribe is to be a primitive, and to know only one's own generation is mentally to remain always a child" (xi).

Stereotypes are fairly easy to spot; mistakes about cultural elements of native life are not. We would quickly reject the superior tone used by Christie Harris in her popular collection of West Coast tales, *Once upon a Totem*: "In the long ago days, ignorance and imagination added even more terrors. . . . Lacking science, the aborigines found fanciful reasons for the mysteries of nature" (59). We might also reject the condescension of Charles Gillham's statements, in *Beyond the Clapping Mountains*, that "long before the whitemen came to Alaska, the Eskimo people had strange ideas about birds and animals. They thought that they were all people and merely dressed to look like the animals whose clothes they wore" (17). It is not difficult to see that both the statements are based on views that European religion and science were correct and that native ones were products of unenlightened minds. In addition, however, Gillham's assertion is erroneous, for what the Eskimos believed was that all living creatures possessed an *inua*, or soul, and that powerful spirit beings could assume human or animal shapes at will. Readers of children's books must understand that statements such as these suggest that the authors are not in full sympathy with the cultures whose traditional stories they are adapting.

Two recent picture books indicate that factual errors continue to appear in children's books. Marcus Crouch's *Rainbow Warrior's Bride* is a fairly accurate adaptation of a well-known Micmac-Malacite tale from the East Coast. However, in one of William Stobbs's accompanying illustrations, a man stands by the sea wearing a West Coast blanket, while behind him is a West Coast totem pole and a Great Plains tipi. In a newly illustrated version of Longfellow's *Hiawatha*, with pictures by Chris Molan, the youthful hero stares pensively into the distance as three dancers wearing false face (or medicine) masks stand behind him.

However authentic the Hiawatha story itself may (or may not) be, it is based on Ojibwa legends from northern Ontario, Michigan, and Minnesota; the false face masks were worn by the Iroquois people of southern Ontario and upstate New York. Finally, in *Song of Sedna*, a recent retelling of an Inuit legend known across the Canadian Arctic and into Greenland, artist Daniel San Souci, brother of author Robert D. San Souci, shows the tall and willowy heroine standing near some very large evergreen trees and a West Coast totem pole. Later, a supernatural being rides a serpent that resembles an Asian dragon and bears rattlesnake markings on its scales. By not worrying about cultural accuracy, such illustrators reinforce the stereotype that all native peoples were the same. They fail to understand the cultural specificity of each story and, therefore, fail to convey the important fact that each story was a very significant outgrowth of a distinct native group and environment.

Two picture books that do accurately reflect traditional cultures are Gerald McDermott's *Arrow to the Sun* and Paul Goble's *Girl Who Loved Wild Horses*, both Caldecott Medal winners. The former is based on the Pueblo tale of the rejected boy who goes on a long journey in search of his divine father, the Sun. The latter deals with a Sioux girl who feels a strong affinity with horses and, at the conclusion of the tale, becomes a horse and the mate of the leader of the wild horses. While both author-illustrators have adapted their traditional materials, each has used his illustrations to keep the story close to the original cultural meanings.

McDermott not only combines traditional Pueblo design and color patterns with his own graphic style, he specifically uses aspects of Pueblo iconography to communicate the story's symbolic significance. Thus the four trials the boy faces in the kivas must be understood if readers are to see his triumphant return as an important cultural event. He has shown himself worthy of bringing the life-giving rain to his people. In the tests, he has brought peace by taming the mountain lions (traditional symbols of the war), he has demonstrated his reverence to the rattlesnakes (used in the sacred rain ceremonies), and he has created conditions favorable to pollination by forming the bees into a functioning hive. Now he is capable of receiving his father's power, given him by the supernatural lightning.

In presenting the movement toward integration in *The Girl Who Loved Wild Horses*, Goble draws on the widespread native belief in the interrelatedness of all living things, a belief expressed in the Sioux phrase *mitakuye oyasin* 'we are all related.' The marriage that concludes the narrative symbolizes this theme, as do many of the illustrations. A brief discussion of two of these will explain the point. For the traditional Plains people, the circle symbolized the unity of existence. The first illustration, found on the half-title page, contains a famous representation of the circle, the radiating sun. Contained within the outer rim is the neck of the male horse; however, the girl is not part of the circle. At the story's opening, human beings and animals, symbolized by the two figures, have not achieved unity. At the conclusion of the story, with the girl's transformation into a mare and her mating with the stallion, harmony has been achieved. Both her neck and her mate's now form part of the circle.

Good illustrated adaptations of traditional tales can be used in two ways in children's literature courses: To reinforce the point generally made in analyzing picture books—that both words and illustrations must be studied to grasp the full meaning of the narrative—and to help students understand the ways in which native narratives reflect the cultures that created them. These two picture books can be directly related to other works often studied, so their similarities to and differences from books in the European tradition can be better perceived. The search for the father in *Arrow to the Sun* is similiar to that traced in Lloyd Alexander's *Taran Wanderer*. Both follow the type of narrative structure outlined by Campbell in *The Hero with a Thousand Faces*. *The Girl Who Loved Wild Horses* can be contrasted to ''Beauty and the Beast'' (Lang) and ''East o' the Sun and West o' the Moon'' (Dasent). In those European tales, transformation into bestial or animal form is seen as a curse, a thwarting of the characters' drive to fulfillment in marriage, whereas in Goble's book, the reverse is true. Because animals are not viewed as inferior beings, the girl's transformation is a positive first step toward her marriage.

Traditional myths, legends, and folktales provide an excellent introduction to the cultural diversity of native peoples. We should first recognize that, whether or not they are accurate, all written versions are, in a sense, artificial. Unlike European folktales, which have been published as fairy tales for children for at least two centuries, the dominant form of the native tale was, and often still is, oral. Its telling was a public performance, and the occasion gathered the people together not only physically but also psychologically. Telling and listening to stories was a communal act. Many of the narratives were sacred, explaining the mysteries of creation and the reasons for the world's present characteristics; several were designed to teach appropriate social values; others celebrated great events from fairly recent history; and some merely provided entertainment, often humorous.

Versions of traditional tales adapted and published for children are generally two or three steps removed from the native originals as they may have been performed orally. From the original language, they may have been translated either by an interpreter or the recorder; translations have probably been edited, even if only slightly, into prose form; finally, the printed forms have served as the basis for the children's versions. Of course, European folktales adapted for children are often several steps removed from the oral traditions, and there are many inferior and bowdlerized versions of them. However, these adaptations generally remain within the European tradition of their origin and reflect the values (changing though they may be) of that tradition.

Often native tales are retold for children in ways that make them as much like European fairy tales as possible. An example is Charles Godfrey Leland's frequently anthologized late-nineteenth-century adaptation of the East Coast story "How Glooskap Found the Summer," which begins:

> In the long ago time before the white men came to live in the New World, and when people lived always in the early red morning before sunrise, a mighty race of Indians lived in the northeastern part of the New World. Nearest the sunrise were they, and they called themselves Wawaniki— Children of the Light. Glooskap was their lord and master. He was ever kind to his people, and did many great works for them. (523)

These opening lines create a tone that influences the reading of the story. "In the long ago time" sounds not unlike the "Once upon a time" opening of European tales. (Later there are references to fairies!) The phrases "white men," "New World," and "the northeastern part" set the narrative in a geographical perspective determined by a European point of view. Glooskap's being called "lord and master" gives him a role like that of a medieval feudal lord.

Native legends and myths are also frequently expanded and reshaped so that they acquire the length and characterization of short stories. Inner conflicts and motivations are delineated in a way simply not found in traditional tales. Harris, in her collection *Mouse Woman and the Vanished Princesses*, uses such an approach. Finally, they are often bowdlerized. Coyote, the best-known of the native tricksters, had an enormous ego and libido. Always wandering along, he occasionally did good deeds but more often performed acts designed to fulfill his selfish desires. Violence and sexual events that often formed integral parts of the original Coyote stories and other tales are either changed or omitted in children's versions.

It is important that students comprehend the distance that frequently separates the versions of native tales they read from the oral originals. Such awareness will alert them to the ways in which nonnative points of view have influenced the ways native peoples are regarded. It will also make them realize that any literary analysis they do should be considered more for how it illuminates the written version of a story than for what it may (or may not) tell about the originating culture. It is probably best to introduce traditional materials in reputable editions not specifically published for children. Alice Marriott and Carol K. Rachlin's *American Indian Mythology*, available in an inexpensive paperback edition, is useful for this purpose. The editors, both respected anthropologists, collected the majority of the tales directly from native informants. Grouping the stories under the headings "The World beyond Ours," "The World around Us," "The World We Live in Now," and "The World We Go To," they provide a representative sampling from a wide variety of cultures and, in their headnotes, place individual stories within specific cultural contexts. Reading a number of selections, students will see the different types of stories and realize the diversity of outlooks of different cultural groups. They can compare tale types and motifs of native literature with those of the European folktales most widely presented to children, and they can consider why nonnative cultures might avoid retelling certain native tales for children and might drastically alter others.[1]

In presenting novels dealing with native peoples, instructors should notice a basic paradox. Traditional literatures were essentially communal. Tricksters, legendary heroes, and historical personages were important as they reflected cultural values rather than as individuals. Novels, on the other hand, deal with individual personalities. Thus we should be aware that, no matter how factually accurate an author may be in the treatment of physical and cultural traits of the characters, in dealing with the inner lives of specific characters and in methods of presentation, the writer of a children's novel about native peoples may be more influenced than he or she realizes by the attitudes and conventions of Western literature. This point may be demonstrated by comparing two novels by nonnative writers with two native writers.

Scott O'Dell's *Island of the Blue Dolphins* is the account of a California native girl's eighteen years of isolation on an offshore island. In *Julie of the Wolves*, Jean Craighead George describes a modern Alaskan Eskimo girl surviving an arctic winter with the aid of a pack of wolves. Both are based on extensive research into the cultural and geographical aspects; however, in structure and presentation of the main characters, both use conventions of the Western novel. As survival novels, they follow the pattern of separation, survival, rescue, and reunion. The greater part of each focuses on the physical and psychological endurance of the central character. "How to do it" chapters detail the ways the isolated individual remembers and utilizes the techniques of her culture to obtain physical necessities. Chapters centering on the inner life often reveal the character recalling the spiritual elements of the social group and understanding their value.

Inherent in the conventions of the survival novel as they are used in these two books are adventure and psychological analysis. In life-threatening situations, the central characters must display considerable physical ability and inner courage. However, by the very nature of their situations, they are unique. They face inner and outer pressures not normally encountered by members of the culture. Thus, unlike traditional native narratives, the characters are not representative. As the central figures in their novels, they are the subject of detailed study and their inner conflicts are fully presented. Filled with hatred of the Aleuts, who killed her father and brother, Karena, in *Island of the Blue Dolphins*, must learn to overcome her intense loathing. Julie, who is fleeing to San Francisco in George's novel, comes to understand the value of the old ways, which she had originally scorned.

In addition to conventions of the survival novel, George includes in *Julie of the Wolves* elements of pastoralism. The contrasts between a sullied, artificial, complex urban world representing progress, greed, anxiety, and ambition, and a rural world that is natural, pure, and calm, are reflected in that between San Francisco, Barrow, and Kangik, on the one hand, and the seal camp and the tundra, on the other. In the end, the heroine discovers that she cannot recover the ideal world and must return to her father, who has capitulated to the values of civilization. George also incorporates aspects of the problem novel, a genre widely used in young adult fiction of the past two decades. Julie's difficulties are increased by government intervention, which disrupts her happy life by sending her to school and by attempting to send her father to Vietnam; by her uncle's alcoholism; by peer pressures to accept the modern ways; and by the failure of her father to maintain his cultural integrity.

Neither O'Dell nor George would claim to be presenting insiders' narratives; they are knowledgeable and sympathetic outsiders. Two authors who do write from the inside are Markoosie, an Inuit from arctic Canada, the author of *Harpoon of the Hunter*, and Jamake Highwater, the author of *Anpao: An American Indian Odyssey*, who until recently claimed to be of Blackfoot-Cherokee heritage. In both these works we see a mixture of novelistic techniques and conventions of traditional narratives. *Harpoon of the Hunter* is a naturalistic survival story in which Kamik, a young Inuit, travels with several other villagers in pursuit of a rabid polar bear. Although the other members of the party are all killed, he survives and is rescued. However, when several members of his family and his new wife drown crossing broken river ice, he commits suicide, running himself onto his harpoon. *Anpao* is a highly symbolic, almost surrealistic account of a young man's journey to the Sun. If the Sun, who is his father, will remove the scar the youth wears on his face, he may return to earth to marry. However, when Anpao returns to his village, he finds that the arrival of the white man signals destruction to his people. With his bride and a faithful few, he travels beneath the waters of a nearby lake, where life everlasting can be found.

Both *Harpoon* and *Anpao* portray heroes who are representative rather than individualized, and both are based on earlier legendary material. In *Harpoon*, Markoosie makes use of simple cinematographic techniques, switching abruptly between scenes of the solitary hunter and the advancing rescuers. He also adds to traditional survival stories a modern romantic interest, although Kamik and his bride sometimes speak like teenagers in a B-grade 1960s teen movie. *Anpao* is far more complex. The story, which begins in medias res, is narrated by Wasicong, a holy man who changes from human to owl shape. Within the narrative there are several surrealistic dream scenes and a number of grotesque symbolic characters. Highwater, drawing an analogy to techniques of contemporary native painting, has stated that he blends traditional narratives into a unified whole by using the resources of modern fiction and cinematography to create a pan-Indian epic embodying the essence of all native character and history (Stott).

Both works are highly ironic. Unlike the traditional survival story, *Harpoon of the Hunter* does not conclude with the reunion scene. After the joy of the reunion, disaster and death strike. However, subtle foreshadowing throughout the narrative indicates that the outcome is inevitable—an indication of Inuit fatalism. And although it apparently concludes with the hero leading his people to safety, *Anpao* can be read as a testament of failure. Throughout the novel, Anpao has revealed his inability to take advice or learn from mistakes and his failure to confront, decisively, threatening forces. His submarine retreat may well be an example of withdrawal based on misunderstanding of the right course of action (Stott).

These four novels may be effectively taught in children's literature courses in several ways. They reflect a range of native experiences, mythical, historical, and contemporary, as depicted by both native and nonnative writers. It is illuminating to see to what extent the four authors incorporate traditional and novelistic techniques. In the treatment of character development and relationships, the works can be read in conjunction with other children's novels on similar topics. *Island of the Blue Dolphins* can be studied alongside Armstrong Sperry's *Call It Courage*. The relationships between father and daughter in *Julie of the Wolves* and Madeleine L'Engle's *A Wrinkle in Time* are both similar and different. Anpao's journey can be compared with Taran's in Alexander's story or with Alice's experiences in Carroll's *Alice's Adventures in Wonderland*, and his role as culture hero with those played by such Western heroes as Robin Hood, King Arthur, Beowulf, and Paul Bunyan. And the treatment of death in *Harpoon of the Hunter* is markedly different from that in most children's novels.

The central theme of this essay is awareness. Students of children's literature have the opportunity to discover the cultural realities of an important element of North American life. Through the study of picture books, folktales, and novels, they can achieve such understanding. In addition, they should recognize the ways in which published versions of traditional stories and novels can alter or even distort these realities. Finally, they can examine how these narratives relate to those they are most familiar with, both in their similarities and differences. Only by developing a multicultural framework will they be able to help children understand the rich diversity of the world they read about and in which they live.

University of Alberta

Note

[1] Fortunately, more native writers are now retelling the traditional stories of their peoples. While most often written for native children, these stories are certainly accessible to other children. Unfortunately, they are often distributed by small regional presses. Four particularly readable collections are *Arikara Coyote Tales. A Bilingual Reader*, edited by Douglas R. Parks; *Iroquois Stories: Heroes and Heroines, Monsters and Magic*, by Joseph Bruchac; *Tales the Elders Told: Ojibway Legends*, by Basil Johnston; and *Tonweya and the Eagles and Other Lakota Indian Tales*, by Rosebud Yellow Rose. Intended primarily for schoolteachers and librarians, *Books without Bias: Through Indian Eyes*, edited by Beverly Slapin and Doris Seale, contains articles by native writers and readers, bibliographies of books by native authors, and a directory of Native American publishers.

Works Cited

Alexander, Lloyd. *Taran Wanderer*. New York: Holt, 1967.

Bruchac, Joseph. *Iroquois Stories: Heroes and Heroines, Monsters and Magic*. Illus. David J. Ripley. Trumansburg: Crossing, 1985.

Campbell, Joseph. *The Hero with a Thousand Faces*. Princeton: Princeton, 1949.

Carroll, Lewis. *Alice's Adventures in Wonderland*. London: Macmillan, 1865.

Crouch, Marcus. *Rainbow Warrior's Bride*. Illus. William Stobbs. London: Pelham, 1981.

Dasent, George Webbe. "East o' the Sun and West o' the Moon." *East o' the Sun and West o' the Moon*. Edinburgh: Douglas, 1888.

George, Jean Craighead. *Julie of the Wolves*. New York: Harper, 1972.

Gillham, Charles. *Beyond the Clapping Mountains*. New York: Macmillan, 1943.

Goble, Paul. *The Girl Who Loved Wild Horses*. Scarsdale: Bradbury, 1978.

Harris, Christie. *Mouse Woman and the Vanished Princesses*. Toronto: McClelland, 1976.

——— . *Once upon a Totem*. Toronto: McClelland, 1963.

Highwater, Jamake. *Anpao: An American Indian Odyssey*. Philadelphia: Lippincott, 1977.

Johnston, Basil. *Tales the Elders Told: Ojibway Legends*. Illus. Shirley Cheechoo. Toronto: Royal Ontario Museum, 1981.

La Barre, Weston. *The Peyote Cult*. New York: Schocken, 1969.

Lang, Andrew. "Beauty and the Beast." *The Blue Fairy Book*. London: Longmans, 1889.

Leland, Charles Godfrey. "How Glooskap Found the Summer." *The Riverside Anthology of Children's Literature*. Ed. Judith Saltman. Boston: Houghton, 1985.

L'Engle, Madeleine. *A Wrinkle in Time*. New York: Farrar, 1962.

Longfellow, Henry Wadsworth. *Hiawatha*. Illus. Chris Molan. London: Methuen, 1984.

Markoosie. *Harpoon of the Hunter*. Montreal: McGill–Queens, 1970.

Marriott, Alice, and Carol K. Rachlin. *American Indian Mythology*. New York: Harper, 1968.

McDermott, Gerald. *Arrow to the Sun*. New York: Viking, 1974.

O'Dell, Scott. *Island of the Blue Dolphins*. Boston: Houghton, 1960.

Parks, Douglas R. *Arikara Coyote Tales: a Bilingual Reader*. Illus. David J. Ripley. Roseglen: White Shield School District 89, 1984.

San Souci, Robert D. *Song of Sedna*. Illus. Daniel San Souci. Garden City: Doubleday, 1980.

Slapin, Beverly, and Doris Seale, eds. *Books without Bias: Through Indian Eyes*. Berkeley: Oyate, 1988.

Sperry, Armstrong. *Call It Courage*. Philadelphia: Winston, 1940.

Stott, Jon C. "Narrative Expectations and Textual Misreadings: Jamake Highwater's *Anpao* Analyzed and Reanalyzed." *Studies in the Literary Imagination* 16 (Fall 1985): 93–106.

Yellow Rose, Rosebud. *Tonyweya and the Eagles and Other Lakota Indian Tales*. Illus. Jerry Pinkney. New York: Dial, 1979.

Teaching Banned Children's Books

Mark I. West

History of Censorship Cases

Censorship is generally equated with the banning of books from libraries, but this is only one form of censorship. Restrictions are often imposed on books long before they ever reach library shelves. Such restrictions have strongly influenced the history of children's literature. As early as the late seventeenth century, distinctions were drawn between subjects that could be dealt with in children's books and those that could be addressed only in books for adults. In 1693, for example, the English philosopher John Locke argued that ghosts and goblins should not appear in stories for children (MacDonald 105). Once the idea of childhood innocence took root, restrictions of this sort greatly increased.

To ensure that children's books conformed to the idea of childhood innocence, publishers sometimes engaged in blatant censorship. Many nineteenth-century publishers, for example, decided that some of the bawdy passages from Jonathan Swift's *Gulliver's Travels* were inappropriate for children and excised them from juvenile editions of the book. The most frequently censored passage, according to a survey conducted by Sarah Smedman, was the one in which Gulliver extinguishes a fire in the Lilliputians' palace by urinating on it. This incident was deleted or rewritten in nearly every children's edition published during the second half of the nineteenth century (84–85).

For the most part, however, nineteenth-century publishers had no need to engage in such overt forms of censorship. Children's authors generally censored their own books; they were well aware of the taboos and automatically observed them. This tradition of self-censorship continued well into the twentieth century. Until quite recently, children's authors simply assumed that they could not refer to sexuality, graphically describe violent acts, portray adults in a negative light, use curse words, or address controversial social problems. If, for some reason, they deliberately or unwittingly violated one of these taboos, their editors would strongly recommend that they revise the offending passage. Once in a while, of course, books intended for young readers were published that did break taboos, and some of these became the focus of censorship attempts. For example, Mark Twain's *Adventures of Tom Sawyer* was banned from many public libraries during the 1870s and 1880s largely because the child characters are seldom punished for misbehaving (Jordan 34–35). In the 1950s and 1960s, J. D. Salinger's *Catcher in the Rye* attracted the attention of censors who disapproved of its profanity (Nelson and Roberts 182–83). Still, most children's books published before the 1960s sparked little controversy.

The only children's authors who systematically violated taboos before the 1960s were writers for publications that children generally purchased on their own, such as dime novels, series books, and comic books. Since they were more concerned with meeting the demands of children than with winning approval of parents, they tended to write about subjects that children found interesting even if the result was the breaking of certain taboos. For instance, the creators of both dime novels and comic books frequently portrayed violence, while series books tended to ignore accepted norms concerning adult-child relationships. In many series books, children were described as being equal or even superior to adult characters. Because these forms of popular culture broke so many taboos, they often came under attack by self-appointed censors.

Anthony Comstock (1844–1915) had led the campaign against dime novels. As head of the New York Society for the Suppression of Vice, he frequently called for the banning of all these works, especially those that dealt with violent crimes. Such stories, he argued in *Traps for the Young* (1883), were a primary cause of juvenile delinquency. When children started to buy more series books than dime novels, librarians mounted their own censorship campaign, which began in the 1880s and continued until the 1920s. In addition to attacking series books in their professional journals, they published lengthy lists of books that were "not to be circulated" in respectable libraries (West, *Children* 20–30). The movement to ban comic books was led by Fredric Wertham, a prominent New York psychiatrist. In his book *Seduction of the Innocent* (1954), Wertham argued that comic book reading could lead otherwise normal children to become criminals, sadists, or homosexuals. He lobbied for the enactment of anti–comic book laws and nearly succeeded in getting such legislation passed in New York State.

For the most part, the campaigns against dime novels, series books, and comic books focused on genres rather than on particular titles or authors. It was not until the 1970s that censors began waging major battles against individual children's books.

Modern Censored Books

The tradition of self-censorship continued to exert a strong influence on children's literature until the late 1960s. However, the social changes that occurred during that decade gradually helped break down the practice. As Americans became more accepting of sexuality and less confident in the infallibility of authority figures, a number of authors and editors questioned the legitimacy of the taboos that had encumbered children's literature for so many years. As a result, the early 1970s saw the emergence of a new breed of children's books. The works of Judy Blume, Norma Klein, and Maurice Sendak dealt with the issue of sexuality, while other authors, such as Louise Fitzhugh, Paul Zindel, and Robert Cormier, depicted adult characters unflatteringly. At the same time, S. E. Hinton, Alice Childress, Isabelle Holland, and several others wrote about controversial social issues, such as gang violence, drug abuse, and homosexuality. Scholars and critics began referring to these types of books as the new realism in children's literature.

While several works of new realism raised eyebrows when they first appeared, few were censored during the first half of the 1970s. This situation started to change as the Moral Majority and other conservative religious and political groups gained power and influence. As the leaders of these organizations urged their followers to speak out against sex education, the teaching of evolution, and "sinful" children's books, the new realism in children's literature came under serious attack. Parents demanded that numerous children's books be banned from libraries and not be taught in public schools. This trend accelerated dramatically in the early 1980s, and it shows no signs of abating.

The most frequently censored children's author is Judy Blume. The censors have focused their attacks on five of her books: *Are You There, God? It's Me, Margaret; Then Again, Maybe I Won't; Deenie; Blubber;* and *Forever.* During the first half of the 1980s, over sixty attempts to ban these works were reported to the *Newsletter on Intellectual Freedom,* and it is estimated that many more went unreported. With the exception of *Blubber,* the censorship of Blume's books is the result of their sexual content. The censors dislike *Are You There, God?* because it discusses menstruation and breast development. *Then Again, Maybe I Won't* and *Deenie* are vilified for mentioning wet dreams and masturbation, and *Forever* gets in trouble because it deals with sexual intercourse and describes the use of birth control devices.

Norma Klein, the second most frequently censored children's author, also comes under fire for including sexually related material in her books. Klein's first children's book, *Mom, the Wolf Man, and Me,* is sometimes censored because it contains a single mother who remains sexually active. A number of her other books are targeted for similar reasons. Critics attack *It's Not What You Expect* for including a character who has an abortion, *Naomi in the Middle* for explaining how conception occurs, and *It's Okay If You Don't Love Me* for portraying a teenage girl who initiates a sexual relationship.

Blume's and Klein's stories are certainly not the only children's books that have been declared taboo. Maurice Sendak's *In the Night*

Kitchen is often censored because it contains pictures of a nude boy. *My Darling, My Hamburger* and *The Pigman*, by Paul Zindel, are sometimes attacked by people who dislike Zindel's disparaging comments about parents and teachers. Robert Cormier's *Chocolate War* and *I Am the Cheese* come under pressure from those who feel that they undermine parental, institutional, and governmental authority. Another book that is frequently censored is *A Hero Ain't Nothin' but a Sandwich*, by Alice Childress. Censors do not approve of this book's discussion of drug abuse or its use of street language. While these titles are favorite targets, a complete list of censored children's books would run on for pages.

In addition to attacking individual books, contemporary Comstocks frequently condemn textbooks. This practice has attracted attention in recent years in part because of three prominent court cases involving disputes over the use of textbooks in the public schools. The first case surfaced in Louisiana, where, in 1981, religious fundamentalists pushed through a state law requiring public school science courses in which evolution is taught to use textbooks that discuss creationism. In June 1987, however, the Supreme Court struck down the law on the grounds that it introduced religious dogma into the public school curriculum. The second case originated in eastern Tennessee, where fundamentalists argued against the use of a standard set of reading textbooks that they deemed "anti-Christian." In August 1987, the United States Circuit Court of Appeals for the Sixth District ruled that the school board had not infringed on the religious freedom of these parents by requiring the use of the textbooks. The third case took place in Alabama, where several hundred fundamentalists argued that dozens of commonly used textbooks should be banned for promoting the "religion" of "secular humanism." In August 1987, a few days after the Tennessee decision, the Circuit Court of Appeals for the Eleventh District declared that secular humanism is not a religion and that therefore the textbooks could not be banned. Although the outcome of these cases has weakened the current censorship movement, there is no indication that it is coming to an end.

Treating Censored Books in the Classroom

Because censorship has become such a serious problem in children's literature, a number of teachers of children's literature are now including discussions of censorship in their classes. Such discussions, however, are most helpful when students read some of the targeted books. While it would be impossible to acquaint students with every controversial children's book, it is certainly feasible to have them read a few of Blume's or Klein's censored works. Without firsthand knowledge of at least a few censored titles, students may find it difficult to make sense of the intense rhetoric that is often used by those who wish to ban these books from libraries and classrooms. Several censors, for example, have proclaimed that *Deenie* is a how-to manual about masturbation when in reality the subject is mentioned on only two or three pages.

Requiring students to read a few of these books can also help them understand some of the reasons for a seldom discussed but omnipresent tension within the field of children's literature. It is not simply a coincidence that the two most controversial children's authors are also two of the most popular among children and teenagers. Throughout the history of children's literature, the books that children have selected on their own have often met with disapproval from adults. Conversely, children's books that have won praise from adults have often been ignored by children (Norby). Students of children's literature should be aware of this pattern and ask themselves why it exists.

If students research this question, they would soon find that the most common explanation is that children's literary tastes are underdeveloped. However, an examination of the controversy surrounding Blume's and Klein's books indicates that this idea is something of a ruse. In the end, it is not the books' literary qualities that trouble adults; it is their contents. Even among adults who disapprove of censorship there is a tendency to frown on the inclusion of sexuality in children's books (Rees 173–84). Most scholars specializing in children's literature, for example, do not advocate the banning of Blume's books, but few actively defend her right to discuss sexuality.

Students who probed deeper might arrive at another explanation for why adults and children tend to like different children's books. Students might discover that some grownups enjoy children's literature because it allows them to escape the complexities of adult life and relive the perceived pleasures of childhood. For these readers, children's literature has a nostalgic appeal. Many children, by contrast, are anxious to grow up and thus seek books that help explain the mysterious worlds of adolescence and adulthood. Consequently, while children often appreciate Blume's and Klein's willingness to write openly about menstruation, masturbation, and other taboo subjects, adults who want to read about childhood innocence may feel repulsed or even betrayed by the writers' frankness. In a sense, children and adults have conflicting tastes because they approach children's literature with different expectations. This is an important point for students to think about, for it might help them come to a clearer understanding of their own expectations of children's literature.

The insights that students can gain through reading controversial children's books are greatly enhanced if they also do some writing on the subject of censorship. One possible assignment is to ask students to write a personal response paper about a censored children's book. In their papers, they should address such questions as the following: Why is the book controversial? Do you think it is objectionable? Would you have been interested in reading this book as a child? Would you allow your own children to read it? Do you think the book should be banned?

In addition to describing their reactions to a book, students could be asked to include research findings in their papers. A simple project is to require students to look through a number of issues of the *Newsletter on Intellectual Freedom* and read about the censorship cases involving the book they have chosen. At the beginning of each issue of the *Newsletter* there is a guide for finding information about particular titles. Another fairly simple research project is for students to interview a local children's librarian about censorship. Many librarians have had to deal with censorship pressures, and some are quite willing to talk about their experiences. Both of these research projects provide students with concrete information they can go on to interpret in their papers.

Supplementary Readings on Censorship

Students who take a serious interest in the censorship of children's literature should be encouraged to do some outside readings on the subject. *Dealing with Censorship*, an NCTE publication edited by James E. Davis, is a good place for students to start. The fact that the book came out in 1979 makes it a bit dated, but most of the book's eighteen chapters remain stimulating and useful. *Protecting the Freedom to Learn*, by Barbara Parker and Stefanie Weiss, is another good source of information about censorship trends. It also provides material on how to prevent censorship from occurring. This book, published by People for the American Way, can be purchased only through the organization's office. The address is 1424 16th Street, NW, Suite 601, Washington, DC 20036. One other book students might find helpful is Nicholas Tucker's *Suitable for Children*. Although this book was published in 1976, many of its essays raise issues that pertain to ongoing controversies.

Numerous articles about censorship have been published in recent years. The *Newsletter on Intellectual Freedom* occasionally publishes full-length articles about censored children's books; one of these articles deals specifically with the censorship of Blume's books (Goldberger). The *Children's Literature Association Quarterly* has published a number of articles on censorship, including two excellent overviews by Amy McClure entitled "Limiting the Right to Choose" and "Intellectual Freedom and the Young Child." For a discussion of recent censorship involving books for young adults, students should turn to Ken Donelson's "Almost 13 Years of Book Protests." Students should also read about censorship from the perspective of an author whose works have been banned. A helpful source in this area is *Trust Your Children* (West). This book contains interviews with Judy Blume, Norma Klein, Robert Cormier, Betty Miles, Harry Mazer, Nat Hentoff, Roald Dahl, Daniel Keyes,

Maurice Sendak, and John Steptoe. It also includes interviews with children's book publishers and anticensorship activists.

There are two children's novels about censorship that students might find especially interesting. Nat Hentoff's *Day They Came to Arrest the Book* is aimed at teenagers. The story revolves around an attempt to ban *The Adventures of Huckleberry Finn* because it contains the word *nigger*. The major proponents of censorship in this story are a black student, this student's father, and a young feminist. Hentoff is well aware that these characters are not typical book censors, but he uses them to show that the urge to ban books is not limited to the Moral Majority crowd. Although Hentoff's plot is a bit contrived, the book provides a thoughtful introduction to the meaning of the First Amendment. *Maudie and Me and the Dirty Book,* by Betty Miles, is intended for a somewhat younger audience than Hentoff's book, but it is the stronger of the two novels. The major characters in the story, two eleven-year-old girls, begin working as aides in a first-grade class. Their job is to select picture books and read them aloud to the class. One of the girls chooses a book that deals with the birth of a puppy. After hearing the story, a first-grade boy asks how the puppy got inside the mother dog, and the girl gives him a simple but honest answer. A few parents hear about this incident and demand that the book never be used again. In addition to providing an accurate description of how censorship cases typically develop, Miles does an excellent job of capturing the children's reactions to the whole affair. She makes it clear that the children feel much more confused and threatened by the parents' near hysteria than they do by the contested book.

These various books and articles on censorship can supply students with valuable background information and help them realize what a severe problem censorship has become. If, however, students read only secondary sources, their understanding would be superficial. In the end, the best way to teach students about censorship is to have them read the banned books along with the related material. This approach prevents students from viewing censorship as an abstract problem and helps prepare them to resist future censorship efforts.

University of North Carolina, Charlotte

Works Cited

Comstock, Anthony. *Traps for the Young.* New York: Funk, 1883.

Davis, James E., ed. *Dealing with Censorship.* Urbana: NCTE, 1979.

Donelson, Ken. "Almost Thirteen Years of Book Protests . . . Now What?" *School Library Journal* Mar. 1985: 93–98.

Goldberger, Judith M. "Judy Blume: Target of the Censor." *Newsletter on Intellectual Freedom* May 1981: 57.

Hentoff, Nat. *The Day They Came to Arrest the Book.* New York: Delacorte, 1982.

Jordan, Alice M. *From Rollo to Tom Sawyer and Other Papers.* Boston: Horn, 1948.

McClure, Amy. "Intellectual Freedom and the Young Child." *Children's Literature Association Quarterly* 8.3 (1983): 41–43.

———. "Limiting the Right to Choose: Censorship of Children's Reading." *Children's Literature Association Quarterly* 7.1 (1982): 39–42.

MacDonald, Ruth K. *Literature for Children in England and America from 1646–1774.* Troy: Whitston, 1982.

Miles, Betty. *Maudie and Me and the Dirty Book.* New York: Knopf, 1980.

Nelson, Jack, and Gene Roberts, Jr. *The Censors and the Schools.* Boston: Little, 1963.

Norby, Shirley. "Kids as Book Critics." *Proceedings of the Eighth Annual Conference of the Children's Literature Association.* Ed. Priscilla A. Ord. 27 March 1981. Boston, 1982. 136–40.

Parker, Barbara, and Stefanie Weiss. *Protecting the Freedom to Learn: A Citizen's Guide.* Washington: People for the American Way, 1983.

Rees, David. *The Marble in the Water.* Boston: Horn, 1980.

Smedman, Sarah. "Like Me, Like Me Not: *Gulliver's Travels* as Children's Book." *The Genres of Gulliver's Travels.* Ed. Frederik N. Smith. Newark: U of Delaware P, 1990. 75–100.

Tucker, Nicholas, ed. *Suitable for Children: Controversies in Children's Literature.* Berkeley: U of California P, 1976.

Wertham, Fredric. *Seduction of the Innocent.* New York: Rinehart, 1954.

West, Mark I. *Children, Culture, and Controversy.* Hamden: Archon, 1988.

———. *Trust Your Children: Voices against Censorship in Children's Literature.* New York: Neal-Schuman, 1988.

CRITICAL APPROACHES

Perspectives on Children's Literature: An Overview

Susan R. Gannon

What is children's literature? How is it different from other kinds of literature? These are good questions, but there are no easy answers. As Perry Nodelman has suggested:

> Children's literature is not just literature written with children in mind, nor is it just literature that happens to be read by children. It is a genre, a special kind of literature with its own distinguishing characteristics. Identifying those characteristics and defining that genre are the major tasks immediately confronting serious critics. (*"Beyond Genre"* 81)

If children's literature is a genre, it is certainly a strange, elusive form and—like the novel—hard to define. Yet each term I ask my students to join in the task of identifying its distinguishing characteristics. As they read, they do a good deal of "thick description," that patient accumulation of data about the literature—observed, analyzed, interpreted from a variety of perspectives—that is the necessary preliminary to any attempt at definition. They begin also to read appreciatively the work of practical critics in the field and to acquire the rudiments of a critical vocabulary in which what children's literature "has to say about itself" might be expressed (Geertz 27).

By the end of the semester, however, my students come to realize that to "uncover the conceptual structures that inform" the texts they have studied and to "construct a system of analysis in whose terms what is generic to those structures . . . will stand out" is likely to be the work of a lifetime, not a college term (27). Nevertheless, during their semester course they will have begun to construct their own working poetics of children's literature, a pluralistic, tentative "system of analysis" infinitely revisable in the light of experience and not likely to produce pat answers to difficult questions. What follows are simply some suggestions about the sort of critical reading that can help college students begin to identify the distinguishing characteristics of children's literature, to acquire an appropriate critical vocabulary, and to think seriously about the literature, by asking useful questions from a variety of perspectives. The individual works cited here are not necessarily the best readings available but have been chosen because they illustrate the possibilities of certain lines of inquiry.

The critical approaches described here involve a careful look at the text itself to clarify its structural properties, to set it in a variety of contexts, to note how the demands of an audience can shape it, and to consider the way authorial motivation has affected its production. Therefore, I will discuss the approaches under four headings: "The Text," "The Context," "The Audience," and "The Author." A fifth section, "Classroom Practice," comments on the way critical theory can be translated into practical activity in the undergraduate classroom.

The Text

Mansucript study, generic inquiry, close reading, and various kinds of structural analysis raise questions about form and meaning in children's literature that should be central to the college course. Manuscripts of many children's books are available for study by critics and have great value for those who would define the literature. The recent work done on E. B. White's *Charlotte's Web* by Peter Neumeyer and by Perry Nodelman is a good case in point. Neumeyer's close study of White's heavily revised manuscript clarifies the crucial choices White made while shaping his book. The final text of *Charlotte's Web*, it seems, was achieved only through considerable effort, including twelve different attempts at openings for the story. Picking up the clues provided by Neumeyer's analysis of the manuscript, Nodelman inquired into the function of those troublesome first chapters in his study "Text as Teacher." He suggests that the first two chapters of White's book prepare young readers "for the complexities that follow by presenting a simpler, more easily identified with, more wish-fulfilling version of the same story." Drawing on Neumeyer's manuscript study as well as on the work of cognitive psychologists like Piaget and reader-oriented critics like Wolfgang Iser, Stanley Fish, and Louise Rosenblatt, Nodelman identifies the double function of those first two chapters: they not only "satisfy the narrative competence of naive readers" but "they act as a cognitive map, a pattern to be changed and enriched by what follows" (125). *Charlotte's Web* is a surprisingly complex story, demanding some fairly sophisticated reading skills, yet with the preparation provided by those first chapters, Nodelman suggests, "even readers with the most primitive of narrative competencies have the opportunity to make a transition and cope with the complexities of the rest of the novel" (125–26). Clearly, here manuscript study has led to the kind of observations about the structure of a children's novel that might be of great interest to critics trying to determine the difference between fiction for children and for adults.

The purpose of genre criticism, as Northrop Frye has said, is to clarify and bring out "a large number of literary relationships that would not be noticed as long as there were no context established for them" (247–48). Criticism by genre, then, can help us understand not only the force of tradition but the nature of a particular artist's response to the tradition. Children's literature offers special challenges to genre criticism, challenges grounded in the concern of the literature with external events rather than their implications, with feeling rather than appearance, and in its penchant for fantasy and thematic dwelling on a process that "describes the move from a 'frustrated' world of innocence to a 'desirable' world of experience"—an interesting reversal of the familiar tragic pattern of experience represented in adult literature (Nodelman, "*Beyond Genre*" 82).

Of course, the same characteristics that render children's literature problematic to systematic genre-centered criticism make it likely that such study can illuminate the ways writers for children have modified traditional forms to appeal to younger readers and to embody patterns of experience especially relevant to them. Students curious about the way a writer can adapt established forms to create a new work might look at "Tradition and the Individual Talent of Frances Hodgson Burnett," in which Phyllis Bixler contends that Burnett's achievement as a children's writer can be understood if her novels are examined within the context of a long literary tradition. In *Little Lord Fauntleroy* and *A Little Princess* Burnett produced a combination of fairy tale and exemplum. In *The Secret Garden* "she continued to use themes and motifs from these genres, but she gave symbolic enrichment and mythic enlargement to her poetic vision by adding tropes from pastoral tradition" (191).

The single objective critical approach with which most undergraduates are familiar is the formalist close reading. Today such readings, like Virginia Wolf's subtle yet accessible study "The Symbolic Center: *Little House in the Big Woods*," are likely to draw on a variety of critical strategies. Wolf sees this book, by Laura Ingalls Wilder, as embodying a vision of "harmony within the individual, the family, the community, and nature." Touching on its "tension in style and structure," she finds its "antithetical balance of opposites" "the key to the novel" (65). Wolf shows how Wilder's cumulative style is built of "contrasting words, phrases, and clauses in parallel constructions" (66) and how a similar antithetical balance marks the structure of each chapter, in which "work, routine, security, and family contrast with play, wonder, danger, and nature" (67). The novel, according to Wolf, is structured not by plot but by the vision of opposites it projects, by its use of the cycle of seasons, by its suggestions of a "circular pattern of descent and ascent, a movement from an idyllic world to a demonic one and back again," and by its evocation, through the image of the little house, of a "perfect centeredness" (68). Students sensitive to the conventional use of such symbolic oppositions in literature may agree with Wolf's conclusion that "this first Little House book is more nearly romance than realistic fiction" (69).

Few purely structuralist or semiotic approaches to children's literature have appeared as yet, however promising the idea of such study might seem, given the prominence of genres like fantasy and the folktale, which have been successfully analyzed from this perspective. There are, however, a couple of useful introductory surveys of the critical possibilities of such study.

In 1982 the *Children's Literature Association Quarterly* published a set of papers from a special MLA session, Structuralist Approaches to Children's Literature. These papers are a set of rather eclectic and experimental applications of structural models to the reading of various texts in children's literature. Anita Moss offers readings of *Tom Sawyer* and *The Enchanted Castle* based, as Elizabeth Francis puts it, "on structuralist notions of code, sign, and referentiality as well as the critique of 'bourgeois' narrative":

> If Tom Sawyer uses literary conventions to manipulate the behavior of the society in which he lives, Nesbit's characters use literary conventions to explore the question of meaning itself. Moss deftly shows us that Nesbit questions the autonomy of signs and the fixity of their signifieds, that Nesbit is aware of the contingency of meaning, even as she builds her narrative on respect for the child's ability to absorb and transform rules and literary conventions.   ("Appropriating" 52)

A recent issue of *Studies in the Literary Imagination*, edited by Hugh Keenan and devoted to Narrative Theory and Children's Literature, includes eight essays that apply recent critical theory to specific texts, including Robert Louis Stevenson's David Balfour novels, Burnett's *Secret Garden*, Mary Norton's Borrowers books, and Kenneth Grahame's *Wind in the Willows*. Lines of inquiry are derived from reader-response criticism, from narrative theory, and from the work of individual critics like Northrop Frye, Hillis Miller, Peter Brooks, W. R. Irwin, and Frank Kermode. The essays, taken as a group, offer students an interesting exploration of some central concerns in recent children's literature criticism, especially the difficulty of making critical assessments of books in a field in which so many works are so similar both in their core of meaning and in their structural patterns. The articles examine, as well, the problems created by the existence of a primary defining audience (children) and a secondary critical audience (adults). In the words of editor Keenan, as these essays show, "children's literature is not simple. It is often more sophisticated than we have allowed." It may be that alternate readings must be seen as "a valid part of its ambiguity," and "our descriptions of children's literature may well need to be rethought." Certainly literary theory—as this collection of essays shows—can be an important resource for critics of children's literature. "And conversely, children's literature may have much to contribute to literary theory as a proving and testing ground" (2).

The Context

Various critics have made the case for knowledge of historically important children's literature by students. Some urge that students learn to measure modern works against the historical models that have become canonical so that "standards of excellence" can be "grounded in an acknowledgment of our inherited tradition" (Demers 143). Others are more interested in assessing the values children's literature has proposed at various times and places. Isaac Kramnick, for example, sees children's literature of the late eighteenth century as self-consciously expressing the values of the middle class and serving "as an important vehicle for the socialization of children to these values" (211). Jack Zipes, in his study *Fairy Tales and the Art of Subversion: The Classical Genre for Children and the Process of Civilization*, also explores the way literature has been used to socialize children. Zipes's "concern is largely with the fairy-tale discourse as a dynamic part of the historic civilization process, with each symbolic act viewed as an intervention in socialization in the public sphere" (11). Other scholars pursuing a similar line of inquiry have read the Babar series as books of courtesy (Hildebrand) or as ideological propaganda (Payne). Students interested in examining children's literature for its hidden social agenda can also look at the many feminist studies of the cultural stereotypes and archetypal patterns so often embodied in fiction. Or they might apply the strategies of various feminist critics to their own study of historical children's literature (Francis, "Feminist Versions").

Archetypal and mythic criticism can be considered mimetic in the sense that it assumes that myth arises from recurrent human responses to significant events that then become the basis for permanent patterns in a culture. Virginia Wolf has observed that "children's novels displace myth much less than many adult novels and make one wonder if the children's novel as a genre should not be defined in terms of its reliance on myth" (Wolf, "Paradise Lost?"). And her further suggestion that "the less displaced myth is in a novel, the younger the audience will be to whom the novel will be accessible" (63) echoes Frye's observation that the cycle of literature ranging from the mythic through the romantic and the highly mimetic requires an increasingly sophisticated reader.

For college students, identifying the mythic models and archetypal patterns that have been displaced in a children's novel often is a major step toward grasping the basic structure of the work. A good model for this sort of study can be found in James T. Henke's discussion of the mythic and fairy tale allusions in Voigt's *Homecoming*. "Voigt," he notes, "has taken an unpleasant reality of contemporary America and endowed it with fairy tale and epic qualities. The story of Dicey Tillerman and her brothers and sister is the story of Hansel and Gretel and the saga of Homer's wily hero" (45).

Students may also be struck by the way mythic and archetypal patterns concerned with symbolic maturation recur in children's fiction and especially in fantasy. Ursula Le Guin's unusually deliberate and self-conscious use of the "Jungian concept of universal archetypes and the Taoist idea of balance or equilibrium between complementary forces throughout creation" (Jenkins 21) might provide a good focus for students' study of this phenomenon. In "Growing Up in Earthsea" Sue Jenkins shows how Le Guin's books deal with themes the author feels are especially important for young people: coming of age, and coming to terms with sexuality and with death.

In *Adventure, Mystery, and Romance* John G. Cawelti explores the way in which universal archetypes that fulfill the reader's needs are embodied in the formulas of popular fiction in "figures, settings, and situations that have appropriate meanings for the culture which produces them" (6). In their capacity to assimilate new meanings, the great variety of popular literary formulas "ease the transition between old and new ways of expressing things and thus contribute to cultural continuity" (36). The study of the way conflicts in society are represented and mediated through such formulas has had provocative results when applied to literature for young readers. For instance, students might read a thoughtful consideration of a new genre, "Sweet Dreams for Sleeping Beauties: Pre-Teen Romances," in which Lois Kuznets and Eve Zarin, quoting John Cawelti, see such stories as offering the reader an opportunity to "explore in fantasy the boundary between the permitted and the forbidden and to experience in a carefully controlled way the possibility of stepping across the boundary" (29; see Cawelti 35).

The Audience

The effect of children's literature on its primary audience has been of much interest to recent critics. Studies of the child's act of reading address a variety of issues including questions about the progress of aesthetic development, the nature of reader response to literature, the acquisition of symbolic competence, the development of narrational skill, the nature and role of pictorial perception in literary experience, and the relationship between metaphoric and cognitive capacities.

(Cochran-Smith, "Toward an Understanding" 22)

Students will find helpful guidance on some basic reading in Cochran-Smith's "Toward an Understanding of Children's Literary Experiences: An Annotated Bibliography of Selected Theory and Research" and in Peggy Whalen-Levitt's "Literature and Child Readers," which brings together a group of essays on the way literary communication theory might be useful in the criticism and teaching of children's literature.

In an effort to supplement clinical research with more informal surveys, scholars have compiled long-term descriptive studies based on observations of children and their relationships with literature in natural contexts, largely by parent-diarists. Students who want to try similar observational study might profit from reading "The Parent Diary as a Research Tool," by Marilyn Cochran-Smith.

Some academic criticism of individual books reflects a communication perspective. One study of Robert Cormier's *I Am the Cheese*, for example, draws on Wolfgang Iser's idea that the reader actively participates in bringing out the meaning in a book. Cormier's novel, by misleading its readers into believing what later turn out to be lies, forces them to undergo the same experience the protagonist, Adam, does: "Adam's discoveries are more horrifying, and the disorientation that results from them more intense, because Adam provides readers that same faith in untruths that Adam has, the same discoveries, and the same awesome sense of having trusted too much" (Nodelman, "Robert Cormier" 100).

Rhetorical criticism explores the various strategies available to the writer for controlling audience response. Though some rhetorical critics write from a traditional perspective, classifying the various moves an author can make according to an elaborate terminology, others—like Wayne C. Booth—use ordinary language. Booth's subject in *The Rhetoric of Fiction* is the "technique of non-didactic fiction viewed as the art of communication with readers—the rhetorical sources available to the writer . . . as he tries consciously or unconsciously to impose his fictional world upon the reader" (xiii). Booth's treatment of the various kinds of realism might be useful to students of children's literature, and his analysis of the way the "implied author" can affect reader sympathies and convey the "norms" of a work might be helpful in assessing the didactic element in children's fiction. Further, Booth's discussion of "unreliable" narration can help critics to deal more effectively with problems of authority, reliability, irony, distance, and sympathy in fiction that uses young children as narrators or focal characters or that is designed to be read by a mixed audience of adults and children.

Lois Kuznets, in "Permutations of Frame in Mary Norton's 'Borrowers' Series," attempts "to delineate the nature of the rhetorical situation within each of Norton's Borrower books separately." The essay speculates on the reasons for the rhetorical changes in form that emerge in the series, changes Kuznets sees as "connected with a deepening commitment on Mary Norton's part to the notion of making her Borrower characters independent of *all* human beings—even those sympathetic to them—while at the same time she increasingly develops and emphasizes the allegorical significance of the Borrowers' story as an embodiment of the human condition in danger and prosperity" (67).

Reader-response and rhetorical criticism have also, of course, a good deal of potential as approaches to the history of children's literature, of child audiences, and of authorial strategies in past periods as well as for analysis of modern texts. For example, Kirsten Drotner has studied the response of English children to periodicals written for them from 1751 to 1945, and Mitzi Myers has demonstrated the way the female pedagogue in children's fiction by eighteenth-century women writers prepares "her audience of child and parent readers to export Georgian faith in moral regeneration through education into the real world" (39).

The Author

Critics interested in the way artists express themselves in their work have often examined authorial biography for the clues to meaning it can offer. Leon Edel has said that "literature and biography are intimately related." What the literary biographer seeks to discover about the author are "all those characteristic modes of thought, perception, emotion" that may be embodied more honestly in his work "than in the conscious statements he makes about himself" (66).

Sometimes "characteristic modes of thought" appear in the work of a group of writers from a particular period or milieu, and critics will explore the common elements in their work and their thought. Thus Humphrey Carpenter in *Secret Gardens: A Study of the Golden Age of Literature* suggests that writers like Charles Kingsley, Lewis Carroll, George MacDonald, Kenneth Grahame, and A. A. Milne rejected the values of their contemporary world in favor of an "Arcadia, A Good Place, A Secret Garden" (13) in which their own reservations about the real world could be safely, if subversively, expressed. Carpenter's approach raises questions students might like to pursue about the changing nature of the dialogue between children and adults and the ways such change may affect the kind of children's books it is possible to write.

Biographical work of a psychological nature has been done on many children's authors, though perhaps for obvious reasons such work has concentrated on authors whose lives present evidence of pathology. For a short but revealing study of an individual artist's motivation to write a children's story, students might read U. C. Knoepflmacher's "Resisting Growth through Fairy Tale in Ruskin's *The King of the Golden River*," which sees the story as

> addressed to a double audience of child and adult by a writer whose delayed adolescence caused him to continue to hover between the opposed states of innocence and experience. Despite his eagerness to obtain the approval of this dual readership through the story of an obedient and effeminate boy rewarded for charitable behavior, Ruskin was not wholly able to prevent quite contrary emotions from piercing his fable's emphasis on acquiescence. The rebelliousness that would surface in his later career lurks in *The King of the Golden River* as half-submerged as those threatening black rocks over which the swirling waters "rose wildly into the night." (5–6)

Students may profit from an acquaintance with a variety of psychological approaches to literature. The chapter "Literature and Psychology," by Murray M. Schwartz and David Willbern in *Interrelations of Literature* (ed. Barricelli and Gibaldi), outlines the uses of psychology in the interpretation of literary texts: to open up the thematics and symbolism in a work, to understand it as the expression of the individual artist's psyche, or to reveal the dynamics of the literary response of a particular audience.

The way in which desire operates dynamically in fictional narrative for both authors and readers has been studied by Peter Brooks, who focuses on the logic that is at work in story, leading from an initial incident to the final outcome, mediating or resolving the central problem. Story for him is a narrative way of thinking through a situation. Plot "is the logic and dynamic of narrative, and narrative itself a form of understanding and explanation" (10). Brooks's approach to traditional story, folktale, myth, and imaginative fiction is of great potential use to students of children's literature. In particular, his treatment of the dynamic of parent-child relationships in the nineteenth-century novel should be of interest to students of adolescent literature, whose central concern is the conflict between individual freedom and legitimate authority (Gannon).

Classroom Practice

A practicing teacher and critic has observed that

> in the past twenty years, literary theory has achieved a recognized, if sometimes feared, place in our curricula. What has rarely happened is its

transition into pedagogy. That process is necessary if theory is to become more than elitist speculation. If the questions theory raises are important, they must have consequences in praxis. (McCormick 849)

Critical reading such as that outlined above will, for many students, provide a useful vocabulary and a variety of models for independent inquiry into children's literature. The population of the college children's literature course, however, can be quite diverse. And some students may need to be introduced to critical theory in a more mediated form, perhaps as it is embodied in the questioning strategies that structure class discussion or in the design of assignments, critical apparatus, journal protocols, research topics, examinations.

For such students, in particular, keeping a reading journal with carefully designed response assignments may be helpful. Through such an exercise they can become aware of their own implicit critical assumptions and, perhaps, come to appreciate—rather than be overwhelmed by—the variety of critical options open to them.

In her article in *College English*, Kathleen McCormick suggests structural response assignments for general literature courses that could focus the attention of students keeping reading journals on various aspects of their experience. Such assignments can easily be adapted to the children's literature class, so that students can be alerted to the role their literary competence plays in determining the systems and structures they discover in texts and to the way their understanding of literary convention is affected by their own personal and cultural background.

The reading of Pirandello, McCormick believes, can enable students to see how expectations and reading strategies affect the way they respond to a particular text. That students of children's literature might do much the same thing in a close study of Cormier's *I Am the Cheese* is evident in Phyllis Bixler's detailed account of her own classroom experience. Bixler's students recorded their responses to two separate readings of Cormier's novel and wrote essays reflecting on what they had learned from the experience. Among the outcomes of this exercise is Bixler's recognition of one limitation in using teacher-constructed apparatus. She notes the way her protocols constituted an attempt to shape her students' responses. Yet she observes that such shaping is probably inevitable: "As literature teachers we are quite appropriately introducing our students to what Stanley Fish calls 'interpretive communities' larger than a particular classroom. We will do so more responsibly, however, if we are fully conscious of what we are doing and if we also learn to encourage the imaginative energy of student interpretations, which are too often dismissed as 'wrong-headed' or 'insensitive to the text.' " Bixler's students were future teachers, and she felt this assignment made them "more conscious of how they themselves read literary texts, and of how they might enhance their own students' responses to literature" (16).

What is children's literature? How is it different from other kinds of literature? My students and I (even when using critical readings like those described here) often find that "progress" toward the answers we seek is, as Clifford Geertz has observed in a different context, "marked less by a perfection of consensus than by a refinement of debate." As Geertz points out, "What gets better is the precision with which we vex each other" (29). We may not, by the end of our semester, be able to define children's literature or to establish its distinguishing characteristics, but we usually find ample and immediate rewards for all our effort in the "dialogue of the classroom itself" as we explore individual texts together, "trying in genuine dialogue with each other about the texts we are questioning to determine what meanings and experience make sense—a plurality of senses—in this shared conversation" (Booth, "Pluralism" 479).

Pace University

Works Cited

Bixler, Phyllis. "*I Am the Cheese* and Reader-Response Criticism in the Adolescent Literature Classroom." *Children's Literature Association Quarterly* 10.1 (1985): 13–16.

Bixler [Koppes], Phyllis. "Tradition and the Individual Talent of Frances Hodgoon Burnett: A Generic Analysis of *Little Lord Fauntleroy, A Little Princess,* and *The Secret Garden.*" *Children's Literature* 7 (1978): 191–207.

Booth, Wayne C. "Pluralism in the Classroom" *Critical Inquiry* 12.3 (1986): 468–79.

———. *The Rhetoric of Fiction.* 2nd ed. Chicago: U of Chicago P, 1983.

Brooks, Peter. *Reading for the Plot: Design and Intention in Narrative.* New York: Knopf, 1984.

Carpenter, Humphrey. *Secret Gardens: A Study of the Golden Age of Children's Literature from* Alice in Wonderland *to* Winnie-the-Pooh. Boston: Houghton, 1985.

Cawelti, John G. *Adventure, Mystery, and Romance: Formula Stories as Art and Popular Culture.* Chicago: U of Chicago P, 1976.

Cochran-Smith, Marilyn. "The Parent-Diary as a Research Tool." *Children's Literature Association Quarterly* 5.3 (1980): 3–5. Rpt. in Dooley 51–53.

———. "Toward an Understanding of Children's Literary Experiences: An Annotated Bibliography of Selected Theory and Research." *Children's Literature Association Quarterly* 4.4. (1980): 17–21. Rpt. in Dooley 22–25.

Demers, Patricia. "Classic or Touchstone: Much of a Muchness?" *Children's Literature Association Quarterly* 10.3 (1985): 142–43.

Dooley, Patricia, ed. *The First Steps: Articles and Columns from the* ChLA Newsletter/Quarterly, *Vol. I–VI.* West Lafayette: Children's Literature Assn., 1984.

Drotner, Kirsten. *English Children and Their Magazines, 1751–1945.* New Haven: Yale UP, 1988.

Edel, Leon. "Literature and Biography." *Relations of Literary Study: Essays on Interdisciplinary Contributions.* Ed. James Thorpe. New York: MLA, 1967. 57–70.

Francis, Elizabeth. "Appropriating the Theory: Structuralism and Children's Literature." *Children's Literature Association Quarterly* 7.3 (1982): 52–58.

———. "Feminist Versions of Pastoral: *The Madwoman in the Attic* and *The Lay of the Land.*" *Children's Literature Association Quarterly* 7.4 (1982–83): 7+.

Frye, Northrop. *Anatomy of Criticism.* New York: Atheneum, 1969.

Gannon, Susan. "Repetition and Meaning in Stevenson's David Balfour Novels." *Studies in the Literary Imagination* 18.2 (1985): 21–33.

Geertz, Clifford. *The Interpretation of Cultures: Selected Essays by Clifford Geertz.* New York: Basic, 1973.

Henke, James T. "Dicey, Odysseus, and Hansel and Gretel: The Lost Children in Voigt's *Homecoming.*" *Children's Literature in Education* 16.1 (1985): 45–52.

Hildebrand, Ann M. "Jean de Brunhoff's Advice to Youth: The *Babar* Books as Books of Courtesy." *Children's Literature* 11 (1983): 76–95.

Jenkins, Sue. "Growing Up in Earthsea." *Children's Literature in Education* 16.1 (1985): 21–31.

Keenan, Hugh. "Editor's Comment." *Narrative Theory and Children's Literature.* Spec. issue of *Studies in the Literary Imagination* 18.2 (1985): 1–2.

Knoepflmacher, U. C. "Resisting Growth through Fairy Tale in Ruskin's *The King of the Golden River.*" *Children's Literature* 13 (1985): 3–30.

Kramnick, Isaac. "Children's Literature and Bourgeois Ideology: Observations on Culture and Industrial Capitalism in the Later Eighteenth Century." *Culture and Politics from Puritanism to the Enlightenment.* Ed. Perez Zagorin. Los Angeles: U of California P, 1980. 203–40.

Kuznets, Lois. "Permutations of Frame in Mary Norton's 'Borrowers' Series." *Studies in the Literary Imagination* 18.2 (1985): 65–78.

Kuznets, Lois, and Eve Zarin. "Sweet Dreams for Sleeping Beauties: Pre-Teen Romances." *Children's Literature Association Quarterly* 7.1 (1982): 28–32.

McCormick, Kathleen. "Theory in the Reader: Bleich, Holland, and Beyond." *College English* 47.8 (Dec. 1985): 836–50.

Moss, Anita. "Makers of Meaning: A Structuralist Study of Twain's *Tom Sawyer* and Nesbit's *The Enchanted Castle.*" *Children's Literature Association Quarterly* 7.3 (1982): 30–45.

Myers, Mitzi. "Impeccable Governesses, Rational Dames, and Moral Mothers: Mary Wollstonecraft and the Female Tradition in Georgian Children's Books." *Children's Literature* 14 (1986): 31–59.

Neumeyer, Peter. "The Creation of *Charlotte's Web:* From Drafts to Book." *Horn Book* Oct. 1982: 489–97; Dec. 1982: 617–25.

Nodelman, Perry. "*Beyond Genre* and Beyond." *Children's Literature Association Quarterly* 6.1 (1981): 22–24. Rpt. in Dooley 81–83.

———. "Robert Cormier Does a Number." *Children's Literature in Education* 14 (Summer 1983): 94–103.

———. "Text as Teacher: The Beginning of *Charlotte's Web.*" *Children's Literature* 13 (1985): 109–27.

Payne, Harry C. "The Reign of King Babar." *Children's Literature* 11 (1983): 96–108.

Schwartz, Murray M., and David Willbern. "Literature and Psychology." *Inter-relations of Literature.* Ed. Jean-Pierre Barricelli and Joseph Gibaldi. New York: MLA, 1982. 205–24.

Whalen-Levitt, Peggy, ed. "Literature and Child Readers." *Children's Literature Association Quarterly* 4.4 (1980): 9–28. Rpt. in Dooley 17–29.

Wolf, Virginia. "Paradise Lost? The Displacement of Myth in Children's Novels Set on Islands." *Studies in the Literary Imagination* 18.2 (1985): 47–63.

——— . "The Symbolic Center: *Little House in the Big Woods.*" *Children's Literature in Education* 13 (1982): 107–14. Rpt. in *Children and Their Literature: A Readings Book.* Ed. Jill May. West Lafayette: Children's Literature Assn., 1983. 65–70.

Zipes, Jack. *Fairy Tales and the Art of Subversion: The Classical Genre for Children and the Process of Civilization.* New York: Wildman, 1983.

Approaching the Illustrated Text

George R. Bodmer

Even though we are admonished not to judge a book by its cover, we begin responding to a work of literature as soon as we pick it up. Likewise, a strong instinctive or emotional reaction sets in as soon as pictures are encountered. Although the pictures are, ideally, meant to be "read" at that point in the text where they are positioned, no one can help leafing through the book, soaking up the sense of the story through the illustrations.

Illustration serves to expand, explain, interpret, or decorate a written text. In addition, the illustration offers a "text" in itself, which always tells a slightly different story, just as two words are never totally synonymous. As such the illustration is also a "reading" of the written text, creating a tension between picture and word, as the viewer-reader springs back and forth between the two. In older books, picture and text were clearly separate; the picture, in color or black and white, came on its own page or its own distinct part of the page. More recently, words and pictures have tended to bleed into each other, with the text sometimes printed atop the image, for instance.

There is always, however, a distance between pictures and words, often between the artists who create each. They are sometimes separated by distance or by time—for example, the modern illustrator Barry Moser created drawings for Lewis Carroll's *Alice's Adventures in Wonderland*. Often the text is shaped by the illustrator, as in the case of John Tenniel's suggestions to Carroll for *Alice*. Even when the visual artist and text artist are the same person, there is a gap; both contemporary artist-writers Maurice Sendak and Dr. Seuss have often said that the words have come first, before the pictures.

Obviously there is considerable diversity in the extent to which a story can be illustrated. Often collections of short works like fairy tales are limited to one picture for each story. Each page of a picture book usually has an illustration, which is larger than the accompanying text. There are even picture books with no words, although a text or storyline obviously exists, in the writer's mind and for the reader-viewer to recreate. For the work to be successful, a balance must be reached, a deal struck. Interesting pictures cannot save a dull story, although a good story can pull some drab artwork along. Likewise, too elaborate art can overpower a small story. Part of a picture book's appeal is that, for a young audience, it helps bridge the gap before a child learns to read; a picture's more abstract and emotional appeal is a doorway to the literal communication of the written words.

Another deal is struck between how much of the actual storytelling is done by the words and how much is done by the pictures. The pictures may add important facts that the text doesn't give, or they may simply, for example, show what a character or scene looks like. The illustrations may also undermine the written story, providing an ironic subtext.

A picture is limited in the way it can impart information. For instance, as E. H. Gombrich points out, pictures cannot make a simple declarative statement (82), cannot say, "Come here, Mr. Watson, I need you." Likewise, a single picture is usually limited, in time, to a single event. Chronology and changing events can be shown through a film-strip or comic strip–like sequence. Or future or past events can be shown emblematically, with objects symbolizing what the reader knows will happen. As in all illustration, the artist must pick a turning point or, as Edward Hodnett calls it "a moment of choice," an instant that focuses an event, a theme, or a character (7).

In Sendak's picture for the Grimm fairy tale "Rapunzel," in *The Juniper Tree,* we see Rapunzel staring sadly out a tower window, her long hair streaming out the window also. In the lower left-hand corner of the picture, a large chain hangs down; although it is not attached to Rapunzel, we see it symbolizing her captivity. On the right side of the picture, her sinister witch-guardian observes her, a pair of scissors in her hand. The young woman waits for some salvation, while the scissors prominently jump ahead in the story, indicating what will happen when Rapunzel finds her young lover.

"Rapunzel" is a familiar story, but, viewed in another context, Sendak's picture would be difficult to read. Since the point of view is inside the room, we cannot see how long the woman's hair is. The witch looks vaguely threatening, but not especially so. The picture is framed, by a wooden jamb and drapery, and so cluttered that the young woman appears to be leaning toward the open window for a breath of air. Perhaps assuming that his viewer has seen many pictures of Rapunzel with her hair streaming out of the tower window, the artist has chosen to show the psychologically restrictive nature of Rapunzel's relationship with the "mother" who doesn't want to let her grow up and move out. This picture interprets and encapsulates the fairy tale, but the reader could not unravel the story without the accompanying text.

The history of book illustration has largely been shaped by the technology for reproducing artwork. As John Rowe Townsend points out, when books were hand-written and hand-copied, the manuscripts were limited only by what the artist could draw (142–43). The first mechanically produced books were illustrated by relatively crude woodcuts, a technology that required the drawing to be cut into a block. For instance, William Caxton's version of Aesop's *Fables* (1483) had 186 woodcuts, mostly copied from an earlier French edition. Even though the technique of wood engraving, developed in the nineteenth century, produced a sharper image, a separate artisan cut the woodblock from a freehand drawing that was either traced directly onto the block by the original artist or transferred from paper. Obviously there was some dropoff in the process, although artisans at shops like those of the Dalziel brothers in Victorian England were capable of great beauty and fluidity of line. For example Tenniel's drawings for *Alice's Adventures* were cut into woodblocks. Nevertheless, reliance on woodcuts lasted for four hundred years.

Lithography and photography developed in the nineteenth century also, and the latter provided a means to reproduce the artist's freehand drawing. Originally, color was either added by hand after the printing, or, more rarely, several blocks were made to overprint the picture. In our own time, whether the artist makes the final draft in pencil, chalk, charcoal, collage, lithograph, woodcut or wood engraving, paint, or pen and ink, the work is photographed and printing plates are made from the original image. Although illustrations, especially elaborate and colorful ones, increase the production costs of the book, the artist is freer than ever before to produce beautiful and thoughtful illustrated works. Some of the most elaborate and sophisticated of these, however, seem designed to attract adult buyers rather than child readers.

Much credit for the popularity of picture books belongs to Dr. Seuss (Theodor Seuss Geisel), who wrote and illustrated more than forty-five works. Seuss began cartooning in college, at a time when humor magazines, and especially college humor magazines, were in abundance; after studying literature in Europe, he returned to the United States to write and draw advertising copy. After being turned down by many publishers, his first book for children, *And to Think That I Saw It on Mulberry Street*, came out in 1937. His books combine wild color, a loose-limbed, whimsical style of drawing animals and people, and an irresistible poetry that children take to immediately. In the 1950s, with *The Cat in the Hat*, he adapted his writing to offer children easy-to-read books with limited vocabularies. At a time of cheaper means of production and even financial incentives from the government (libraries were funded in a Sputnik-era move to improve education), Seuss was at the center of an explosion of American illustration and picture books for children.

Seuss's chief literary device is that of progression, inward, outward, mathematical or geometrical. For instance, the taking off of one hat produces another hat and another, in *The Five Hundred Hats of Bartholomew*

Cubbins and *The Cat in the Hat Comes Back*. The alphabet doesn't stop with Z, but continues *On Beyond Zebra*. A bad idea is carried to its logical and frightening conclusion in *The Lorax*, *The Butter Battle Book*, and *Yertle the Turtle*. In *Horton Hatches the Egg*, the diligent elephant Horton is suckered into sitting on an egg for Mayzie, a lazy bird, and sticks to it even after he is tied up, carted off, and put on exhibition across the sea. Seuss's illustrations for this fifty-three-page book are typical, pencil line drawings filled in minimally with turquoise and reddish orange (Seuss has painted some illustrations, for *McElligot's Pool*, but usually includes line drawings with solid blocks of color). The subdued turquoise is almost entirely used for sky, water, and rain, while the bright orange highlights small details, like a bow tie, tail feathers, the egg, antlers, tongues; this is not one of Seuss's bright books. In another technique characteristic of the artist, the scene, especially the sky, is printed to the edge of the paper without margin (that is, *bleeds*), usually up to the right corner. This format emphasizes the extensive use of diagonals in the book; as the lazy bird escapes upper page right, the rain falls at an angle on the sitting Horton, and the elephant is often pictured pushing off the top right corner of the page. Horton is a funny-looking, woebegone elephant, and by often drawing him half off the page, Seuss exaggerates the irony of a heavy elephant sitting on a bird's egg. The image also creates a sense of being trapped, as the surrogate mother Horton is by his egg and his principle: "An elephant's faithful / One hundred per cent!"

The text of *Horton Hatches the Egg* is kept separate from the pictures; often the words appear on an all-white page facing an illustration. In nine out of the ten instances of such a two-page spread, the words fall on the left page and are encountered first, suggesting a subordinate position for the pictures. Sometimes the picture extends diagonally across two pages, but the words always appear on blank white. The pictures portray Horton, all knees, big feet, curves, and cartoon features, as a silly-looking creature, dwarfed by his problems. The artist has chiefly, through the expression in Horton's eyes, portrayed the emotions of the scenes—his shock, his sadness, his fear and suffering, and finally his joy at being rewarded with the hatching of a little elephant-bird. Obviously, having the words without the pictures would rob the book of much of its appeal, but the story is completely told in the text; the illustrations offer no new facts.

Dr. Seuss returned to his character fourteen years later in *Horton Hears a Who!*, and here Horton is again diligent in protecting a dust speck holding a minuscule civilization of Whos that only he can hear. Once more he is put upon by skeptical animals, who take the speck from him; they are convinced only when the combined shouting of the Whos is made loud enough at last by the addition of the voice of the smallest, Jo-Jo. In this seventy-one-page book the line drawings are in ink and are harder-edged than in its predecessor, with less shading. The colors, vivid orange, pink, and blue, are brighter and tend to dominate more explosively. The illustrations tend toward roundness and curves, especially Horton's belly and the round globe of a dust speck, and the story is more inward, as Horton concentrates on the tiny civilization he cannot see. Again, the pictures highlight the theme as well as the reality of the contrast between the size of an elephant and the Whos on a mite. The message here is "A person's a person, no matter how small."

In *Horton Hears a Who!* the text and pictures usually overlap, with the words printed on top of color and even on Horton's belly at one point. This technique was used previously—for instance, when the words in L. Frank Baum's first Oz book, *The Wonderful Wizard of Oz,* were printed over W. W. Denslow's drawings (1900). In *Horton Hears a Who!* it underscores the mood. As Horton chases a bird who has stolen the dust mite over a mountain top through the night, the entire double-page spread, including the text, is blue with darkness. The mite is hidden in a gigantic pink clover patch, and again the words are printed on top of the pink, showing us the endlessness of the field and Horton's task of finding it again. The words and pictures flow together, and Seuss allows the pictures to do more of the work. He has said, "If I'm supplementing the words with pictures and if I can substitute the adjectives with a picture, I'll leave them out of the text" (Cott 21). What makes this book appealing is Horton's expressions, as well as his wrong-way knees and jutting feet that no real elephant would have. But Seuss has also developed what Horton and the other animals cannot see—that is, the Whos and their world—in incredibly busy pictures of activity and humor. The text doesn't describe what the Whos look like, and Seuss pictures them as upright, doglike characters, with wild tufts of hair and incredulous eyes. Even at the most exciting parts of the story, the reader is sidetracked, looking at the double-page spreads of the Who cities, all arches and steps, full of bustling Whos. This is a story of imagination, of unseen worlds within worlds, and the illustrations keep us moving between the external world and the movement inside.

There is something comforting about the consistency of Dr. Seuss's style over forty years; his books and pictures are immediately recognizable. Not so with Maurice Sendak (b. 1928), who has illustrated approximately seventy books for other writers and produced fifteen of his own, in a vast variety of styles, including very simple black and white line drawings, lush color paintings, and quiet crosshatched scenes. His styles are at times cartoonlike, sometimes sketchy or photographic. He has also experimented with the rich possibilities of picture books and the relation of text and pictures.

Sendak has often used the pictures to undercut the written text, even when that text is his own, and to produce an ironic subtext to the book. For instance, *Pierre* is one of four tiny boxed books in the Nutshell Library. Titled *Pierre: A Cautionary Tale in Five Chapters and a Prologue*, it tells the story of a contrary little boy who answers every question with a smug "I don't care!" Left at home by his parents, he is eaten by a lion. He is dumped out of the upended lion and "learns" his lesson: "Yes, indeed I care!!" Drawn in pen and ink and colored in mostly with light washes of yellow and blue, the pictures show a bratty-looking boy and a friendly-looking, toothless lion. Probably because of the smallness of the book, the text always appears on the left page facing a picture. The pictures have no background other than the white page and include only the furniture needed for the scene (a bed, for instance, as the lion gets sick from eating Pierre). That a boy swallowed by a lion can be saved is consistent with fairy tale logic, as in "Little Red Riding Hood," but the story might be frightening to a child without Sendak's pictures of a cuddly, nonthreatening lion, who stays for the weekend after giving up his meal. Along with a series of other Sendak antiheroes, Pierre is so arrogant a child, as we see him again after his transformation, that, as viewers, we know not to believe that he would give up his rotten ways. The pictures let us know not to fall for this simple moral.

Sendak's greatest book, *Where the Wild Things Are*, stars Max, a similarly independent and wayward boy. Wearing a white wolf costume, Max is sent to bed without his supper for mischief and imagines himself sailing across water to "where the wild things are." These creatures he tames, just as it is suggested he can learn to tame the wild animal in himself. To tell his story, Sendak uses only 338 words, usually appearing as a strip at the bottom, or on an otherwise blank left page. In the middle of the book, in the climax of the story, Max commands, "Let the wild rumpus start!" and what follows are three double-page unnarrated pictures, of glorious dancing by the wild things, certainly the most praised scenes in contemporary picture books.

The pictures in *Wild Things* are mostly pen and ink, filled in with cross-hatching, and backed by subdued pale blues, browns, and reds. This darkish quality, along with an almost always present moon and stars, reminds us of night and allows the reader to see Max's journey as a dream. The pictures also begin small and expand (the first is about $5\frac{1}{2} \times 4$ inches; the second, $6\frac{1}{4} \times 5$ inches; the third, $7\frac{1}{4} \times 6$ inches) until they bleed to the edge of the page and explode in the wild rumpus. Perry Nodelman, in "How Picture Books Work," has pointed out that the words describe the wild things as frightening creatures, with "terrible roars and . . . terrible teeth and . . . terrible eyes and . . . terrible claws." Yet the pictures comfort the reader, showing chubby childish animals who just want to play (4). The pictures do most of the work here, in presenting a story of the struggle for control in a child's life and the value of imagination. When Max returns from his underground journey, he finds his dinner waiting for him; the final line, "and it was still hot," faces a blank page and throws the story back to the reader.

In these two books, and in his illustrations for Grimm's *King Grisly-Beard* (1973), Sendak offers stories with parallel texts in the words and pictures that the reader alternates between. Neither is complete without the other, but we can see Sendak being the truer in his pictures.

The previous examples have largely dealt with artists' illustrations for their own works. Let me conclude by briefly considering an artist working with material he didn't write, Garth Williams's pictures for the 1953 edition of Laura Ingalls Wilder's *Little House* series. The first three books were originally illustrated by Helen Sewell in the 1930s; the later ones by Sewell and Mildred Boyle. Williams did much research for his artwork, including visiting the locales of the stories and conferring with Wilder. Even though the volumes themselves don't say so, it is possible to determine that Pa Ingalls and the other family members in Williams's drawings look like the historical figures on whom the characters are based.

Williams (b. 1912) produced pencil drawings that appear integrated without color into the text (approximately 74 for 238 pages of text in the first, *Little House in the Big Woods*). Only the title picture covers a full page, and clearly the pictures are secondary to Wilder's text. They stress the human aspects of the story, the togetherness of the family. The pictures focus on a child's view of life on the frontier, in terms of being protected by a family, but it is not a romantic view, since danger and hard work are actively presented. At times, Williams clears up confusing passages in the writing, as when he sketches the smoke house Pa builds out of a hollow tree, or shows how one could mistake an old log for a bear (although the latter picture appears before the story, diffusing the suspense). These pictures are realistic, though it is important to remember that they represent Williams's point of view, rather than Wilder's. The pictures enhance the novels, but the reader is always thrown back to the words.

Students should be aware that there is a tension between the pictures and the story in the books they read. To examine the ways an illustrated text works, the reader should consider these questions:

1. Does the illustration tell the same story as the words? What has been added or changed?
2. Can the words tell the story without the pictures?
3. Can the pictures tell the story without the words?
4. What is the style of the artwork? How is color used? What do style and color contribute to mood, description, or storytelling?
5. What is the physical relationship between pictures and printed text? Do they overlap, or are they separate?

6. What is the tone or mood of the pictures?
7. What is the goal of the illustration?

The pictures in an illustrated book show us how one person read the story. The artist becomes a critic, explainer, enhancer, and interpreter, presenting a version of the story in the pictures offered. The relationship between words and pictures is a creative one for us as viewers, as we shift back and forth, responding to the two in different ways. It is a process that involves us in the text and makes us participants in the story.

Indiana University Northwest

Works Cited

Cott, Jonathan, "The Good Dr. Seuss." *Pipers at the Gates of Dawn: The Wisdom of Children's Literature.* New York: Random, 1981. 3–37.

Gombrich, E. H. "The Visual Image." *Scientific American* Sept. 1972: 82–96.

Grimm. *The Juniper Tree.* Trans. Lore Segal and Randall Jarrell. Illus. Maurice Sendak. New York: Farrar, 1973.

Hodnett, Edward. *Image and Text: Studies in the Illustration of English Literature.* London: Scolar, 1982.

Nodelman, Perry. "How Picture Books Work." *Image and Maker: An Annual Dedicated to the Consideration of Book Illustration.* Ed. Harold Darling and Peter Neumeyer. La Jolla: Green Tiger, 1984. 1–12.

Sendak, Maurice. *Pierre: A Cautionary Tale in Five Chapters and a Prologue.* New York: Harper, 1962.

———. *Where the Wild Things Are.* New York: Harper, 1963.

Seuss, Dr. [Theodor Seuss Geisel]. *Horton Hatches the Egg.* New York: Random, 1940.

———. *Horton Hears a Who!* New York: Random, 1954.

Townsend, John Rowe. "Pictures That Tell a Story." *Written for Children.* 2nd rev. ed. Harmondsworth, Eng.: Penguin, 1983. 142–59.

Wilder, Laura Ingalls. *Little House in the Big Woods.* Illus. Garth Williams. New York: Harper, 1953.

Shadows in the Classroom: Teaching Children's Literature from a Jungian Perspective

John Cech

> *I have a little shadow that goes in and out with me*
> *And what can be the use of him is more than I can see.*
> > —*Robert Louis Stevenson*

Something unusual often occurs in the classroom when the discussion moves to the psychological dimensions of a work of literature. Once-comfortable chairs become uneasy pews. A lively, talkative class can quite suddenly grow quiet and tentative, if not stop its comments altogether. Part of what makes many students so hesitant about entering into such a discussion is that the realm of the psyche is, for most of them, uncharted territory. But another reason for their uneasiness is related to what they *do* know about psychology—especially some of the basic tenets of Freudian theory, like the Oedipus complex—and their anxiety about the possibilities of discovering, like that ill-starred king of Thebes, some unexpected and unpleasant secret about themselves. My students often indicate the importance they accord to psychological functions when they refer to the unconscious as the "subconscious," as though it were a nether world in which one stores away the junk that has outlived whatever usefulness it may have had or that was never very important in the first place. Whether this rejection of the unknown and, with it, anything that can't be empirically tested or measured in pragmatic terms has had a peculiar flourishing in America—as Constance M. Rourke argues in *The Roots of American Culture*—is a complicated question and one for another time. But what seems clear is that many of our students regard discussions of the psychological dimension of literature with feelings that range from indifference to distrust to disbelief. We may be able to talk about a character's motivation: Why, for instance, does the reckless Toad in *The Wind in the Willows* set off in his motorcar, against all better judgment and the lessons he has learned from his own experience? We may eventually arrive at such adjectives as "obsessive" or "compulsive," but there is often resistance to probe, more deeply than the purely descriptive level, the psyche of a character, a work, or a writer; and this seems to hold whether we are talking about Oedipus in a world masterpieces class or about Toad in children's literature.

In fact, students in children's literature courses are generally more interested in preserving what they believe to be the "innocence" of "kiddie lit." The fallen world, one that is aware of the darker side of human experience (those things that adults write about for other adults), many students feel should not be allowed to pollute what they believe ought to be the pristine world of children's books. Most students are baffled and many become angry when they are asked to consider, for example, the psychosexual interpretive possibilities of works written for or inherited by children. "What pervert could make up this stuff?" one student fumed during a discussion of Bruno Bettelheim's Freudian analysis of "Little Red Riding Hood." Even after hearing Charles Perrault's version, in which he explicitly makes it a cautionary tale about sexuality, seduction, and sexual abuse, many students are still unwilling to grant this possible reading to the story. Once a student scoffed that Perrault was, after all, French. Others have insisted that this is not the "correct" version of the story. "Sex and violence," one student complained. "Why does every fairy tale have to be about sex and violence?" In our current conservative climate, many more of my students agree with the child psychiatrist Richard Gardner, who advocates purging fairy tales of any potentially anxiety-producing elements, than with Leslie Fiedler, who maintains that fairy tales offer us ultimately healthy moments of "privileged insanity" (27).

Though Freud visited the United States in 1909 and many of his ideas about children have been incorporated into our conceptions of the child and our approaches to child rearing, there continues to be a puritanical suspicion of his theories of psychosexual development. Many of my students are as shocked to see Maurice Sendak's little Mickey fall out of his clothes, and frontally nude, across the pages of *In the Night Kitchen* as some of Sendak's critics were when the book first appeared in 1970. Students often denounce as prurient the idea that Mickey exemplifies Freud's genital stage of development—despite Sendak's obvious acknowledgment of that level of meaning. Why, of all the things Mickey could shout at the climactic moment of the story, does Sendak have him crow "Cock-a-Doodle Doo!" in 48-point type across the page?

There is also genuine surprise when I ask students to listen, with their older ears, to a rhyme they may themselves have chanted, in which the singer takes sadistic, wish-fulfilling relish in watching her baby brother, Tiny Tim, perish through a series of misadventures in the bathtub. Despite the sexual revolution, it is startling to find that psychological subjects like Judy Blume's treatment of biological and emotional coming of age in *Are You There God? It's Me, Margaret* and the natural curiosity about sexuality that surfaces in a work like John Neufield's *Freddie's Book* continue to set off such alarm bells in classrooms— and not only among students whose religious beliefs do not permit them to tolerate such subjects in a book a child might read. Even though there appears to be a greater public understanding and recognition of the effects of psychological trauma on children, this awareness does not necessarily lead to a sympathetic acceptance of works for older children and young adults that examine these emotionally upsetting experiences sensitively and honestly. Thus, *I Am the Cheese*, Robert Cormier's depiction of a boy's mental disturbance, for example, is dismissed as a "weird" or "negative" book that should not be recommended to children.

One explanation for these reactions may be that, as a culture, we tend to be literal-minded about so many things, including literature and particularly children's literature. If, for instance, a fairy tale contains violence, we assume it will "teach" violence to the child who reads it. If a fairy tale portrays a stepmother in a negative light, we fear that the child may learn to think badly of his or her own or someone else's stepmother. Hearing or reading a fairy tale that deals with subjects about which children are already anxious—such as being lost or abandoned—may, according to this line of reasoning, only fuel this fear. Of course, if we wished to avoid bringing children into contact with any book that might ignite their anxieties or raise important moral or ethical issues, there would be few books left on the shelf and scarcely any chances for children to engage those problems in the safe environment that a book creates. But literalism is even more psychologically limiting because, as James Hillman notes, it blocks emotional growth and causes us to lose "the imaginative metaphorical perspective to ourselves and our world" (*Loose Ends* 2). Such rigidity leads to a kind of categorical thinking that stereotypes the characteristics of children and adults, placing them into those bicameral pigeonholes in which "childhood tends to mean wonder, imagination, creative spontaneity while adulthood, the loss of these perspectives" or, conversely, that dismisses the imaginative and nonrational as "childish," while the rationality of the adult world is valorized. What is imperative, to borrow Hillman's response to the problem, is "restorying the adult—the teacher and the parent and the grandparent—in order to restore the imagination to a primary place in consciousness in each of us, regardless of age" (*Loose Ends* 4).

Whether as part of the therapeutic process or as a regular regimen for maintaining one's psychological balance, Hillman prescribes those highly imaginative works that are usually regarded as children's literature: myths, legends, folktales, fairy tales. These stories keep the adult from becoming "adulterated" and at the same time offer "a person images as containers for future experiences" ("Children" 6). In essence, these genres, which make up so much of children's literature, provide us with a mythical map, like the one of the Dreamtime that is created for every Australian aboriginal child who comes of age, that "initiates us into psychic reality, by telling about the creatures and perils of the soul and the heart's possibilities of blessing in images of universal intelligibility." This "higher education" elevates what has come to be known as children's literature to a central importance in our development because it is "a poiesis, a crafting or artificing of the imagination itself . . . a psychic breeding ground for an individual's own poetic process, the fantasy imagery that is the basis of religious, artistic, scientific, and social life" (5–6).

It is difficult, however, to convince students that they have such a poetic unconscious, one that should be explored, regardless of their majors. Most students remain guarded—understandably so. For to traverse this terrain is risky. It means leaping into a part of one's self that is unknown, shadowy, and, thus, frightening. But one doesn't usually jump without looking. Like Bilbo Baggins in *The Hobbit*, we need to be somehow forced into taking a voyage of self-discovery. Sometimes a book can act to spur such an inward journey, as Kafka observed in his famous remark about reading—that a book should be like an "axe which smashes the frozen sea within us" (qtd. in Chambers 17).

One of those ice-breaking works that can open students in an immediate way to the psychological power of literature in general and children's literature in particular is Ursula Le Guin's *Wizard of Earthsea*. This fantasy novel is a bildungsroman about Ged, a young wizard, and his encounter with his own dark side, which Le Guin calls and gives shape to as the Shadow. In an act of youthful, reckless bravado, Ged has summoned this creature from the Land of the Dead—the metaphorical underworld of the psyche—in order to show off his precocious powers as a magician. But he does not know how to control the formidable presence he has set loose in his world, upsetting its balance and nearly destroying himself in the process. After a series of successively more dangerous encounters with this dark force, Ged has only one remaining option: to turn to face it. In fact, he must become the hunter of the terrifying, shadowy form that has been pursuing him, tracking it to the farthest reaches of Earthsea if necessary in order to overcome its elusive, relentless power.

In *Man and His Symbols*, a collection of essays on Jungian psychology, Marie-Louise von Franz discusses the importance of this encounter with the shadow, one of those "primordial images" that Jung calls archetypes, those "symbolic images" that "are without known origin" and that "reproduce themselves in any time or in any part of the world." (Jung 68–69). The "realization of the shadow," von Franz notes in quoting Jung, is the beginning of individuation, the lifelong process of coming to know our own unconscious and its "regulating center," the Self. The shadow represents "those qualities and impulses [an individual] denies in himself but can plainly see in other people" (von Franz, "Process" 168).

For Le Guin, a careful reader of Jung,

> [t]he Shadow is the other side of our psyche, the dark brother of the conscious mind. It is Cain, Caliban, Frankenstein's monster, Mr. Hyde. It is Virgil who guided Dante through hell, Gilgamesh's friend Enkidu, Frodo's enemy Gollum. It is the Doppelganger. It is Mowgli's Grey Brother; the werewolf; the wolf, the bear, the tiger of a thousand folktales; it is the serpent, Lucifer. The shadow stands on the threshold between the conscious and the unconscious mind, and we meet it in our dreams, as sister, brother, friend, beast, monster, enemy, guide. It is all we don't want to, can't, admit into our conscious self, all the qualities and tendencies within us which have been repressed, denied, or not used. . . . The less you look at it . . . the stronger it grows, until it can become a menace, an intolerable load, a threat within the soul.   ("Child" 63–64)

Thus, on one important, thematic level, *A Wizard of Earthsea* can be seen as a dramatization of one young person's discovery of and reconciliation with his own shadow. However, this realization does not stop there: it leads to the broader, more mature psychological perception that

> the shadow is not simply evil. It is inferior, primitive, awkward, animal-like, childlike; powerful, vital, spontaneous. It's not weak and decent . . . it's dark and hairy and unseemly; but without it, the person is nothing. What is a body that casts no shadow? Nothing, a formlessness, two-dimensional, a comic-strip character. The person who denies his own profound relationship with evil denies his own reality. He cannot do, or make; he can only undo, unmake.   (64–65)

To begin to draw these connections between Le Guin's novel and the wider realm of the psyche to which her novel is alluding, one of course needs to introduce Jung's ideas into the discussion. I reserve this discussion until after the class has read the novel, to let the students experience what Jung calls the "peculiar fascination" that arises from contact with the archetypes evoked by a work like *A Wizard of Earthsea* (79). For the archetypes, Jung explains,

> are, at the same time, both images and emotions. One can speak of an archetype only when these two aspects are simultaneous. When there is merely the image, then there is simply a word-picture of little consequence. But by being charged with emotion, the image gains numinosity (or psychic energy); it becomes dynamic, and consequences of some kind must flow from it.   (96)

Among the more tangible consequences that occur when students read *A Wizard of Earthsea* is that a good many are, to a greater or lesser degree, upset by it. Some will admit to being terrified by the book; others vociferously reject it as a work of "children's" literature, preferring to see it as an anxiety producer for children in an already sufficiently tense world. Once they have read Le Guin's essay on the shadow, which I also assign, many are even more agitated: What could she possibly mean, they ask, by suggesting that children—even preadolescents—should become more aware of their own dark side, of their own "profound relationship with evil"? What does she mean when she writes:

> Unadmitted to consciousness, the shadow is projected outward, onto others. There's nothing wrong with me—it's *them*. I'm not a monster, other people are monsters. All foreigners are evil. All communists are evil. All capitalists are evil. It was the cat that made me kick him, Mummy.
>
> ("Child" 64)

Why should we become conscious, students will often say, of all this negative stuff? Again, literalism has clicked on.

However, class discussions of the shadow can also be among the most exciting of the course, because students are asked to examine a symbol that not only has a literary manifestation but that, because of the capacity of archetypes to affect us emotionally, cannot help but have a personal relevance and resonance. From an exploration of Ged's motives and actions—his arrogant unwillingness to look beyond himself, his proud hatred of his rival, Jasper, and his projection onto Jasper of his (Ged's) own dark qualities—the class quickly acknowledges how we all use others as a kind of screen onto which we cast our own shadowy projections. From these recognitions, we can begin to explore the wider implications of the shadow archetype and what Jung referred to as the "living reality" of these symbols in our own lives and in our culture. We often look at other examples of the shadow as well—from reigning nasties of the media to contemporary hysterias about national political "enemies," from nursery rhymes or poetry for younger children (like Stevenson's "My Shadow") to the legislation of apartheid. The point in drawing on such wide-ranging and often extraliterary examples is to create a context in which the students can see the vital presence that an archetype has and thus gain a sense of its ability to influence us at every age and on a number of levels of experience. Jung insists that we should not "treat archetypes as if they were part of a mechanical system that can be learned by rote." Rather, Jung believes, "they are not mere names, or even philosophical concepts. They are pieces of life itself—images that are integrally connected to the living individual by the bridge of the emotions" (96).

During class discussions, I present a general overview of Jung's ideas, noting some of the basic differences between his model of the psyche and that of his early teacher Freud. For instance, it is necessary to point out how, for Jung, the unconscious is regarded not as simply the center for instinctive impulses and drives (id) but rather as the source for those "symbolic images," the archetypes, that have inhabited humankind's dreams, mythology, and art for millennia. A major idea that I work with is Jung's belief that the development both of individuals' understanding of themselves and of a culture's understanding of itself entail increased consciousness of the unconscious, which "contains all aspects of human nature—light and dark, beautiful and ugly, good and evil, profound and silly" (103). Civilization and personal enlightenment, for Jung, both depend on our ability to pay attention to and come to know about those "inner motives" that "spring from a deep source that is not made by consciousness and is not under its control." The spirits of ancient mythology "are as active as they ever were," Jung insists. In modern society, "gods and demons have not disappeared at all; they have merely got new names," and they demand of us, as they required of the ancients, a commitment to introspection, must as we might like to avoid this difficult task (82).

Individuation is the name Jung uses to refer to the lifelong process of becoming more aware of the unconscious. Von Franz describes individuation in *Man and His Symbols* as a "slow, imperceptible process of psychic growth . . . the conscious coming-to-terms with one's own inner center . . . or Self" ("Process" 161, 166). The Self is "an inner guiding factor . . . the regulating center that brings about a constant extension and maturing of the personality" (163). Through a study of our dreams and their archetypal content, we become, in essence, more Self-conscious, more able to integrate the archetypal material of the unconscious into our conscious life. "The study of individual, as well as of collective, symbolism is an enormous task, and one that has not yet been mastered," Jung writes (103). But the important thing is to begin to recognize that "seemingly unending web of archetypal patterns" that give meaning to our individual and collective lives (81).

Although I introduce a number of Jung's ideas formally in the context of discussing *A Wizard of Earthsea* because of the novel's particularly Jungian nature, it would be equally possible to do so at virtually any point in the course—with nursery rhymes, picture books, fairy tales, mythology, folklore, or realistic fiction. In fact, a whole course could be structured around a Jungian approach to children's literature, focusing on the archetypal images and themes that are woven into the fabric of individual works and that also appear in a wide spectrum of genres, historical periods, and cultures. Thus in *A Wizard of Earthsea*, it is important to look not only at the motif of the shadow as it emerges in the book but also at the larger, archetypal pattern that the novel brings alive: that of the hero and his guest. For Ged's story is a variation on the theme of the archetypal symbol that Joseph Campbell has called the "hero with a thousand faces." According to this theme, such heroes are called on an adventure in which they leave the security of home for a perilous series of trials that test their mettle. Ultimately, they must confront a superhuman or supernatural power over which they manage to triumph in the end; they can thus return transformed, themselves the agents of future transformation, to the world or society they left at the

outset. There are other archetypal elements in *A Wizard of Earthsea*—
for instance, those of the *puer aeternus* and the *senex*, the figures of the
eternal child and the wise elder. These figures represent those eternal
oppositions between youth and age, innocence and experience, impet-
uousness and caution, future and past, immortality and mortality. The
book is also a working out and a bringing into balance of this conflict:
Ged, the gifted but brash young wizard, realizes that he cannot deal
with his shadow alone. He needs the help of the aged Archemage of
Roke, who sacrifices his life saving Ged from destruction in one of his
early encounters with the Shadow. Then Ged must have the wise coun-
sel of Ogion, his old teacher, who instructs the young man in how to
come to terms with the enemy that is slowly destroying him.

In the end, the novels in Le Guin's *Earthsea* trilogy reflect, in their
complex interweaving of archetypal material, the process of individuation, of Self-awareness that Jung sees as central to the development of
human spirit from which the psyche takes its name. In the process, the
reader, like the hero Ged, is also asked to pass through the gates of horn
and ivory that separate the relatively safe, waking world from the unfamiliar and often dangerous realm of the unconscious. Ged's adventure
is, on some fundamental level, our own as well, and it provides us with
a powerful means for bringing the psychological dimension into the discussion of children's literature.

There are, of course, other approaches for introducing students to
the shadow and, thus, to an exploration of the unconscious. In *Sharing
Literature with Children*, for instance, Francella Butler organizes the readings of one of her chapters around the archetypal theme of the shadow,
including such widely ranging genres and works as Aesop's fable "The
Dog and the Shadow"; African and American Indian folktales; short
fantasies like Hans Christian Andersen's "Shadow" and Virginia
Hamilton's "How Jahdu Ran through Darkness in No Time at All";
and "shadowy" poetry from such writers as J. R. R. Tolkien ("The
Mewlips"), Rachel Field ("My Inside-Self"), and John Ciardi ("Sometimes I Feel This Way") (192–264). As Butler and others have pointed
out, the shadow occurs in many other works for younger and older children and for adolescents—so much so, in fact, that its frequent mani-
festations demand our attention. The shadow lurks around the edges of
the "more intimate and personal images" of nursery rhymes (Carter
25). Its presence is palpably present in picture books like Sendak's *Where
the Wild Things Are* or the recent translation by Marcia Brown of Blaise
Cendras's primordial celebration of the archetype in *Shadow*. Nor are the
shadow's appearances limited to fantasy; it is an important element in
such realistic novels as Cormier's *Chocolate War* in the figure of Archie
Costello, one of adolescent fiction's most villainous characters. Cormier
develops this dark side even more consciously in the sequel to that
book, *Beyond the Chocolate War*, in which he has Archie tell one of the

boys who has tried, unsuccessfully, to kill Archie, "You'll always have me wherever you go and whatever you do. . . . Because I'm you. I'm all the things you hide inside you. That's me" (264).

Jung's ideas speak immediately and personally to me; they hold for me certain fundamental truths about human psychological nature, and they offer a productive, expansive way for discussing literature, one that is suited to the symbolic, metaphorical nature of language, literature, and the arts as a whole. Jungian approaches to literature do not preclude other interpretations and they do not lead, it seems to me, to reductive or absolute readings of a text. Though she is writing about fairy tales, von Franz is also describing a basic principle of any Jungian reading of a text when she insists that there is no one correct interpretation of a work, since, ultimately, "there is no possibility of translating its content into intellectual terms." Rather, "the best we can do is to circumscribe it on the basis of our psychological experience and from comparative studies, bringing into the light, as it were, the whole net of associations in which the archetypal images are enmeshed" (*Fairy Tales* 1). The process of analysis thus becomes, at least in part, an act of personal discovery as the psyche of the reader draws in the net it has cast to catch a glimpse of those bright, elusive elements of that shadowy, secret Self.

University of Florida

Works Cited

Butler, Francelia. *Sharing Literature with Children: A Thematic Anthology.* New York: McKay, 1977.

Carter, Robert. "The Tao and Mother Goose." *Parabola* 5.4 (1981): 19–26.

Chambers, Aidan. *Booktalk: Occasional Writing on Literature and Children.* New York: Harper, 1985.

Cormier, Robert. *Beyond the Chocolate War.* New York: Knopf, 1985.

Fiedler, Leslie. "Fairy Tales—without Apologies." Rev. of *The Uses of Enchantment,* by Bruno Bettelheim. *Saturday Review* 15 May 1976: 24–27.

Hillman, James. "The Children, the Children." *Children's Literature* 8 (1980): 3–6.

———— . *Loose Ends: Primary Papers in Archetypal Psychology.* Zurich: Spring, 1978.

Jung, Carl Gustav, ed. *Man and His Symbols.* New York: Doubleday, 1954.

Le Guin, Ursula K. "The Child and the Shadow." *The Language of the Night: Essays on Fantasy and Science Fiction.* New York: Putnam's, 1979.

———— . *A Wizard of Earthsea.* New York: Bantam, 1975.

Rourke, Constance M. *The Roots of American Culture and Other Essays.* 1942. Westport: Greenwood, 1980.

von Franz, Marie-Louise. *Interpretation of Fairy Tales.* Zurich: Spring, 1973.

———— . "The Process of Individuation." Jung 158–229.

GENERIC ISSUES

Reading Fairy Tales

Maria Tatar

Those who write about fairy tales are often accused of casting evil spells on the world of fantasy or, worse yet, of breaking magic spells. We are entitled to search for the hidden meanings of literary texts, but fairy tales count as sacred stories meant to enchant rather than to edify. To analyze them is to destroy them. It is easy to take a cynical view and adopt the position taken by the King of Hearts in *Alice in Wonderland*. "If there's no meaning in it," he asserts, "that saves a world of trouble, you know, as we needn't try to find any" (Carroll 94). Most critics, however, have favored the position embraced by the Duchess: "Everything's got a moral, if only you can find it" (67). There is something to be said for the view that fairy tales have no meaning (and that they move in the mode of the absurd) as well as for the view that they are charged with meaning (and can be read as allegories). But there are numerous other positions and possibilities—these will be explored as we look at the evolution of the tales and at their interpretive history.

Tolkien tells us that fairy tales did not always belong to the culture of childhood—they were retired only relatively recently to the nursery, just as "shabby or old-fashioned furniture is relegated to the play-room, primarily because the adults do not want it" (34). For centuries, folktales served the cause of adult entertainment. At fireside gatherings, around the kiln, in the spinning room, or in workrooms, tales were told to while away a long winter evening or to shorten the hours devoted to domestic and agricultural chores. Peasants told many of the tales, but aristocrats also found them amusing and depended on them, sometimes to relieve boredom, at times to induce sleep (Ariès 95–98). The storytelling tradition survives today in pockets of rural culture—folk raconteurs still entertain villagers with their tales of mystery and magic in the backwaters of many countries (Dégh 163–264).

The precise historical juncture at which folktales, in particular fairy tales, transformed themselves from adult entertainment into children's

OUACHITA TECHNICAL COLLEGE

literature is difficult to identify. The frame story of Giambattista Basile's
Pentamerone (1634–37) describes the Neapolitan narratives in that collection as "those tales that old women tell to amuse children" (1: 9).
Yet the stories in the *Pentamerone* must have been aimed primarily at
adults: it is hard to believe that a tale (I cite only one of many possible
examples) in which a boy calls an old woman a "blood-sucking witch,
baby-smotherer, lump of filth, fart-face" was really intended as bed-
time reading for children. Charles Perrault's *Tales of Mother Goose*
(*Histoires; ou, Contes du temps passé*), published in 1697, is often seen as
pivotal with respect to the question of the audience. As Robert Samber,
its first English translator, observed, "not only Children, but those of
Maturity" would find in the tales "uncommon Pleasure and Delight."
Perrault offered "morals" right along with entertainment, and they
were often framed with both adult and child in mind. Consider, for
example, the double lesson of "Bluebeard." I present each "moral" in
abbreviated form:

> Curiosity in spite of its charms
> Often brings with it many regrets . . .

and for "those of Maturity":

> The time of strict husbands has passed,
> And none will demand the impossible,
> Even if plagued by jealousy and doubt.
> He whispers sweet things in his wife's ear;
> And no matter what color his beard may be,
> It is not hard to tell who is the master.
> (*Contes* 128–29; my trans.)

The story is clearly directed at two audiences. The first of its two morals
teaches children a lesson about a vice that can be an endless source of
aggravation to parents. The second is not really a moral but a witticism
designed to keep adults from nodding off.

Perrault's collection straddles almost perfectly the line between
adult entertainment and children's literature. Later collectors may initially have conceived their volumes of folktales, legends, and folk songs
with the amusement of adults in mind but found themselves, whether
intentionally or not, responding to a growing demand for children's
books. As the audience changed, the tales changed, eliminating off-
color episodes and adding didactic elements. The Grimms' *Nursery and
Household Tales* (1812–15), for example, began as a scholarly project that
was to serve as a contribution to the "history of poetry" for the entire
nation, but it turned into an anthology of tales directed almost exclusively
at children. The same holds true for many of the other great nineteenth-
century collections, a large number of which were inspired by the

Grimms' pioneering work in the field of folklore (Afanasev; Jacobs; Asbjørnsen and Moe).

Not all folktales became a part of the culture of childhood. Adults bequeathed to children specific types of stories, primarily magical tales that placed heroes and heroines on the road to high adventure. "Hansel and Gretel," "Little Red Riding Hood," "Jack the Giant Killer," "Cinderella," and "Tom Thumb," which have all become classics of children's literature, pit the weak against witches, ogres, giants, and other menacing supernatural presences. No matter how helpless the victims seem at the start of these tales, they nearly always succeed in triumphing over their wicked adversaries. That these tales would prove especially satisfying to children, who perceive themselves without the requisite strength or power to challenge the adult world, is a point well made by the psychologist Bruno Bettelheim in his *Uses of Enchantment*.

Many of the magical tales cited above have also been turned into cautionary tales. "Little Red Riding Hood," for example, which started out as a bawdy folktale with a heroine who performs a striptease for the wolf, was turned by Perrault, the Grimms, and others into a stern lesson on the importance of obedience. Some versions of the tale show Red Riding Hood escaping from the wolf by telling him that she must go outdoors to relieve herself. When she tarries too long, the wolf wants to know exactly what she is up to: "Are you making a load out there? Are you making a load?" (Delarue). As folktales moved from workrooms and fireside gatherings into the nursery, they generally lost much of their earthy humor (both bawdy and scatological) even as they retained and sometimes strengthened their exposition of violence. Neither Perrault nor the brothers Grimm show us the protagonist of "Little Red Riding Hood" stripping before the wolf or relieving herself, but both work hard to build tension in the scene that unfolds in the bedroom right before the wolf pounces on his victim. And both turn the story into a cautionary tale, the one warning about the dangers of listening to strangers (Perrault), the other about the perils of straying from the proper path (Grimms). Magical tales, which show the heroes and heroines defeating ogres and outwitting giants, generally follow the pattern of victimization and revenge. Cautionary tales, by contrast, defeat the protagonists by staging a transgression and its punishment (with a rescue scene often appended to soften the blow). These stories, with their strong disciplinary edge, have a certain undeniable appeal to parents who seek to teach lessons as they tell stories (Tatar 179–92).

The term *fairy tale* has gained the widest currency for designating the two (overlapping) types of stories described above. Although the term is misleading (there are very few fairies in most such tales) and is used in a notoriously imprecise fashion (to designate everything from rough-hewn traditional tales to stylized literary texts), I will use it here to identify those folktales that have, by common consensus and convention, become children's literature.

The avenues for approaching fairy tales and for understanding the complexities of their simplicity are legion. The history of folklore scholarship began, however, not with the interpretation of tales but with the task of defining, collecting, and classifying them. Let us start with the most basic question: Just what is a folktale? Purists might insist that the genre exists only as part of an oral tradition passed on from one generation to the next—preferably by rugged peasant narrators seated around the fire husking corn and mending scythes on chilling autumn nights. In this case, the experts actually know better. The folktale is a notoriously elastic genre, accommodating all manner of prose narratives, both written and oral. Stith Thompson reminds us of the folktale's most salient feature: "The teller of a folktale," he observes, "is proud of his ability to hand on that which he has received" (*Folktale* 4). Rather than priding themselves on their creative genius and inventive spirit, folk raconteurs bank heavily on traditional materials (themes worked and reworked over a period of centuries) to shape their stories. For this reason, the tales they tell are often referred to as *traditional tales* or *traditional literature*. Recording an oral narrative does not necessarily deprive it of its status as a folktale. The recorded version may fall flat; it may be retold nearly beyond recognition of the original; and it may fail to capture the interpretive elements (facial movements, gestures, changes in intonation) that often accompany an oral narrative. Still it remains a folktale, even if it moves from the realm of folklore into the area of what Richard Dorson and Alan Dundes have defined as "fakelore."

Unlike the literary text, the folktale knows no stable form. For nearly every tale, we have hundreds, and in some cases thousands, of extant forms. Each text could be called a corrupt version of the original (if it ever existed at all), but it could also be seen as one of an infinite number of legitimate variant forms. Soon after the term *folklore* was coined by William Thoms and the field became established as a scholarly discipline, folklorists set themselves the task of collecting and classifying the vast array of materials that constituted their domain. *The Types of the Folktale* (*Verzeichnis der Märchentypen*), a landmark study of 1910 by the Finnish scholar Antti Aarne, set up a classification system of tale types that, despite criticism from various quarters, today still provides the basic point of reference for the study of folktales. In its final form Aarne's catalog, which was translated and enlarged by Thompson, contains 2,499 tale types divided into five categories: animal tales, ordinary folktales, jokes and anecdotes, formula tales, and unclassified tales. For each type, Aarne and Thompson provide a summary of the tale, a breakdown of the chief motifs (the smallest possible narrative units), and bibliographical references. The tale-type index is supple-

mented by Thompson's *Motif-Index of Folk-Literature*, a six-volume reference work classifying the basic elements that constitute the plots of
traditional literature from around the world.

The work of Aarne and Thompson laid the foundation for folktale
scholarship and made clear the importance of comparative analysis.
Henceforth it would be impossible—or at least methodologically un-
sound—to study a tale in isolation. It may have seemed astonishing that
Aarne and Thompson could reduce the countless numbers of extant
folktales to only 2,499 tale types, but by contrast with the calculations of
their Russian colleague Vladimir Propp, that number seemed down-
right astronomical. In *The Morphology of the Folktale*, published in 1928,
Propp declared that "all fairy tales are of one type in regard to their
structure." Rather than classify tales by themes (a "dangerous" mistake
made by Aarne), the Russian folklorist preferred to show how the building blocks (he identifies thirty-one functions and seven spheres of action) of all fairy tales remain constant and help us understand the
predictability of fairy tale plots.

In recent years, folklorists have heeded the call of Alan Dundes not
to abdicate the important work of analysis to those unschooled in their
discipline ("Study of Folklore"). They too have begun to produce readings that, along with those of anthropologists, feminists, theologians,
psychologists, historians, literary critics, and others, have enriched and
deepened our understanding of the tales. Dundes himself, an avowed
Freudian, has urged his colleagues to focus on the family conflicts dra-
matized in fairy tales ("Psychoanalytic Study of Folklore"). Incest, child
abandonment, sexual jealousy, sibling rivalry, mutilation, murder, and
cannibalism: these are just a few of the preferred themes of fairy tales.
In many instances, especially when studying unbowdlerized tales, it
make no sense to search for latent meanings, because the tales in fact
conceal so little. They openly dramatize the kinds of events that are ordinarily suppressed in children's literature: erotic intrigue, physical suffering, violent deaths, and grim acts of revenge. Freud's description of
myth as "psychology projected onto the external world" (6: 258) could
be said to hold true for folktales as well. Fairy tales, in particular, give
us exaggerated and distorted (one might even say uncensored) forms of
internal conflicts played out in the context of family life.

Although psychoanalysis remains one of the best optics we have for
looking at the dynamics of family life in fairy tales, psychoanalytic criticism seems to raise a red flag wherever it goes—not entirely without
reason. In the name of psychoanalysis, red caps have been turned into
symbols of menstruation, houses made of gingerbread into the bodies of
mothers, and golden eggs into anal ideas of possession. Our faith in
psychoanalytic readings of fairy tales is quickly undermined once we
begin comparing the interpretations and discover how different they
are, even when they have all emerged from the same school. It is not

only the larger contours of the tale's plot that generate disagreement but even the fine points of detail. Let us look at the case of the dwarfs in "Snow White." For Bettelheim, these seven hardworking fellows represent the days of the week, and also the seven metals and the seven planets. In addition, these little men, "with their stunted bodies and their mining occupation—they skillfully penetrate into dark holes—all suggest phallic connotations" (210). Bettelheim's obvious discomfort with these creatures (since he cannot find one satisfactory explanation for their existence, he reaches for several) will be shared by anyone who reviews various assessments of the dwarfs' role in the tale. One critic sees the seven men as siblings of the heroine, another finds that they represent Snow White's unconscious mind, while a third views them as a group of homosexuals (Spörk 176–78). When we turn to another analysis and discover that the dwarfs symbolize Snow White's genitals, it becomes difficult not to flinch in disbelief (Gmelin 41).

While even the most astute psychoanalytic critics can go wrong when it comes to details, less restrained interpreters are perfectly capable of doing violence to an entire text. Consider the following recent observations on "Rumpelstiltskin":

> The miller's boasting of his daughter's gold-spinning ability conveys as well as conceals the threat of a son's powerful rivalry toward his father (the King). Thus, on a preoedipal level of understanding, the miller cedes his great power (gold-feces) to his father, a manic-restitutive defense conveyed verbally by his boastfulness. On an oedipal level of understanding, he thereby also denies his incestuous wish to impregnate his own daughter, to have a baby by her. Also inherent in his offer are the elements of a covert *menage-à-trois*, a sharing of one female between two males which, together with the anal aspects of the miller's offer, point toward his self-abnegatory homosexual desire toward his King-father.
>
> (Rinsely and Bergmann 7)

When we further hear that Rumpelstiltskin's stomping is "symbolic of masturbation" and learn that his gold spinning suggests "a child playing with his own feces, a masturbatory precursor," it becomes difficult to suspend disbelief. These are the kinds of uncontrolled interpretations that give psychoanalytic criticism of both folktales and literary texts a bad name. There are enough such examples around to make psychoanalytic interpretations an easy target for ridicule.

These documented cases of overinterpretation or misinterpretation would be enough to discourage most people from adopting psychoanalysis as a tool for analyzing fairy tales. More serious, however, are the undocumented cases of misguided psychoanalytic discourse. These virtually all begin in the same way: "Psychoanalytic critics would say . . ." That opening phrase, or a variant of it, is followed by a preposterous statement equating one character, motif, or object in a tale with an anatomical part or a psychoanalytic concept. The very ring of the phrase "psychoanalytic critics would say" is now a negative one, and few fail to cringe in anticipation of the far-fetched statements that inevitably follow. Two examples must suffice. In an analysis of "The Juniper Tree," Lutz Röhrich observes that "psychoanalytic critics would see in the motif of dismemberment a symbol of castration or castration anxiety" (194; my trans.). The child psychologist Carl-Heinz Mallet notes, with regard to the male hero of "The Juniper Tree," that "psychoanalytic critics would immediately see the boy as the phallus of the husband" (216). These hypothetical psychoanalytic critics lead a strange, ghostly double life in the literature on fairy tales: they serve as both straw men and as whipping boys for other critics. Anyone who accepts the label "psychoanalytic critic" has to take on the burden of all the actual errors made by such critics along with all the potential mistakes attributed to them.

Psychoanalytic critics can be dogmatic; they can misread the details of a text; and they can even get an entire text wrong. But their errors are no graver than those found in sociohistorical readings, in feminist interpretations, and even in folkloristic analyses. At the same time, psychoanalysis can put us on the right track for understanding a number of prominent fairy tale themes. In stories ranging from "The Juniper Tree" through "Tom Thumb" to "Sleeping Beauty," for example, cannibalism figures as a significant motif. A woman chops up the corpse of her stepson and serves him up to her husband in a stew; an ogre relishes the thought of eating seven brothers for dinner; a woman develops an appetite for her grandchildren. It would not be terribly useful in any of these cases to consult handbooks on the actual practice of cannibalism. Here, psychoanalysis, with its attempt to investigate such matters as the fear of being devoured and oral fixation, can be far more useful than the study of historically documented incidents of cannibalism (*Destins du cannibalisme*; Fenichal).

Because the fairy tale privileges descriptions of family life, it lends itself eminently well to psychoanalysis. But fairy tales also operate like magnets, picking up bits and pieces of everyday reality so that they come to be littered with cultural debris. As Italo Calvino has put it, "The folktale, regardless of its origin, tends to absorb something of the place where it is narrated—a landscape, a custom, a moral outlook, or else merely a very faint accent or flavor of that locality" (xxi). In an Italian version of "The Three Spinners," for example, the heroine downs endless amounts of lasagna in order to take the edge off her nervousness about spinning endless quantities of flax. Such culturally determined details can be found in any folkloric item, though it is not always as easy as in this case to assign a place to them.

To state that fairy tales give us psychological drama set in culturally determined scenes is to make an almost trivial point. But even our best interpreters of fairy tales have a way of choosing up sides in the debate over the degree to which fairy tales reflect psychic or cultural realities. We have seen how psychoanalytic critics can take tales and treat them as if they were "flattened out, like patients on a couch, in a timeless contemporaneity" (Darnton 13). But historians slide with ease to the opposite extreme when they argue, as Eugen Weber does, that these tales may be about "real people" and then proceed to treat these literary tales as if they were historical documents (96). To be sure, most historians take a more measured view and study fairy tales in search of clues about the facts of everyday life in past ages and about the *mentalité* of a specific culture. But even if one assumes that history was "immobile" at the village level during the age in which these tales flourished in oral form and just before they were recorded in the large collections of the nineteenth century, it becomes difficult to sort out fact from fantasy and to determine exactly which details can be seen as timeless universals and which can be read as specific to a culture.

The battle between psychoanalysis and history on the terrain of folklore should not divert our attention completely from various skirmishes of less central methodological importance. It is astonishing to observe how scholars from virtually every discipline and of every methodological persuasion have a contribution to make when it comes to fairy tales. "Little Red Riding Hood" has been read by historians as a realistic text based on accounts of werewolves attacking and devouring children. Psychiatrists have found in the story an exposition of "human passions, oral greediness, aggression, and pubertal desires" (Bettelheim 182). But there are also studies of the tale by legal experts (who offer disquisitions on the wolf's punishment) and by solar mythologists (who liken Little Red Riding Hood to the sun, which is engulfed by darkness at the end of its journey). Ideologues of the Third Reich hailed Red Riding Hood as a symbol of the German people, terrorized but finally liberated from the clutches of a Jewish wolf, and feminists have found in the story a parable of rape that teaches young women about ferocious male beasts. Once we decide to move from a literal reading to a symbolic interpretation, we perform an operation that frees us to substitute virtually any power perceived as predatory for the wolf and any entity perceived as innocent for Red Riding Hood. Each fairy tale text has a certain polysemic quality to it, rendering it capable of generating an almost endless number of interpretations (Turner 41–42).

Readings of Perrault's "Bluebeard" tell us something about the hazards of moving too swiftly from the literal to the symbolic plane. When the key that Bluebeard's wife used to open the door forbidden to her becomes stained with the blood of Bluebeard's dead wives, it is not Bluebeard who comes under fire as a serial murderer, but his wife as an adulteress. The bloodied key has been read as a sign of "marital infidelity"; it marks the heroine's "irreversible loss of her virginity"; it stands as a sign of "defloration." For one critic, the forbidden chamber is "clearly the vaginal area," while the bloody key is a "symbol of the loss of chastity" (Dundes, "Psychoanalytic Study of the Grimms' Tales" 56). If one recalls that the bloody chamber is strewn with the corpses of Bluebeard's previous wives, this reading becomes more than odd. And it is difficult to understand exactly why the heroine's opening of a door should be equated with sexual betrayal (Tatar 156–70).

The proper interpretation of fairy tales remains a hotly debated subject. Just as controversial has been the question of the pedagogical value of these tales. Bettelheim's claim that listening to fairy tales can provide children with powerful therapeutic benefits has been challenged by many critics, but that has not prevented it from becoming dogma in many circles. The graphic descriptions of cruel and unusual punishments in many fairy tale anthologies may in fact not provide children with the best possible nighttime fare. In Italian tales, witches are regularly coated with pitch and burned to death; German tales show them being rolled down hills in barrels studded with nails; in Russian tales they freeze to death. Fairy tale heroes and heroines also do not always serve as ideal models for children. When faced with a crisis, they typically respond by sitting down and having a good cry. Rather than rely on their own resources, they often depend on magical means and supernatural helpers to gain their ends. Lying, cheating, and stealing also become perfectly acceptable, so long as such practices enable them to move further down the road to wealth and social promotion through a good marriage.

Jack Zipes has argued persuasively that fairy tales play an influential role in socializing children. Most of the tale collections canonized by our culture, however, fail his test of the right values. Perrault, for example, shows us women who demonstrate "reserve and patience," who remain passive until "the right man comes along." For the male figures alone, Perrault reserves "remarkable minds, courage, and deft manners." The "ideal types" fashioned by Perrault were used to reinforce "the standards of the civilizing process set by upper-class French society" (25–26). Zipes concedes that "it would be foolish to reject the entire classical canon as socially useless or aesthetically outmoded" and advocates reappropriation of the tales by more liberal and enlightened minds. His concerns are shared by feminist critics in particular, for so many fairy tale heroines suffer silently until released from a humble state by a male figure (Stone; Bottigheimer). Heroes are not always as courageous and dashing as some would have us believe—but they generally take a more active role than their female counterparts in shaping their destinies.

Fairy tales have left a mark on nearly every childhood. Scholars in pursuit of their deeper meanings and their hidden messages may risk breaking their magic spell, but they also help us understand something about the values and assumptions embedded in a story. There is nothing sacred about any specific fairy tale. Each is of value as a document true to its time and place. But since we may not necessarily want a child to hear how the Grimms' wicked queen demands Snow White's lungs and liver or to witness the thrill that Walt Disney's Snow White gets from housekeeping, there is nothing wrong with preserving the old versions as historical documents and creating new ones for the entertainment of children. Keeping the storytelling tradition alive requires changes in words and variations in detail.

Children may have appropriated fairy tales, turning the childhood of fiction into the fiction of childhood, but they did not leave adults entirely empty-handed. George Dasent, a renowned scholar of Old Norse, congratulated the brothers Grimm in particular on elevating "what had come to be looked on as mere nursery fictions and old wives' fables—to a study fit for the energies of grown men, and to all the dignity of a science" (xix). Now, one hundred years after these observations, the need to legitimize the study of fairy tales is no longer so urgent. It has become both an art and a science—for young and for old, for male and for female.

Harvard University

Works Cited

Aarne, Antti. *The Types of the Folktale: A Classification and Bibliography.* Trans. and enlarged by Stith Thompson. 2nd ed. Helsinki: Academia Scientiarum Fennica, 1981.

——— . *Verzeichnis der Märchentypen.* Helsinki: Academia Scientiarum Fennica, 1910.

Afanasev, Alexander Nikolaevitch. *Russian Folktales.* 1855–64. New York: Pantheon, 1945.

Ariès, Philippe. *Centuries of Childhood: A Social History of Family Life.* Trans. Robert Baldick. New York: Vintage-Random, 1962.

Asbjørnsen, Peter Christen, and Jørgen Moe. *Norwegian Folk Tales.* 1845. Trans. Pat Shaw and Carl Norman. New York: Pantheon, 1960.

Basile, Giambattista. *The Pentamerone.* Trans. Benedetto Croce. Ed. N. M. Penzer. 2 vols. London: Bodley, 1932.

Bettelheim, Bruno. *The Uses of Enchantment: The Meaning and Importance of Fairy Tales.* New York: Vintage-Random, 1977.

Bottigheimer, Ruth B. *Grimms' Bad Girls and Bold Boys: The Moral and Social Vision of the Tales.* New Haven: Yale UP, 1987.

Calvino, Italo. Introduction. *Italian Folktales.* Selected and retold by Italo Calvino. Trans. George Martin. New York: Pantheon, 1980.

Carroll, Lewis. *Alice's Adventures in Wonderland and Through the Looking-Glass.* New York: Bantam, 1981.

Darnton, Robert. "Peasants Tell Tales: The Meaning of Mother Goose." *The Great Cat Massacre and Other Episodes in French Cultural History.* New York: Basic, 1984. 8–72.

Dasent, George. Introduction. *Popular Tales from the Norse*. New York: Putnam's, 1888.

Dégh, Linda. *Märchen, Erzähler und Erzählgemeinschaft*. East Berlin: Akademie, 1962.

Delarue, Paul, ed. "Le Petit Chaperon Rouge." *Le Conte populaire français*. Vol. 1. Paris: Maisonneuve, 1967. 373–74.

Destins du cannibalisme. Spec. issue of *Nouvelle Revue de Psychanalyse* 6 (1972).

Dorson, Richard M. "Fakelore." *Zeitschrift für Volkskunde* 65 (1969): 56–64.

Dundes, Alan. "Nationalistic Inferiority Complexes and the Fabrication of Fakelore: A Reconsideration of Ossian, the *Kinder- und Hausmärchen*, the *Kalevala* and Paul Bunyan." *Journal of Folklore Research* 22 (1985): 5–18.

———. "The Psychoanalytic Study of Folklore." *Annals of Scholarship* 3 (1985): 1–42.

———. "The Psychoanalytic Study of the Grimms' Tales with Special Reference to 'The Maiden without Hands' (AT 706)." *Germanic Review* 62 (1987): 50–65.

———. "The Study of Folklore in Literature and Culture: Identification and Interpretation." *Journal of American Folklore* 78 (1965): 136–42.

Fenichal, Otto. "The Dread of Being Eaten." *Collected Papers*. New York: Norton, 1953. 158–59.

Freud, Sigmund. *The Psychopathology of Everyday Life*. Vol. 6 of *The Standard Edition of the Complete Psychological Works*. Trans. James Strachey. London: Hogarth, 1960.

Gmelin, Otto F. *Böses kommt aus Kinderbüchern: Die verpassten Möglichkeiten kindlicher Bewusstseinsbildung*. Munich: Kindler, 1972.

Jacobs, Joseph. *English Fairy Tales*. 1890. London: Bodley, 1968.

Mallet, Carl-Heinz. *Kopf ab! Gewalt im Märchen*. Hamburg: Rasch, 1985.

Perrault, Charles. *Histoires, ou, Contes du temps passe*. Ed. Gilbert Rouger. Paris: Garnier, 1967.

Propp, Vladimir. *The Morphology of the Folktale*. 1928. Trans. Laurence Scott. 2nd ed. Austin: U of Texas P, 1968.

Rinsley, Donald B., and Elizabeth Bergmann. "Enchantment and Alchemy: The Story of Rumpelstiltskin." *Bulletin of the Menninger Clinic* 47 (1984): 1–14.

Röhrich, Lutz. "Die Grausamkeit im deutschen Märchen." *Rheinisches Jahrbuch für Volkskunde*. Bonn: Dümmler, 1955. 176–224.

Samber, Robert. Dedication. *Histories or Tales of Past Times*. By M. Perrault. Trans. Robert Samber. London: Pote, 1729. Rpt. in *The Authentic Mother Goose Fairy Tales and Nursery Rhymes*. Ed. Jacques Barchilon and Henry Pettit. Denver: Swallow, 1960.

Spörk, Ingrid. *Studien zu ausgewählten Märchen der Brüder Grimm: Frauenproblematik, Struktur, Rollentheorie, Psychoanalyse, Überlieferung, Rezeption*. Königstein: Hain, 1985.

Stone, Kay F. "Feminist Approaches to the Interpretation of Fairy Tales." *Fairy Tales and Society: Illusion, Allusion, and Paradigm*. Ed. Ruth B. Bottigheimer. Philadelphia: U of Pennsylvania P, 1986. 229–36.

Tatar, Maria. *The Hard Facts of the Grimms' Fairy Tales*. Princeton: Princeton UP, 1987.

Thompson, Stith. *The Folktale*. 1946. Berkeley: U of California P, 1977.

———. *The Motif-Index of Folk-Literature*. Rev. ed. 6 vols. Bloomington: Indiana UP, 1955–58.

Thoms, William. "Folklore." *The Study of Folklore*. Ed. Alan Dundes. Englewood Cliffs: Prentice, 1965. 4–6.

Tolkien, J. R. R. "On Fairy-Stories." *The Tolkien Reader*. New York: Ballantine, 1966. 3–84.

Turner, Victor W. *The Ritual Process: Structure and Anti-Structure*. New York: Aldine, 1969.

Weber, Eugen. "Fairies and Hard Facts: The Reality of Folktales." *Journal of the History of Ideas* 42 (1981): 93–113.

Zipes, Jack. *Fairy Tales and the Art of Subversion: The Classical Genre for Children and the Process of Civilization*. New York: Wildman, 1983.

Fairy Tales and Children's Literature: A Feminist Perspective

Ruth B. Bottigheimer

Introduction: Common Misperceptions

It is widely believed that fairy tales represent the culmination of hundreds, even thousands, of years of uninterrupted oral tradition. Seen as embodying timeless and ageless truths, they are considered particularly suitable as reading material during children's formative years. Exposure to fairy tales is said to both help and hasten a child's maturation. It is repeatedly asserted that the voice of the folk speaks through fairy tales, despite convincing evidence of thoroughgoing reformulation by their bourgeois editors. Fairy tales, according to this view, spring particularly from the province of women and thus put the reader into immediate contact with ancient matriarchal cultures and practices. And, finally, fairy tale motifs are said to symbolize deep-seated cultural and personal experiences and characteristics, whose analysis opens the door to the individual or collective psyche. In short, fairy tales have more often than not been treated as though they existed above the constraints and beyond the analytic procedures of ordinary literary genres.

Fairy Tales as Folk Narrative

Current thinking in folk narrative research offers a very different set of propositions. Here fairy tales are understood to be imaginative constructs that are historically based, culture-specific, oral or written, and produced either by men or by women depending on local circumstances. Although their plots remain remarkably constant over long periods of time, the language, style, and genre in which the plot is cast all can substantially alter the sense of the story. In terms of their continuing life cycle, oral and written sources recharge each other rather than develop in isolated currents. No unbroken oral tradition has to date been proved in communities such as Western Europe, where written tales or tale collections, whether embedded in larger pieces of literature or appearing independently, have been an integral part of both leisure and school reading since the Roman Empire. On the contrary, there appears to have been an active interplay between manuscript tale collections and published texts, on the one hand, and tale teller and real or fictive audiences on the other. The special place that fairy tales currently enjoy within children's literature is a relatively recent phenomenon, dating from the eighteenth century and becoming fully developed in the nineteenth.

None of these propositions is specifically feminist in intent; each of them, however, can be applied productively to topics of particular interest to feminist readers of fairy tales. And unlike the flawed but popular postulates with which I introduced this essay, these propositions also enable the feminist scholar to pursue important questions within a broad national and international framework.

"Cinderella": A Case Study

"Cinderella" makes an excellent test case for these statements. The tale exists in hundreds of versions—in China, Greece, Egypt, Scotland, the Appalachian Highlands of the United States, the Soviet Union, and, of course, Italy, France, and Germany. The last grouping offers a dramatically contrasting set of tales: Giambattista Basile's Italian "La Gatta Cenerentola" of 1634, Charles Perrault's French "Cendrillon" of 1697, and Jacob Grimm and Wilhelm Grimm's German "Aschenputtel" of 1812—and of 1857.

Basile's heroine, Zezolla, like other Cinderella figures, suffers at the hands of her malicious, ill-tempered stepmother. But quite unlike other Cinderellas, she sets about improving her lot independently and purposefully. At her governess's suggestion she invites her stepmother to inspect her clothes, and while the hated woman peers into a trunk, Zezolla lets the heavy lid fall onto her neck. Thus widowed, her father now marries the governess, who eventually produces her own six daughters, to Zezolla's great disadvantage and discomfiture. Although the rest of the story follows a generally familiar course, Zezolla has capacities notably lacking in her counterparts in subsequent Perrault or Grimm versions, for she has the power to enchant. She adjures her father to commend her to the dove of the fairies, but should he forget, she says, "May it be impossible for you to go forward or back" (58). With the help of a fairy who descends from a fig tree, Zezolla is beautified by a band of maidens, and she attends feast-day celebrations at which the King is bewitched by her beauty. A solitary shoe, the single means by which the King can identify his beloved, causes him to invite all the women of the realm to a feast so he can find its owner. Eventually he identifies Zezolla, marries her in great splendor, and the six sisters "crept quietly home to their mother, confessing in spite of themselves that: 'He is mad who would oppose the stars' " (61).

Perrault's Cendrillon is "of an exceptionally sweet and gentle nature" (58), a statement that could hardly be made about Zezolla. Cendrillon endures everything patiently, helps her two stepsisters into their ball gowns, dresses their hair, and buckles their slippers. A fairy godmother transforms her, six mice, a rat, a pumpkin, and six lizards into a beauty with a retinue requisite for appearing at a ball at the court of Louis XIV. The prince falls ever more in love with her; when she disappears, he searches the realm for the one whose foot the tiny slipper fits. Cendrillon herself laughingly asks, "Let me see if it will not fit me." The godmother reappears and once again transforms the girl whose beauty is matched by her goodness, which she proves by finding two gentlemen of high rank to marry her sisters. Two morals close the tale, one of which extols graciousness; the other, godmothers.

The Grimms published two different versions of the Cinderella tale: a German-language version of the Perrault tale in the first edition of *Grimms' Tales* in 1812, and a second version that emerged through successive editions, at the end of which it conformed to Wilhelm Grimm's conception of a German folk-derived tale. In the process the tale underwent fundamental reformulation, particularly in the area of speech. Cinderella came to speak less and less, her father and the prince more. The plot remained the same from 1819 to 1857: the pious wife of a rich man falls ill and dies, and her widowed husband marries a woman with two daughters, "fair of face, but vile and black of heart" (121). Aschenputtel asks him for a hazel branch, which she plants on her mother's grave, and when the branch grows into a tree, birds with magic powers issue from it. They provide her with gowns for the prince's balls, and they help perform the impossible tasks her stepmother sets. The stepmother herself is a marvel of evil, urging her daughters in turn to cut off their heels or their toes so that they will fit the golden slipper by which the prince will recognize the dancer he fell in love with at the ball. When Aschenputtel is finally called to try on the shoe, birds announce that she is the true bride; and when Aschenputtel marries the prince, birds peck out the stepsisters' eyes to punish them "for their wickedness and falsehood" (128).

Although these four tales indisputably have the same plot and belong to the same international tale type, different social and moral systems shimmer through the text. It is significant that Zezolla is decked out by a band of maidens—that she is not isolated within the story—just as it is important that the Grimms' second Aschenputtel loses some of her speech in edition after edition. These four tales offer points of comparison by country, by century, and—in the case of the Grimm tale—by social and educational class. The Grimms' first version was a rags-to-riches tale with a playfully articulate heroine. Its plot and vocabulary translated the courtly French original of Perrault into a German that made sense within the experience of the old woman who told it to Wilhelm in 1810. A far different Cinderella emerged in the second edition, however—more dependent, more silent, more suffering. Speech was used as a character indicator: the bad stepmother rattled on, the good girl was silenced.

The Witch: A Comparative Approach

Locating a particular fairy tale on the spectrum of different versions brings its constituent parts into high relief. When compared with Basile's or Perrault's heroines, the Aschenputtel of *Grimms' Tales* suddenly seems psychologically isolated, personally passive, and functionally silent, characteristics familiar from analyses of other tales from the Grimms' collection.

Similar comparisons can be made interculturally, especially in conjunction with specific fairy tale characters, such as the witch. European feminists understand the fairy tale witch as surviving evidence (through hundreds or thousands of years) of oracular wise women in antiquity. There is little doubt that such cultural figures existed in ancient Europe and the Near East, but they have no demonstrable continuous connection with early modern or modern fairy tale characters. Neo-Freudian psychologists, who have also shown considerable interest in witches, see them as a universal phenomenon mirroring a child's projection of the evil mother. But assertions of this sort are made in a vacuum, for most such analyses ignore fairy tale collections that long outsold the Grimm collection in the nineteenth century and offer a quite different, even contradictory, view and vision of evil characters.

For purposes of comparison, Ludwig Bechstein's *Deutsches Märchenbuch* (1857) is exemplary. Not only did it appear in the same year as the final edition of *Grimms' Tales;* it was also directed at the same audience, bourgeois children. What's surprising, for readers accustomed to *Grimms' Tales,* is the number of villainous males: sorcerers, the devil himself, robbers, male cannibals, violent husbands, a dragon, and even the king. To be sure, there are also mothers-in-law, a second wife who is a sorceress, and the wicked queen of Snow White, but the wicked fairy of "Sleeping Beauty" is called a "wise woman" (242). Balancing the wicked woman in "The Seven Ravens," there's also a *good* mother who didn't really mean to enchant her seven sons. A wicked woman of magic and two witches complete the catalog.

In *Grimms' Tales,* on the other hand, there are a remarkable number of witches. Nearly every bad woman—there are a few exceptions, of course—turns out to have been a witch, a fact that is made to justify the horrid deaths to which they are put, deaths described in loathsome and gloating detail. I need only mention the witch in "Hansel and Gretel" as a prototype, but *Grimms' Tales* offer many more examples.

The contrast in the frequency with which witches appear is even more striking when the comparison is extended cross-culturally to Perrault's tales. Although he wrote in the century of witch hysteria and witch burning, witches are in distinctly short supply. In Perrault's "Sleeping Beauty" an old fairy curses the young child, but the actual agent of her hundred years' sleep is a "goodwoman [who] had never heard speak of the king's proclamation [against spindles]". In this version of "Sleeping Beauty," there is a second part of the story in which the prince's mother behaves like a witch in every respect, having a great hunger both for her grandchildren and for her daughter-in-law. The text, however, accounts for her strange appetites by explaining that she is descended from the race of ogresses. After she orders her cook to prepare her two grandchildren for dinner, she's called "the wicked *queen*" (12; my emphasis), and even at the moment of her horrible death in a vat filled with vipers, toads, snakes, and serpents, this unnatural monster is never once called a witch, but always an ogress.

In Perrault's other fairy tales the author similarly avoids introducing witch figures. "Tom Thumb" has a male ogre; "The Fairies" has a very disagreeable and arrogant mother and a good fairy. "Rickey of the Tuft" has a fairy who makes one of the princesses as stupid as she is beautiful, but she's not described as a witch. "Cinderella" has a stepmother; Red Riding Hood's antagonist is a wolf. The horrifying murderer in "Blue Beard" is a man, and the confused king who wants to marry his own daughter is the wicked figure in "Donkey Skin." Griselda's tormentor is not a witch but her demented husband. Only two tales remain—"Puss in Boots" and "The Ridiculous Wishes," neither of which has a witch.

Cross-cultural and intracultural fairy tale comparisons preclude unreflecting acceptance of categories and interpretations of figures such as the witch. It is extremely important to protect naive readers from received but unexamined, orthodoxies, such as women-as-witches. In the 1970s and 1980s it was principally Freudian writers who confirmed the received orthodoxies, feminist and Marxist perspectives that revised them.

Fairy Tales and Publishing

The fact that fairy tales appear in books introduces an additional category within which the subject of fairy tales and children's literature may be understood. A "book" implies a publisher, and "publisher" traditionally implied a male-dominated and male-directed organizational and conceptual world. Publishing decisions are based on profits and losses, copyrights, pirating, and translating. Marketing choices grow out of assessments of what is offensive or inoffensive, acceptable or not—in a word, salable. Because male narrators tell different stories from female narrators, or tell the same story differently, we are justified in inferring that publishing decisions in the nineteenth and early twentieth centuries were also determined by gender-specific outlooks on the world. One glaring example is the absence of illustrations of a male cannibal figure (although comparable female figures are illustrated in great number and detail) in the German publishing history of *Grimms' Tales*. Such phenomena, though perhaps unintentional and probably unconscious, nonetheless reflect male preference and male prerogative in an age and in a country in which women were confined to "Kinder, Küche, and Kirche."

Texts

Numerous special-purpose collections promote the possibility of teaching fairy tales from a feminist perspective. My preference, however, is to read in national collections to see the strong heroine in context. For these purposes I recommend as particularly useful for literature or comparative literature courses Basile, Perrault, or the Norwegian Asbjørnsen-Moe collection. The gender bias attributed to folk and fairy tales is in many cases simply that of the (nineteenth) century in which they were collected. Basile and Perrault fall outside that influence, while the Norwegian tales are in some respects less colored by nineteenth-century gender values than, for example, *Grimms' Tales*.

The issues I raise here are broadly applicable, both within the field of children's literature and far beyond it. A basic question remains: Should children's access to fairy tales be restricted to those prepared especially for their youthful eyes, or may they also read other tales, formulated not for the nursery but for more robust and worldly venues? The answers to such questions must ultimately rest with the individuals who bear responsibility for the children in their charge. The children's instructors, however, will want to know of the many different Red Riding Hoods who wander through the woods, as well as the variety of Blue Beards waiting in towers. Whether the former escapes and what the latter escapes with are questions whose answers speak volumes about the societies that produced the tales.

The conclusions I have arrived at grow out of feminist interest in and feminist perceptions of a subject long dominated by male perceptions and categories. They parallel conclusions in folk narrative research about the relationship between life experience, tale repertoire, and story content; and they demonstrate, I hope, the fruitful results of working across disciplinary borders.

State University of New York, Stony Brook

Works Cited

Asbjørnsen, Peter, and Jørgen Moe. *East o' the Sun and West o' the Moon*. Trans. George W. Dasent. New York: Dover, 1970.

Basile, Giambattista. *The Pentamerone*. Trans. Benedetto Croce. Ed. N. M. Penzer. 2 vols. 1932. Westport: Greenwood, 1979.

Bechstein, Ludwig. *Deutsches Märchenbuch. Sämtliche Märchen*. Ed. Walter Scherf. München: Winkler, 1983. 5–370.

Grimm Brothers. *The Complete Fairy Tales of the Brothers Grimm*. Ed. Jack Zipes. New York: Bantam, 1987.

Perrault, Charles. *Perrault's Complete Fairy Tales*. Trans. A. E. Johnson. New York: Dodd, 1961.

Recommended Reading

Apo, Satu. "The Structural Analysis of Marina Takalo's Fairy Tales Using Propp's Model." *Genre, Structure and Reproduction in Oral Literature*. Ed. Lauri Honko and Vilmos Voigt. Budapest: Akademiai Kiado, 1980.

Blaubarts Geheimnis. Ed. Hartwig Suluber. Köln: Diederichs, 1984.

Bottigheimer, Ruth B. "The Face of Evil." *Fabula* 29.3–4 (1988): 26–42.

——— , ed. *Fairy Tales and Society: Illusion, Allusion, and Paradigm*. Philadelphia: U of Pennsylvania P, 1986.

——— . *Grimms' Bad Girls and Bold Boys: The Moral and Social Vision of the Tales*. New Haven: Yale UP, 1987.

——— . "Ludwig Bechstein's Fairy Tales: Nineteenth Century Bestsellers and 'Bürgerlichkeit.' " *Internationales Archiv für Sozialgeschichte der deutschen Literatur* 15.2 (1990): 55–88.

Dan, Ilana. "The Innocent Persecuted Heroine: An Attempt at a Model for the Surface Level of the Narrative Structure of the Female Fairy Tale." *Patterns in Oral Literature*. Ed. Heda Jason. Paris: Mouton, 1977. 13–30.

Helms, Cynthia. "Storytelling, Gender, and Language in Folk/Fairy Tales: A Selected Annotated Bibliography." *Women and Language* 10 (1987): 3–10.

Holbek, Bengt. *Interpretation of Fairy Tales*. Folklore Fellows Communications 239. 1987.

Köhler-Zülch, Ines, and Christine Shojaei-Kawan, eds. *Schneewittchen hat viele Schwestern*. Gütersloh: Mohn, 1988.

Lurie, Alison, ed. *Clever Gretchen*. New York: Crowell, 1980.

McGlathery, James M. *Fairy Tale Romance: The Grimms, Basile, and Perrault*. Urbana: U of Illinois P, 1991.

Minard, Rosemary, ed. *Womenfolk and Fairy Tales*. Boston: Houghton, 1975.

Phelps, Ethel Johnston, ed. *The Maid of the North*. New York: Holt, 1981.

Rooth, Anna Birgitta. *The Cinderella Cycle*. Lund: Gleerup, 1951.

Rowe, Karen. "Feminism and Fairy Tales." *Women's Studies: An Interdisciplinary Journal* 6 (1979): 237–57.

Tatar, Maria. *The Hard Facts of the Grimms' Fairy Tales*. Princeton: Princeton UP, 1987.

Zipes, Jack. *Fairy Tales and the Art of Subversion: The Classical Genre for Children and the Process of Civilization*. New York: Wildman, 1983.

———, ed. *The Trials and Tribulations of Little Red Riding Hood: Versions of the Tales in Sociocultural Context*. New York: Bergin, 1983.

High Fantasy, Rites of Passage, and Cultural Value

Jeanne Murray Walker

Fantasy is often ridiculed for its lack of ideas, and readers of fantasy are attacked for their desire to escape. Withdrawal is not a coping strategy most thoughtful adults want to teach children. In fact, if fantasy as a form were merely a way of escaping, it might create problems for children, who need all the practice they can get dealing with a world that grows increasingly complex (see Mobley). But far from isolating children or encouraging them to escape from their social responsibilities, "high fantasy" (Frye 187) unites people into groups and reinforces the values around which those groups cohere. It might be argued, in fact, that if fantasy presents any danger, it is the danger of preparing the reader for obedient, uncritical participation in a comforting, authoritarian system. But the best children's fantasies encourage questioning of commonly held cultural values rather than mere conformity to them. Ursula K. Le Guin's *Wizard of Earthsea*, C. S. Lewis's *Lion, the Witch, and the Wardrobe*, and Norman Juster's *Phantom Tollbooth*, examples of such fantasies, provide good cases to examine in detail.

American Pluralism and Fantasy

Children growing up in American society experience everywhere around them the collision of powerful interests and values. Competing slogans and values bombard their senses daily. Even though they may be nurtured within a family structure, chances are they are not indoctrinated by parents into a clearly defined community of values. As Arnold Van Gennep has argued, many adults can't even formulate their own values, much less pass those values on to their children in any articulate way (189). Many adults feel both a vague discomfort with orthodoxy of any kind and a need to allow their children to make choices in matters of religion and values. As a result, the clearly defined orthodoxies that at one time may have defined whole families for several generations have gone by the boards. American society is increasingly characterized by small, intensely competitive communities of value.

In a society of competing messages, materialism seems to be one clear, unifying value. Money is an externalized, shared standard of value. So far as it goes, this shared value binds people together. It may be that the less unifying the other values are, the more money and materialism come to dominate the imaginations of American children. To own valued possessions is one of the few remaining means of defining and joining a large community.

Fantasy defies materialism by showing that there are, indeed, coherent communities formed around other values. For instance, in *A Wizard of Earthsea* the most important value is equilibrium—awareness of one's self as a part of the whole. Love, according to Madeleine L'Engle's *Wrinkle in Time*, is the power behind all personal and social coherence. *The Lion, the Witch, and the Wardrobe* unveils divine sacrifice as the real force that creates personal and social balance. In *The Phantom Tollbooth*, Juster argues that humanistic wisdom is the essential truth.

Ironically, the very pluralism in America that has created a hunger for the lessons of fantasy has also increased the number of central truths that fantasy tells. It is worth noticing that each of these truths is contrasted with economic and material values. And every fantasy asserts a connection between its own nonmaterialistic value and the pragmatic operations of the social and physical world. Fantasy insists that the material world can be governed best by people who are patient or loving or well educated, not by people who own it.

What matters in fantasy is not so much the value system itself as the investigation of nonmaterialistic values. To read a fantasy is to absorb a particular interpretation of human experience, a kind of psychological or theological lore that claims that readers can change their identity and become powerful in the world. Adult power, fantasy promises, is dependent on bringing one's behavior in line with the reflective, intentional, nonmaterialistic truth that governs the universe. This promise is at once challenging and comforting. Fantasy clears a window in the chaotic world of slogans and ads and religions that compete for the attention of American children. It offers a glimpse of a community ordered by one, univocal value.

The reader can become a member of that community only by questing empathetically with the hero of the fantasy. Although the hero is not a full-fledged member of the community at the beginning, he undertakes a quest on behalf of the entire community. In the process of questing, a hero like Frodo, in *The Hobbit*, begins to conform to the values of the community and, by the end of the quest, has rescued the community from disintegration. This double outcome, shaping the hero and saving the community, represents two sides of the same coin. In order for communities to continue, they must have members; each member can be said to save heroically the community from collapse by adopting its values and interacting with its other members.

Fantasy Patterned by Romance

The quest plot that structures fantasy and the double outcome of the quest—the molding of the hero and the saving of the community—these are also found in romance. As Jane Mobley has shown, fantasy is heavily indebted to the romance tradition. In romance the hero, who seems unworthy at first, sets out on a quest that is of vast importance because the fate of a society rests on its outcome. This quest is always defined by someone of a higher status or greater power—Gloriana in Spenser's *Faerie Queene* or Guinevere in the Wife of Bath's Tale—who speaks with authority for the whole community.

During the quest the hero of romance undergoes a ritual death in a struggle with an enemy who is, as Northrop Frye has argued, "associated with winter, darkness, confusion, sterility"(187). That is why the quest assumes bewilderingly obligatory and crucial proportions. Through questing, the hero's life-giving strengths become clear by the end of the journey. Britomart in the *Faerie Queene*, for example, finds out that she is the mother of the British race, and Gawain discovers that his legendary manners are faulty.

The romance quest pays off not only for the hero but also for the society. Frequently the hero quests so that the social world may be rid of a nagging evil. For example, Redcrosse slays the dragon in the first book of the *Faerie Queene* to relieve Una's father's kingdom of the threat of death. Whether the community is visible throughout a romance or emerges only in a few moments, the hero acts in counterpoint to a defining social structure.

The essential hero, the lonely journey, the wrestling with death, society's stake in the hero's success, the authority who defines and oversees the quest, the wisdom to which the hero (and finally the reader) becomes privy, the dragons and damsels and queens and wicked stepmothers—these are the aspects of romance present in *A Wizard of Earthsea*, *The Lion, the Witch, and the Wardrobe*, and *The Phantom Tollbooth*. Other examples of fantasy patterned on romance include Susan Cooper's books, in which the young hero's task is to collect hermetic signs in order to save a vividly realistic social order. In *A Wrinkle in Time* Meg and Calvin are socially isolated before and during their quest, which, by saving Meg's father, completes the kinship structure of the family. The novels of Lloyd Alexander, Robert Siegel and Katherine Paterson are similarly informed by romance elements.

Fantasy as Rite of Passage

The quest plot has structured fiction for almost a thousand years perhaps because it fills an essential human need. It certainly parallels closely the forms of rites of passage, which have been found by anthropologists in all traditional societies. Van Gennep, who pioneered work on rites of passage, asserted that they "accompany every change of place, state, social position and age." Later anthropologists have confirmed his claim: for example, all tribal cultures that we know about initiate their members into adulthood with such rituals. Yet American culture, which is relatively ritual-poor, lacks any definitive rites of passage to celebrate this transition. It might be argued that reaching the drinking or voting age, getting a driver's license, or graduating from high school mark adulthood in American society. But these events certainly do not inculcate values in the initiate. On the contrary, they themselves lack most of the identifying marks of passage. The centrality of rites of passage in so many, and such diverse, cultures suggests that they are, if not *necessary*, at least very important to human comprehension of the adult state. In fact, the purpose they serve elsewhere may be accomplished in American life by fantasy.

Rites of passage dramatize the transformations that individuals undergo from one status to another. Unlike everyday experience, which socializes individuals into adulthood, the ritual that changes an individual's status is artificially limited in time and space and patterned in action. The ceremony is not to be confused with years of learning. Alone it does not magically transform a thirteen-year-old boy into a warrior (or a responsible, economically powerful man). Rather, it confers a new *status*. What the "newly made" adult makes of the status is a matter for the future. But the ritual symbolically presents an idealized and abstract summary of what an individual's culture says life is (description) and must be (prescription). The particular ways in which the ritual is patterned in action—the artifice of the ritual—implants in the initiates a vision. Only through experience can they realize that it is a vision of life as the culture knows it.

Rites of passage not only dramatize the act of becoming; they *explain* cognitively what happens in status changes. Such changes inevitably require risks and produce anxiety. Why should or will anyone believe that this particular young person will be able to function as an adult? Or, from the point of view of the initiate, where will the new *me* come from? Who is responsible for the change? Where does the young person go? Where does the adult come from? Both the society and the individual need forceful and convincing answers to these questions. If answers are not forthcoming, members of society are confused about one another's positions and roles, while the initiates, like Ged in *A Wizard of Earthsea*, may fail to see themselves as occupying any status position at all.

Risks involved in status change are frequently represented in symbols of death and resurrection. It is possible, after all, that the initiate will not be able to function as an adult. If this should happen, not only the individual but the social structure itself will suffer from the mismatch between the child and the adult status. Conversely, there is also the risk that society will fail to honor a status change and continue to treat the adult as a child. Either of these possibilities leaves the individual stranded in an inappropriate social role, a social limbo—or, in the symbolic expression of many rites of passage, death. Leaving one status equals death—the death of one social person—and arriving at a new status equals resurrection—the creation of a new social person. After leaving the first status and before gaining the second, the person temporarily rests in a state of betwixt and between. If the transformation fails, the person is caught in a marginal state, becoming socially invisible.

Ritual seeks to control the risks inherent in status change by stamping the mind and emotions of the initiate with the values of the group. The child must learn the secrets of adulthood. In traditional cultures, initiates are forced to memorize difficult laws and lore or to contemplate icons known only to members of the new status position. As Meyer Fortes puts it, initiates are like metal that is melted down and then stamped with a new image. Such refashioning requires the mutual permission and cooperation of the initiate and the society. Ultimately, ritual binds the initiates not only to the new status but also to those for whom they accept it—the holders of other social positions. These people—the total society—are represented in the rite of passage by masters who instruct the initiates in values, who prime and groom them for their new role. It is their task to make sure the initiates know how to behave. But the vivid and public symbolism of the ritual is what effectively converts the child to the new status and what convinces both the initiate and the society that a change has been transacted.

The similarities between a rite of passage and a romance are striking. The authority figure in romance corresponds to the initiator in the rite of passage. The hero is the initiate, who becomes reformed by learning the symbols and lore of the group. The quest plot is the passage from life through death and back to a renewed, changed life. These patterns are also found in children's fantasy, the modern cousin of romance.

A Wizard of Earthsea as Rite of Passage

The parallels between rites of passage and children's fantasy are evident in Le Guin's *Wizard of Earthsea*. Not only does *A Wizard* show its readers that the question of the hero's own "name," his own identity, cannot be avoided; it also indicates that his naming is an event attended by the whole society. Moreover, the naming dramatizes the old and inevitable process in which individuals define themselves in relationship to fixed positions in society. The first chapter of *A Wizard* documents the characteristics of the hero's village, analyzes the social position of wizards, describes celebrations, and illustrates the importance of the myths that perpetuate cultural memory and personal fame. This anthropological detail establishes the groundwork of assumptions and values by which the reader can interpret the behavior of the hero, Ged. But the most telling anthropological statement occurs at the conclusion of chapter 1, where Ged's rite of passage occurs.

As individuals interpret their lives through symbols and events, in their rites of passage, so Le Guin's later chapters are but dramatizations of the elements of Ged's initiation. The spring through which Ged wades is an analogue for the ocean on which he later completes his troubled quest for the shadow. The shadows that "slid and mingled" at the initiation anticipate the terrible shadow that later enters the world by Ged's hand. The new name that Ogion whispers to the boy suggests a later incident in which Ged gives the shadow the same name. The central role of Ogion at the initiation predicts his crucial role in healing the wounded sparrowhawk, the form Ged magically assumes in his flight from deadly peril. Ged's isolation during his walk through the spring prefigures his years of physical and psychological loneliness. And, of course, Ged's walking—his passage through the spring—articulates his forward movement through time and experience.

But how can a modern reader who has never gone through a rite of passage comprehend the significance of this ritual in *A Wizard of Earthsea?* It would be nonsense to argue that by experiencing this brief ritual with Ged, a reader can enjoy a status change. As we have seen, however, the work develops in great detail the elements of the rite of passage. Ged's rite of passage is an analogue to the entire plot, and the plot itself functions as a rite of passage for the reader.

Not only do the specific elements of Ged's initiation (water, a master, naming, a shadow) pattern the rest of the plot; they are used to convince the reader of the social theory that makes rites of passage meaningful. The fiction illustrates the interdependence of human beings and the social nature of individual identities, two broad assumptions that underlie rituals of passage. In fact, in its metaphor of equilibrium, *A Wizard* pushes these assumptions further to show the social aspect of all things, even nature. It portrays, too, the enforced isolation through which an initiate must pass while undergoing the change from old to new self. And it articulates forcefully the danger that threatens society in the act of initiating its members. Such themes in the novel constitute the basic social theory a reader must have in order to comprehend the context for rites of passage.

The teaching at the heart of the rite of passage, Le Guin's idea of equilibrium, challenges materialistic assumptions. Not ownership but the proper use of things gives power, Ged learns. The reader who passes through the initiation with Ged understands that "all power is one in source and end. . . . Years and distances, stars and candles, water and wind and wizardry, the craft in a man's hand and the wisdom in a tree's root: they all arise together. . . . There is no other power" (164). To tap into that power, one must patiently master the true name and nature of everything, including oneself. Nothing could more directly contradict the quick material fix.

The Lion, the Witch, and the Wardrobe: Teaching Children to Interpret the World

In fact, *The Lion, the Witch, and the Wardrobe*, C. S. Lewis's first published Narnia story, is patterned by the same structure as that of Le Guin's work. It bears all the salient features of a rite of passage: (1) The children step from a world of ordinary social experience in London, first into the cultural sanctuary of the Professor's old house and then into the artificially defined space, time, and laws of Narnia. (2) The laws in Narnia force the children to experience and so to comprehend an interpretation of the world (value) and thus to act on it. (3) As a result of their action, they undergo a status change. (4) This status change has been prophesied since the beginning of time in Narnia: as the function of a rite of passage is to transform the initiate, so the very definition of Narnia contains the inevitability of the children's becoming adult kings and queens. (5) The wardrobe, the threshold between the ordinary world and the artificial world of Narnia, is repeatedly referred to by the narrator as a potential place of death, the potential failure of the children's status change.

As in a rite of passage, the four heroes' task is to decipher conventional symbols and internalize them. The symbols teach values and laws that govern Narnia. A familiar—indeed, overwhelmingly common Christian—interpretation of reality shapes the novel's secondary world.

Lewis calls attention in *The Lion* to the act of properly reading objects in the world. Once the children get into Narnia, they evaluate the animals and time and weather and all the events according to conventions they have learned in the past: "They're good birds in all the stories I've read. I'm sure a robin wouldn't be on the wrong side." Only Edmund refuses to generalize about values from the conventional images: "If it comes to that, which is the right side? How do we know that the fauns are in the right and the Queen (yes, I know we've been told she's a witch) is in the wrong? We don't really know anything about either"(59).

It is worth examining why Edmund is unable to interpret conventional signs in Narnia accurately. In the first place, he has been badly educated at a "horrid school," where he started to "go wrong" (177). As a result, Edmund has a bad temper. He snickers at people who look unusual, he teases Lucy mercilessly, he refuses to apologize when he is wrong, and he is greedy. The twin Renaissance categories, nature and nurture, are both defective in Edmund, and the defects make it impossible for him to identify the queen, when he first meets her, as a witch. Edmund accepts and eats her enchanted food. Once he has taken her magic into himself, he becomes a traitor to his brothers and sisters, informing the witch of their whereabouts. Eventually he becomes so deluded that he is unable to differentiate between a live animal and an animal that has been turned into stone by the witch.

Interpretation, like misinterpretation, is cumulative, according to *The Lion*. Therefore, as the children explore the symbols they encounter, they act, and with each act they discover more symbols to unravel. By incrementally discovering and construing symbols, the children learn, step by step, the conventional Christian interpretation of the world that lies behind the symbols of Narnia.

This interpretation, the central lore in the novel's rite of passage, repudiates materialism by associating it with the Witch. After Edmund betrays himself to the Witch in exchange for Turkish Delight, she insists that he is her property, to do with as she likes. "And so," she says, "that human creature is mine. His life is forfeit to me. His blood is my property" (139). The system of debt and payment set up in the Dawn of Time requires that the Witch's claim on Edmund be honored. So Aslan substitutes his life for Edmund's and the Witch kills Aslan instead of Edmund. The Witch's possessive, materialistic assessment of human life is, however, finally proved wrong. As Aslan says, "though the Witch knew the Deep Magic, there is a magic deeper still which she did not know" (159). This magic is the reversal of death.

Meaning lies behind every icon, Lewis's novel teaches, but it is possible to misunderstand *what* meaning. The many polemics and symbols, the collision of slogans and voices that compete for attention as the truth—these are mere appearances of value. If properly read, each can be understood as good or evil according to a master value system, the Christian message. It is possible to read both the book of nature and the book of culture without making the sort of mistakes Edmund does, if the reader has a willing heart and is ready to learn. Lewis's voice in the novel is that of an initiator, and the reader is the initiate. *The Lion, the Witch, and the Wardrobe* is Lewis's attempt to give the reader a good, if brief, education.

The Phantom Tollbooth: Didacticism and Fascism in Fantasy

Fantasy attempts to convince, and the voices that tell the stories in fantasy novels are initiator figures, overtly present and omniscient, solemnly counseling the reader through the images of the narrative. As we have seen, fantasy instructs its readers in the norms and truths of an identifiable social community. It portrays those truths as the standard by which adulthood is measured. And adulthood is the valued goal; unlike some other kinds of fiction, fantasy does not pretend to present a snapshot of the world that is value-neutral. Far from it. To read fantasy is to be confronted by the fact that if we, the readers of the book, cannot be shaped into adults with the hero, in some sense we will die. In fantasy, death or assent are the two choices.

It is not surprising, perhaps, that a society increasingly more pluralistic in its values should enthusiastically clasp this didactic genre to its bosom. Crude forms of fantasy are everywhere—Dungeons and Dragons games, slick movies, the Strategic Defense Initiative (Star Wars). In all of them the good hero navigates the dangerous passage at great risk and wins. Good wins. What does that mean? In most popular fantasies, good is nothing more than us, our group, people who dress like us and eat what we eat. Fragmented as American culture is into groups—women, blacks, Jews, the poor, the elderly—with which individuals identify or are categorized by others, the nation appears to need generically good heroes as role models or symbols. Good equals us equals the successful questor. This formulation powerfully urges readers to conform; any reader who dissents dies, either as the unsuccessful questor or as the evil enemy. Fantasy in these popular versions is like a mindless police officer herding everyone into the same parking lot, shooting the resisters and stragglers.

Not all fantasy is so fascistic, of course. The best fantasy, novels like *A Wizard of Earthsea* and *The Lion, the Witch, and the Wardrobe*, presents complex and clearly defined values, not vacant symbols of the powerful versus the powerless. But even among these complex and thoughtful fantasies, *The Phantom Tollbooth* is remarkable because it examines the policelike qualities of its own form. *The Phantom Tollbooth*, like other children's fantasies, is structured as a rite of passage. Like an initiate, Milo, the child hero, steps from his habitual world into a tollbooth, which takes him to an artificially defined space and time, described as a "destination in mind" (14), betwixt and between childhood and adulthood. This world is populated by witches, damsels, dragons, and other iconic characters. The oddity of these images makes Milo think for the first time about why he is bored and slothful in his routine school and home life. He begins to see reading and arithmetic and logic as heroic tasks. As a result he volunteers to penetrate the menacing Mountains of Ignorance so he can rescue the princesses, Rhyme and Reason, and return them to the Land of Wisdom. During his lonely, terrifying quest, he is transformed into a hero, which is to say that he has learned the value of education. And through his heroism, the social order is transformed into a place where mathematics and language return to their proper functions.

This is as didactic as anything in Lewis's fantasy; but unlike the solemn narrators in *A Wizard of Earthsea* and *The Lion, the Witch, and the Wardrobe*, the narrator of *The Phantom Tollbooth* speaks a good deal of nonsense. In the middle of a passage about the evils of loquacity, for example, Milo asks the Duke how a small wooden wagon that has no motor can be made to move. The Duke replies, "Be very quiet . . . for it goes without saying." What is the reader to make of this and the other wordplay in *The Phantom Tollbooth?*

The reader should recognize that the story emerges out of the narrator's struggle with the rules of language and genre. The legitimate rules are represented by the witch, Faintly Macabre. "For years and years" she was the Which "in charge of choosing which words were to be used for all occasions" (67). Confined to a dungeon when Rhyme and Reason were banished, she bides her time, eating sugar-coated punctuation, while the language of Dictionapolis languishes in disorder. Punctuation should order sentences. The prescriptive and conventional forms of language and literary genres should not be locked up; they are necessary to make meaning. Therefore, the Which must be released before Milo can quest.

But if some forms of linguistic didacticism are kin to the questing mind ("You can call me Aunt Faintly"), others are arbitrary and bullying. Officer Short Shrift arrests Milo for spilling a cartload of letters. Shrift throws into Milo's indictment the additional crimes of forgetting his birthday, "having a dog with an unauthorized alarm" (a watch dog), "sowing confusion, upsetting the applecart, wreaking havoc, and mincing words" (62). After arresting and indicting Milo, Officer Shrift turns into the judge and sentences Milo to the dungeon for six million years. Then, becoming a jailer, he locks the poor hero up. Short Shrift is discipline out of control. He is a parody of romance as police action.

To put it another way, part of the subject of *The Phantom Tollbooth* is the way words and syntax and literary genre tyrannize the reader (and presumably the writer) of romance. This fantasy turns the seams out and lets the reader look at the construction of the document itself and, by analogy, other fantasies. It shows what happens when quick and facile uses of form (Short Shrift) get the upper hand. The hero can't move. That is, the hero can't really work through questions about values, and he can't make any progress toward joining a group of adults who behave according to a clearly articulated set of values.

Even more interesting, *The Phantom Tollbooth* shows why forms like fantasy are often used mindlessly or, it may be, intentionally by people who want to dominate a readership hungry for social cohesion. Fantasy helps to order a chaotic world. And even at the level of language, chaos is everywhere. In the first place, a whole cartload of letters lies spilled nonsensically on the sidewalk. In the second place, the narrator can barely discipline the idioms of language well enough to keep the narration following a linear track of reasonable cause and effect ("it goes without saying"). Perversions of logic are everywhere ("watch dog"). And, in general, the world is full of people who are "sowing confusion," et cetera. Into this wealth of confusion a policeman wades to tidy up.

The authority of the policeman derives from his ability to absolve people of the guilt they feel for acting chaotically in a chaotic world. His name means to shrive, or to confess. Officer Shrift is presumably able to listen to confessions, assess guilt or innocence, pronounce sentences, and so clarify social issues. The problem is, he is power-mad, and, therefore, can't make distinctions. He fails to distinguish between guilt and innocence: the Humbug and the Spelling Bee, not Milo, were the ones who spilled the cartload of letters. And he fails to distinguish between the separate actions of policing, judging, and jailing. As a result, he throws out the hero with the mess. *The Phantom Tollbooth* shows that, like Officer Shrift, fantasy can shut up the voices of pluralism and throw in jail everything that doesn't conform. But the better way—the real way of enforcing social order—is Aunt Faintly's way, delicate, tactful, imaginative, and slow.

How can children avoid the tedium of shallow materialism and the cynical need to be entertained? How can they grow into an active and durable adult generation? These are the questions *The Phantom Tollbooth* asks. Humanistic education is the answer—reading, writing, arithmetic, logic—the tremendous quest children must make by themselves to cross the Mountains of Ignorance, bringing back Rhyme and Reason to Wisdom. The novel convinces us of the value of education through a nuanced and complex use of fantasy. Being convinced, we are no longer bored and self-indulgent children who fail to see why these endeavors are necessary. We become communicants of the orthodoxy of humanism.

There may be no way of counteracting the fragmentation that bewilders American society or the materialism that makes its children passive—no way short of police action, which is worse than pluralism itself. Fantasy can't unify society, even though each of the best fantasies for children presents a single value that claims to be the key to adulthood. Fantasy longs for order; it drives toward unity. But finally, as *The Phantom Tollbooth* shows, too much order can bring everything to a halt. It is best to put up with a limited system of order, one that grows out of insight and educated choice. And as for the inevitable remaining disorder, it can be seen as plenitude gone mad. *The Phantom Tollbooth* recommends that it be viewed with affectionate hilarity.

Deprived of public rites of passage, American children nevertheless are able to substitute the rites of passage embedded in texts. But fantasy is still less effective than true rites of passage. That is partly because different fantasies proclaim different values. The deep fragmentation of

American society can be only healed temporarily, that is, while the reader is undergoing the quest described in any given fantasy. But more important, fantasy fails to initiate children because the contractual agreement between the narrator-initiator and the reader-initiate is only a tacit social contract rather than an explicit one, as in rites of passage. The mark of the society is present not in the physical presence of the attending tribal members but in the conventions of the genre, fantasy. Fantasy represents society as an abstract concept; the conventions of reading are abstract. Young readers who depend on fantasy for rites of passage have no tangible community to support their transformation. Nevertheless, fantasy is valuable. It reminds young readers that there are conventions, that there is a society that can arrive at agreements, that even in their anomalous social position, they participate in social forms.[1]

University of Delaware

Note

[1] Thanks to the University of Delaware Research Foundation for a summer research grant that allowed me to write this article.

Works Cited

Fortes, Meyer. "Ritual and Office in Tribal Societies." *Essays on the Ritual of Social Relations.* Ed. Max Gluckman. Manchester, 1962. 53–88.

Frye, Northrop. *Anatomy of Criticism.* New York: Atheneum, 1964.

Juster, Norman. *The Phantom Tollbooth.* New York: Random, 1972.

Le Guin, Ursula K. *A Wizard of Earthsea.* New York: Bantam, 1968.

Lewis, C. S. *The Lion, the Witch, and the Wardrobe.* New York: Macmillan, 1970.

Mobley, Jane. "Fantasy in the College Classroom." *CEA Critic* 39 (1978): 2–6.

——— . "Magic Is Alive: A Study of Contemporary Fantasy Fiction." Diss. U of Kansas, 1974.

——— . "Toward a Definition of Fantasy Fiction." *Extrapolation* 15 (1973–74): 117–28.

Van Gennep, Arnold. *The Rites of Passage.* Trans. Monika B. Vizedom and Gabrielle L. Catte. Chicago: U of Chicago P, 1960.

Childhood and Romanticism

Alan Richardson

Romantic writers did more than redefine childhood; it was in great part through their theoretical and imaginative works that childhood rose to the prominence it continues to hold in the Western cultural tradition. It would be misleading to suggest that there was a single Romantic image of the child: representations of children during the conventionally defined Romantic period in England (1780–1832) range from Wordsworth's "best philosopher" and Lamb's dream children to the overindulged Middleton brats in Austen's *Sense and Sensibility* or the unruly Price brood in *Mansfield Park*. In a number of ways, however, the child took on a centrality in Romantic writing wholly unprecedented in cultural history. The new concern with childhood not only showed up in poetry, children's literature, and the barrage of educational treatises produced during the period but also made possible the development of the bildungsroman, or novel of development (Buckley 19), the modern autobiography, with its central emphasis on childhood and growth, and a new kind of prose essay that portrayed the author's early life and school days. Education, in the sense both of schooling and the broader one of social and intellectual growth, took on a new prominence along with childhood: the Intimations Ode and *Mansfield Park* may present quite different versions of the child, but both are marked by the concern with education and the "development of the perfected, totalized individual" that Judith Plotz finds central to Romanticism (66).

The associationist psychology of Locke, especially as developed by David Hartley, did much to establish the importance of childhood experience. If the infant's mind is a tabula rasa or, as Locke put it in his popular treatise *Some Thoughts Concerning Education*, a "white Paper" (325), early experience and education become all-important in shaping the adult: "the child is father of the man." Working from associationist

premises, social theorists as diverse as Adam Smith, Mary Wollstonecraft, and William Godwin saw early education as crucial in forming (or
reforming) society. Associationism affected Romantic literature as well:
Coleridge writes in "The Nightingale" of his son Hartley (named for
the philosopher): "his childhood shall grow up / Familiar with these
songs, that with the night / He may associate joy" (107–09). "Frost at
Midnight" similarly ends by promising Hartley a childhood of natural
associations, in contrast to Coleridge's own urban school days "pent
'mid cloisters dim," the father "living, vicariously, a Wordsworthian
childhood" through the son (Newlyn 142). And while it may be going
too far to call Wordsworth himself "the associationist poet" (Willey 149),
The Prelude is pervasively concerned with portraying the effect of early
associations and experiences on the "growth of a poet's mind."

While Locke saw the child as "wax, to be molded and fashioned as
one pleases" (325), Rousseau described the child as a "young plant"
(38), virtuous by nature: "there is no original perversity in the human
heart" (92). In the tension between these two metaphors originates
much of the ambivalence characteristic of Romantic writing on childhood and education. Although Rousseau thought education crucial for
men and women in society—"Plants are shaped by cultivation, and
men by education" (38)—his emphasis on original innocence and organic laws of development led him to recommend a "purely negative"
early education (93). This organic and benevolent view of childhood,
which George Boas has linked to primitivist strains in Western thought
and to the eighteenth-century cult of the "noble savage," finds frequent
expression in Romantic literature, as when Wordsworth describes his
"five years' " self in *The Prelude* as a "naked savage, in the thunder-
shower" (1.304) and attests to a predominately "negative" education in
The Excursion: "I, whose favorite school / Hath been the fields, the roads,
and rural lanes" (2.28–29). Rural childhoods with incidental, desultory
formal schooling are standard in the radical novel of the 1790s, such as
Thomas Holcroft's *Hugh Trevor* or Mary Hays's *Emma Courtney;* Robert
Bage goes further and has his hero in *Hermsprong* brought up "amongst
the aborigines of America" (170). Childhood in Romantic literature is
frequently portrayed as Edenic, natural, and asocial. The Romantic child
is, like Adam, unfallen as long as it remains solitary.

If the child is originally innocent for Rousseau, the Augustinian
emphasis on the child's innate depravity was revived in the later
eighteenth century by such groups as the Methodists and Evangelicals.
Wesley held that the "bias of nature is set the wrong way: education
is designed to set it right" (10: 152), an attitude shared by the Evangelical
Hannah More, for whom children "bring into the world a corrupt
nature and evil dispositions, which it should be the great end of education to rectify" (Stone 294). However, the religious hymns for children written during the same period by the Wesleys and Isaac Watts

varied their portrayals of original sin with celebrations of childhood innocence (Laqueur 11–15). This ambivalent religious view of childhood, combined with the sentimental depiction of childhood naïveté typified by Gray's "Eton" ode ("Where ignorance is bliss, 'tis folly to be wise") and characteristic of much later eighteenth-century verse (Babenroth), helped prepare for the idealized "seer blest" of the Intimations Ode. From being viewed as imperfect—literally unfinished—the child comes, in the Romantic period, to exemplify the perfection of as yet undiminished potentialities. Schiller, in his essay *Naive and Sentimental Poetry*, redefines the child as "a lively representation to us of the ideal, not indeed as it is fulfilled, but as it is enjoined; hence we are in no sense moved by the notion of its poverty and limitation, but rather by the opposite: a notion of its pure and free strength, its integrity, its eternality" (87).

All these versions of childhood—the associationist, the organic, the transcendental, even the Augustinian—can be found in the poetry of Wordsworth. In his early lyrics, as well as in parts of *The Prelude*, he celebrates the spontaneous, unsocialized, egotistical child of nature. In "We Are Seven," the eight-year-old child, with her "rustic, woodland air," challenges the adult's conception of mortality with her naive (in Schiller's sense) confidence in a wholly natural life after death. The "Winander Boy," in one of the earliest sections of *The Prelude*, stands alone in woods or by the lake to blow "mimic hootings to the silent owls" (5.398), exemplifying a purely natural education that Wordsworth opposes to the rationalist educational schemes of his time, fit only for creating "a dwarf man" (5.295). In "The Danish Boy" and "Lucy Gray," the child becomes incorporated into the natural landscape, something between a shade and a genius of the wood. Indeed, the frequent association of death with childhood in Wordsworth points up the limitations of his idealized child of nature: like the Danish Boy and Lucy Gray, the Boy of Winander and Lucy in "Three years she grew in sun and shower" must die in order to retain their natural "eternality." Encountering a beautiful and strangely rural "cottage-child" in a London theater, Wordsworth characteristically imagines him "as if embalmed / By Nature—through some special privilege / Stopped at the growth he had" (*Prelude* 7.400–02).

While Wordsworth celebrates his own rural childhood and natural innocence throughout *The Prelude*, he allows himself (although with some reluctance) to grow up. In representing his own childhood, Wordsworth often treats nature less as a ground that might reabsorb the child figured against it than as a rich mine of associations and experiences that contribute to the growth of a "chosen spirit." Similarly in "Tintern Abbey," the narrator moves from the "glad animal movements" of boyhood through a quasi-erotic adolescent fascination with nature to a maturity distanced from but still informed by the natural scenes and experiences of childhood. (His sister Dorothy, however, serves as a still innocent version of William's younger self through whose "wild eyes" the poet can vicariously relive his "former pleasures.") Although Wordsworth stresses the continuity between his childhood and adult selves throughout his autobiographical poetry, at times his childhood strikes him as a radically different and discontinuous state, as though his own child self were somehow "embalmed" in its innocent state:

> So wide appears
> The vacancy between me and those days,
> Which yet have such self-presence in my mind
> That sometimes when I think of them I seem
> Two consciousnesses—conscious of myself,
> And of some other being.   (*Prelude* 2.28–33)

This tension between a developmental faith in the self's continuity and a haunting sense of childhood as distinctly and irrevocably other comes to characterize many autobiographies and bildungsromane of the nineteenth century.

"To H.C., Six Years Old," a poem on Hartley Coleridge, marks Wordsworth's shift toward the transcendentalized vision of childhood of the Intimations Ode. Although "exquisitely wild," Hartley is heavenly as well as earthly, a "faery voyager" whose "fancies from afar are brought," suspended "Where earth and heaven do make one imagery." (Coleridge similarly idealizes Hartley as a "fairy child" in the conclusion to part 2 of *Christabel*.) In the "Ode: Intimations of Immortality from Recollections of Early Childhood," Wordsworth transfers the source of the child's power from the "the eagerness of infantine desire" and the natural integrity of *The Prelude* to its preexistence in a heavenly realm:

> Not in entire forgetfulness
> And not in utter nakedness,
> But trailing clouds of glory do we come
> From God, who is our home:
> Heaven lies about us in our infancy!
> (62–66)

Nature now becomes a "homely Nurse" who beguiles the growing child, socialization is seen as a "prison-house," and adulthood is redeemed by the "Blank misgivings of a Creature" who dimly recollects the radiance of his true home. The idealization of childhood could go no further; the "nineteenth century's inordinate worship of childhood" was born (Garlitz 647). And yet Wordsworth himself would eventually turn to a bleak, orthodox Christian vision of childhood, as in his sonnet "Baptism": "a timely shower / Whose virtue changes to a Christian Flower / A Growth from sinful Nature's bed of weeds!"

William Blake's conception of childhood has been described in terms both of a conviction in "original innocence" comparable to that of

Rousseau (Coveney 33) and of a Calvinistic belief in "the devil in man and nature . . . disguised behind the very innocence Wordsworth glorifies" (Pattison 65). Neither characterization does justice to Blake's complex portrayal of childhood, which (especially in *Songs of Innocence and of Experience*) transforms the ambivalence of eighteenth-century religious poetry for children into a coherent system. Innocence for Blake is neither preferable to nor canceled out by Experience; both represent "States of the Human Soul" rather than ideals, and both must be subsumed into a fuller and more comprehensive vision if intellectual maturity ("fourfold vision") is to be attained. Although Blake's poetry particularly eludes generalization, his representation of childhood might be thought of in terms of a dialectical triad. Initially, childhood appears Edenic, as in Wordsworth or Lamb. Like Wordsworth in *The Prelude*, whose child self feels "A grandeur in the beatings of the heart" (1.441), Blake celebrates the "unrestrained physical delight of children, who manifest a soul life unspoiled and not made self-conscious by institutional interference" (Babenroth 295) in Songs of Innocence like "The Echoing Green," "Laughing Song," and "Infant Joy," and in *Visions of the Daughters of Albion:* "Infancy, fearless, lustful, happy! nestling for delight / In laps of pleasure" (plate 6, lines 4–5). And yet the perspective of Innocence is fundamentally naive and proves ultimately inadequate to the human world. Behind the apparent simplicity of Innocence lurks the harsher perspective of Experience, and as a result individual poems of Innocence tend to be more complex than their counterparts in experience (Pattison 67).

The "Holy Thursday" poem in *Songs of Experience*, for example, offers a fairly straightforward critique of a "cold and usurious" approach to the plight of poor children, as do "The Chimney Sweeper" and "The Little Vagabond." The "Holy Thursday" in *Songs of Innocence*, however, initially seems an uncomplicated celebration of the Charity School children trooping into Saint Paul's with "innocent faces" like "flowers of London town." It is only when one attends to the deliberately hollow piety of the last line ("Then cherish pity, lest you drive an angel from your door"), the forced metaphors (London flowers are cut flowers; the children flow "like Thames waters" *upward* into the "high dome of Pauls"), and to such details as the beadles' disciplinary "wands," that one detects behind the speaker's laudatory accents Blake's critique of the class oppression built into the Charity School system. To remain in Innocence is to remain content with surface pieties and blind to social injustice. The perspective of Experience is itself incomplete, however, as it envisions no alternative to the bleak, Hobbesian world of rational adulthood. It is because we once enjoyed the Edenic vision of Innocence that we can imagine (and thus build toward) an alternative to the limited world of rational empiricism. The charity children in "Holy Thursday" represent a vision potentially more powerful than that of the "wise guardians of the poor": "Now like a mighty wind they raise to heaven the voice of song / Or like harmonious thunderings the seats of heaven among." Although the child must pass out of Innocence or be condemned, like Thel, to barrenness, children are natural visionaries, and the child's naive perception of an innocent world provides the foundation for imaginative life: "Some children are Fools and so are some Old Men. But There is a vast Majority on the side of Imagination or Spiritual Sensation" (703). The perspectives of Innocence and Experience are both incomplete, but both are necessary aspects of the comprehensive vision of Imagination.

The second generation of Romantic poets—Byron, Shelley, and Keats—have far less to say about childhood than the generation of Wordsworth, Coleridge, and Blake and tend to emphasize instead the period of youth. It is in the prose essays of Charles Lamb and Thomas De Quincey that one finds a bridge between the early Romantic poetry of childhood and the Victorian cult of the child. In his own poetry, Lamb emphasizes childhood innocence, as in "The Christening": "Poor Babe, what can it know of Evil?" (Coleridge lent Wordsworth an analogous line for the opening of "We Are Seven": "What should it know of death?") In his more famous prose essays, Lamb develops both an intense nostalgia for childhood recalled as a lost paradise, and a sentimentalized image of Wordsworth's "heaven-born" child as altogether ethereal. In "Recollections of Christ's Hospital," Lamb set a new standard for the regret of childhood: "For me, I do not know whether a constitutional imbecility does not incline me too obstinately to cling to the remembrances of childhood; in an inverted ratio to the usual sentiments of mankind, nothing that I have been engaged in since seems of any value or importance, compared to the colours which imagination gave to everything then" (287). In "Witches, and Other Night Fears," he finds in children's fantasies reflections of "our ante-mundane condition, and a peep at least into the shadowland of pre-existence" (60). But it is "Dream Children: A Reverie," that Dickens, speaking for his generation, called "the most charming essay, which the tender imagination of Charles Lamb ever conceived" (252). The children in this essay, who begin as the naturalistic but strangely silent children of the narrator, become by the end a bachelor's dream children, whose features "without speech, strangely impressed upon me the effects of speech" (93), prose versions of Lucy Gray and the Danish Boy. "The Child-Angel: A Dream" goes further to imagine a half-earthly, half-celestial child in "a kind of fairy-land heaven," an angel whose mortal taint privileges him to remain "a child forever." Lamb brings together in these essays two motifs from Wordsworth's poetry: the "celestial" attributes of the Intimations Ode and the eternal childhood lent through early death to the child of nature.

De Quincey shares Wordsworth's conception of childhood as some-how discontinuous despite its "necessary" continuity with the adult self: "An adult sympathizes with himself in childhood because he *is* the same, and because (being the same) yet he is *not* the same . . . he feels the differences between his two selves as the main quickeners of his sympathy" (*Confessions* 118). Citing the Intimations Ode, De Quincey sees in children a "far closer communion with God" and a "power of contemplating the truth, which departs as they enter the world"; "into all the *elementary* feelings of man children look with more searching gaze than adults" (153). For De Quincey, as for Schiller, the child is more perfect than the adult it will become, because of a greater "apprehensiveness" and a fuller "natural inheritance" that can only become diminished with age; again citing Wordsworth (De Quincey was one of the few to read *The Prelude* before its belated appearance in 1850), he credits the child with a more profound experience of nature as well (*Collected Writings* 1: 122). De Quincey's prose, like Lamb's, is haunted by spectral children: his sister Elizabeth, who dies at age nine and preys on De Quincey's memories and dreams for the rest of his life; his childhood visions of dying children rising slowly into heaven; his adult obsession with Kate Wordsworth, the poet's daughter, who, dying at age three, appears to De Quincey in the fields of Grasmere after he has spent his nights sleeping on her grave.

The Romantics' major contribution to children's literature has traditionally been described (most recently by Summerfield) as their defense of fantasy reading, especially fairy tales. Coleridge wrote concerning his "early reading of Faery Tales" to Thomas Poole: "I know no other way of giving the mind a love of 'the Great,' & 'the Whole' " (*Letters* 1: 354); Lamb wrote in the same vein to Coleridge, promoting fairy tales over the didactic literature represented by Barbauld and Trimmer: "Think what you would have been now, if instead of being fed with Tales and old wives fables in childhood, you had been crammed with Geography and Natural History?" (Lamb and Lamb 2: 82). Criticizing rationalist education in *The Prelude*, Wordsworth addresses Coleridge in similar terms:

> Where had been we two, beloved friend,
> If we, in lieu of wandering as we did
> Through heights and hollows and bye-spots of tales
> Rich with indigenous produce, open ground
> Of fancy, happy pastures ranged at will,
> Had been attended, followed, watched, and noosed
> . . . .
> Oh gives us once again the wishing-cap
> Of Fortunatus, and the invisible coat
> Of Jack the Giant-killer, Robin Hood
> And Sabra in the forest with St. George!
> (5.233–38; 364–67)

It should be kept in mind, however, that these comments, in private letters and the long-unpublished *Prelude*, did little to affect the history of children's literature. The *Arabian Nights' Entertainment* (cited with gratitude by many Romantic writers), available in English since 1706, and Edgar Taylor's translations of *Grimm's Fairy Tales* (1823–26) had secured their own reputations by the end of the Romantic period.

Far more important than the rehabilitation of the fairy tale is the role played by Romantic poets and essayists in shaping the portrayal of childhood in nineteenth-century literature for adults and children alike. U. C. Knoepflmacher has traced the figure of the "Wordsworthian child of nature" throughout the poetry and prose of the Victorian period and connects the "double vision of an adult self beholding its earlier incarnation," so important in the works of Dickens, George Eliot, and other Victorian novelists, to the "double consciousness" of *The Prelude* ("Mutations" 415). What Knoepflmacher does for the child of nature, Garlitz does for the celestial child of the Intimations Ode, showing how this single, immensely popular poem became a major force in shaping a new poetry of childhood as well as religious discourse throughout the nineteenth century. Representations of childhood in nineteenth-century children's literature equally hark back to Romantic images of the child. Lewis Carroll's "dream-child" owes something to Lamb and, as Knoepflmacher suggests, a great deal to Wordsworth ("Revisiting"); Wordsworth's "child of nature" recurs in such figures as Ruskin's Gluck, Kipling's Mowgli ("Mutations" 425) and, somewhat later, Frances Hodgson Burnett's Dickon in *The Secret Garden*. If Carroll seems anxious to freeze Alice, "like Wordsworth's Lucy Gray, into an arrested world of myth" and eternal childhood ("Revisiting" 4), such transformations in fact come about in stories like Lucy Clifford's "Wooden Tony" and George MacDonald's *At the Back of the North Wind*. In Charles Kingsley's *Water Babies*, with epigraphs from Wordsworth and Coleridge and a passage extolling the Intimations Ode, two children die into life: Tom becomes a literal child of nature as a "water baby" and Ellie becomes a child angel (though both "grow up" at the very end). Indeed, the Victorian literary obsession with dead or dying children noted by David Grylls (39–43) owes as much to Wordsworth, Lamb, and De Quincey as to the religious tradition he cites. And the many children's books that feature children obviously wiser than the adults they must deal with—like F. Anstey's *Vice Versa* or E. Nesbit's *Story of the Amulet*—would have been unthinkable without the Romantic revaluation of childhood. If the Romantic defense of the imagination helped validate the forms of the great works of Victorian fantasy, the "golden age" of children's literature owes still more to the new modes for representing childhood developed throughout the poetry and prose of the Romantic period.

Boston College

Works Cited

Babenroth, A. Charles. *English Childhood: Wordsworth's Treatment of Childhood in Light of English Poetry from Prior to Crabbe.* New York: Columbia UP, 1922.

Bage, Robert. *Hermsprong: Or, Man As He Is Not.* Ed. Peter Faulkner. Oxford: Oxford UP, 1985.

Blake, William. *The Complete Poetry and Prose of William Blake.* Rev. ed. Ed. David V. Erdman. Garden City: Anchor-Doubleday, 1982.

Boas, George. *The Cult of Childhood.* London: Warburg Inst., 1966.

Buckley, Jerome Hamilton. *Season of Youth: The Bildungsroman from Dickens to Golding.* Cambridge: Harvard UP, 1974.

Coleridge, Samuel Taylor. *Collected Letters of Samuel Taylor Coleridge.* Ed. Earl Leslie Griggs. 6 vols. Oxford: Clarendon–Oxford UP, 1956–71.

———. *The Poems of Samuel Taylor Coleridge.* Ed. Ernest Hartley Coleridge. London: Oxford UP, 1912.

Coveney, Peter. *The Image of Childhood.* Harmondsworth, Eng.: Penguin, 1967.

De Quincey, Thomas. *The Collected Writings of Thomas De Quincey.* Ed. David Masson. 14 vols. London: Black, 1896–97.

———. *Confessions of an English Opium Eater and Other Writings.* Ed. Aileen Ward. New York: NAL, 1966.

Dickens, Charles. *The Speeches of Charles Dickens.* Ed. K. J. Fielding. Oxford: Clarendon, 1960.

Garlitz, Barbara. "The Immortality Ode: Its Cultural Progeny." *Studies in English Literature* 6 (1966): 639–49.

Grylls, David. *Guardians and Angels: Parents and Children in Nineteenth-Century Literature.* London: Faber, 1978.

Knoepflmacher, U. C. "Mutations of the Wordsworthian Child of Nature." *Nature and the Victorian Imagination.* Ed. Knoepflmacher and G. B. Tennyson. Berkeley: U of California P, 1977. 391–425.

———. "Revisiting Wordsworth: Lewis Carroll's 'The White Knight's Song.'" *Victorians Institute Journal* 14 (1986): 1–20.

Lamb, Charles. *The Complete Works and Letters of Charles Lamb.* Ed. Saxe Commins. New York: Modern Library, 1935.

Lamb, Charles, and Mary Lamb. *The Letters of Charles and Mary Lamb.* Ed. Edwin W. Marrs, Jr. 3 vols. Ithaca: Cornell UP, 1975–78.

Laqueur, Thomas Walter. *Religion and Respectability: Sunday Schools and Working Class Culture 1780–1850.* New Haven: Yale UP, 1976.

Locke, John. *The Educational Writings of John Locke: A Critical Edition with Introduction and Notes.* Ed. James L. Axtell. Cambridge: Cambridge UP, 1968.

Newlyn, Lucy. *Coleridge, Wordsworth, and the Language of Allusion.* Oxford: Clarendon–Oxford UP, 1986.

Pattison, Robert. *The Child Figure in English Literature.* Athens: U of Georgia P, 1978.

Plotz, Judith. "The Perpetual Messiah: Romanticism, Childhood, and the Paradoxes of Human Development." *Regulated Children/Liberated Children: Education in Psychohistorical Perspective.* Ed. Barbara Finkelstein. New York: Psychohistory, 1979.

Rousseau, Jean-Jacques. *Emile: Or, Education.* Trans. Allan Bloom. New York: Basic, 1979.

Schiller, Friedrich von. Naive and Sentimental Poetry *and* On the Sublime: *Two Essays*. Trans. Julius A. Elias. New York: Ungar, 1966.

Stone, Lawrence. *The Family, Sex, and Marriage in England 1500–1800*. Abridged ed. New York; Harper, 1979.

Summerfield, Geoffrey. *Fantasy and Reason: Children's Literature in the Eighteenth Century*. Athens: U of Georgia P, 1984.

Wesley, John. *The Works of the Rev. John Wesley*. 10 vols. New York: Harper, 1827.

Willey, Basil. *The Eighteenth Century Background*. London: Chatto, 1940.

Wordsworth, William. *Poems*. Ed. John D. Hayden. 2 vols. Harmondsworth, Eng.: Penguin, 1977.

————. *The Prelude: 1799, 1805, 1850*. Ed. Jonathan Wordsworth, M. H. Abrams, and Stephen Gill. New York: Norton, 1979.

Little Girls Lost: Rewriting Romantic Childhood, Righting Gender and Genre

Mitzi Myers

> *Reading has two faces, looks in two directions. . . . It is because reading is almost always an affair of at least two times, two places, and two consciousnesses that interpretation is the endlessly fascinating, difficult, and important matter that [it] is.*
>
> —*Robert Scholes*

> *Tales of fashionable life are very good storys. . . . Miss Egwards tails are very good, particulary some that are very much adopted for youth.*
>
> —*Marjory Fleming*

My two epigraphs, the first from an adult scholar writing at the very end of the twentieth century, the second from a naive child reader at the start of the nineteenth,[1] embody in multiple ways a duality perhaps constitutive of children's literature as a discipline—or should the word be polarity, dichotomy, symbiosis? What word we choose and what stance we take toward the child-adult relation and its literary representation ground our critical approach and perhaps offer an entry into thorny generic questions. Some time back Perry Nodelman described children's literature as

> not just literature written with children in mind, nor is it just literature that happens to be read by children. It is a genre, a special kind of literature with its own distinguishing characteristics. Identifying those characteristics and defining that genre are the major tasks immediately confronting serious critics of children's literature. (81)[2]

Most teachers of children's literature wouldn't want to face *that* as an exam question, and since Nodelman's comment occurred in a review essay, he wasn't bound to a definitive answer either; interestingly, however, his generic observations centered on innocence and experience and the relation between the two. Interestingly, also, historical change (or the lack of it) didn't seem to be a variable.

Though scholarship in children's literature is increasing rapidly and becoming more sophisticated, theoretical investigation of work predating the Victorian "golden age" remains both sparse and naive. Indeed, so aware a critic as Peter Hunt still takes it as a given that modern adults find it virtually impossible to enter eighteenth-century literature for children. The implication is that early writing is unenjoyable, indeed unreadable, that it has little relevance to later literature and nothing to teach us about the workings of the genre. Animating this essay is the contrary belief that investigating historical literary structures and cultural assumptions illuminates the present, even as it contextualizes and thus recovers the past. Not only do we learn about continuities and changes in juvenile literature, I would argue, but historicizing child-adult relations and representations also has important lessons to teach us about the interplay of gender and genre and even about the origins and evolution of the novel itself (for example, how the philosophical *conte*, or moral tale, relates to "romance" and "novel").[3] Thus not only did historical writing for and about juveniles have special uses for writers and readers of the time but it can also assist modern critics in their canonic and generic reconceptualizations.

Like most contemporary students of juvenile literature, Hunt is operating within a post-Romantic, quasi-Wordsworthian paradigm of childhood predicated on the opposition of child and adult or, in Hunt's own phraseology, the childist versus the adultist. The intergenerational is literally the cross-cultural, and, evidently, never the twain shall meet. Within the constraints of this conceptual model, Georgian children's fiction operates like a master-slave relationship; the adult writer bears the whip and inculcates the lesson—the juvenile hero (and reader) exists as passive learner. "Didactic" literature comes off reductively straightforward, all possibilities of complexity or subversion edited out. The same flattening process occurs in virtually all theoretical consideration (Jacqueline Rose and Geoffrey Summerfield are other recent striking examples, though, as I indicate later, Rose's pronouncements offer a useful way of thinking about how child-adult relations get textualized).

Dissertations and surveys devoted to historical topics traffic in plot summary and extractable moral lessons.[4] Even reputable literary and cultural historians—the magisterial F. J. Harvey Darton is a classic example—slide past the moral tale as quickly as they decently can. Gillian Avery categorizes the largely female writers of Georgian fictions as typically down-at-the-heels governesses out to make a pound and vent their grievances against girl nature through punitive tales. Nigel Cross's more recent examination of paraliterary London presents a similarly dreary picture of women writers for children under the rubric of the "female drudge." Yet what Cross also observes should give us pause—that the majority of women who made official nineteenth-century authorial lists wrote for children (and most of these for adults too), a finding corroborated by the entries in Janet Todd's dictionary of earlier women writers. And of course such surveys are highly selective, leaving out of account many lesser and anonymous female authors. "A Lady" is the principal author of most anonymous late-eighteenth-century adult fiction, and the same holds true for juvenile narratives.

What do we make of this critical neglect and these sparse facts? Why have women writers so often been drawn to writing for the young, and how have they used children's literature and juvenile protagonists for their own public and private purposes? Resisting casual clichés about female poverty and feminine nurturance, my book in progress considers the historical conjunction of genre and gender, of child and adult, through analyzing central patterns in the life and juvenile writing of Maria Edgeworth, inarguably the best of the Georgian moralists. Hunt speaks of "the difficulty that most adults have in sustaining interest in . . . eighteenth-century children's books—which represent a cultural gap not just in their content, but in their mode of transmission" (37). Contextualizing Edgeworth's content and mode of transmission, I've discovered, bridges the gap between past and present, child and adult, revealing patterns that continue to shape writing for children despite the surface difference. Paradoxically, thoroughly historicizing Edgeworth in familial, public—and my key topic here—generic context shows her at once a product of her time and precursor of ours, a writer whose work for both juveniles and adults hovers obsessively around developmental processes, intergenerational communication, and cross-cultural connection.

Edgeworth studies inevitably make the writing daughter's relation to the inspiring father central to consideration of her work. Whether Richard Lovell's influence is viewed as harmful or helpful, the educational ideas he and his second wife pioneered are always viewed as the sufficient cause of Edgeworth's huge body of children's books and pedagogic theory. Scholarship typically considers to what extent Edgeworth's ideas do or do not conform to the family educational philosophy. Usually misread, that theory focuses on empowering the child; that is, adult authority is directed toward teaching the child to reflect, feel, and judge for itself, a process depicted in the stories. But Edgeworth's tales for the young are far more than a fictionalized educational program, however positive; they simultaneously enact *and* interrogate that program. Writing for the young allowed Edgeworth to be her father's virtuous daughter, to play the child while writing as adult author, to be at once the heroine and the mother of her own text. Given the family background, the odd thing about the Edgeworth canon is the comparative dearth of lively, wise father figures and the abundance of powerful maternal figures, some wise and many anything but. Equally surprising perhaps are the numerous orphans, émigrés, and displaced persons; the appalling parents who manage to be blessed with children wiser than themselves despite mismanaged educations; the power plays, rivalries, tensions, communication breakdowns, and explosive intimacies that punctuate the work of the writer who established the family idyll before Louisa May Alcott and who indeed lived it with a harmony and happiness denied her successor. Edgeworth fictionalized the juvenile protagonist and the domestic circle in a variety of subtle ways that continually rework and re-solve the problems of her troubled formative years and that also allow her to comment on the larger power relationships of her period—familial and extrafamilial. Situated against the French Revolutionary background, Edgeworth's richly allusive tales regain their original ideological charge.

The patterns I've outlined shape Edgeworth's whole output, but I'll take for example the multiple mother-daughter relations and their literary form in *Emilie de Coulanges*, a novelette in her second series of *Tales of Fashionable Life* (1812). Written for adults as well as adolescents, the story illustrates Edgeworth's lifelong fascination with youthful protagonists who evade the binary opposition of child and adult. Much more subtly than hitherto recognized, Edgeworth's oeuvre considers issues of adult authority and child empowerment and explores what it's like for juveniles who seek both separation and relation, young people who must develop their own sense of self, yet maintain the affiliative network that defines social being: a developmental process much more difficult for girls than for boys, now as well as then. Readers who feel that examining an "adult" tale fudges the argument a bit are reminded that Marjory Fleming was seven when she wrote the journal cited in my epigraph and that her reading, like most of ours when we were young, was catholic: Mrs. Trimmer's robins rub wings with Mrs. Radcliffe's heroines, Hannah More's tracts, the Arabian Nights Entertainments, Pope, Swift, Gray, the Newgate Calendar, and more—juxtapositions that should make us wonder if childist and adultist culture can ever be so hermetically sealed as Peter Hunt's work implies. Indeed, I chose this story to query just that assumption, for the "adult" tales directed to the fashionable world, like the "adult" *Popular Tales* (1804) intended for those lower in rank, were read by a mixed audience of child and adult, like Scott, like Dickens. Similarly, nineteenth-century domestic stories pleasured a dual audience of mother and daughter, much to the chagrin of Henry James, who wanted fiction to signify the male-defined high art novel for mature adults and sneered at "lady" writers "romping through the ruins of the Language" for their ambiguity of audience: "an attempt to provide a special literature for women and children, to provide books which grown women may read aloud to children without either party being bored" (*American Scene* 242; "Schönberg Cotta" 78).[5]

James and other male aesthetes, of course, won that literary war to define genre, just as Wordsworth and other male Romantics had won the earlier battle to define—and gender—the Romantic child. The territory of literary childhood had no sooner been tentatively mapped than it became contested turf. Indeed, one might argue that gender contestation was built into Jean-Jacques Rousseau's pioneer charting. Rous-

seau addresses *Emile* (1762) to mothers because he wishes them to
suckle their own children, but the tutor and pupil of his educational
romance are male and the "development" of the infantilized heroine
destined for the boy's reward is tacked on like an afterthought. And no
sooner had a female tradition of writers for the young adapted and
subverted Rousseau's revolutionary insights than Wordsworth, Lamb,
and other Romantic ideologues branded them a "cursed . . . Crew,
those *Blights & Blasts* of all that is *Human* in man & child.—" (Marrs
2: 82). So quotable is Charles Lamb's diatribe that no juvenile literary
history can resist it, and so compelling is his dichotomy of Science
and Poetry that it helped established the paradigm that still shapes historical discussion: the bad old enlightened eighteenth century versus
the imaginative Romantics. Paradigms, so Thomas S. Kuhn argues,
creak on and on, forestalling investigation until at last they collapse of
their own dead weight.

The Romantic paradigm, however, shows no signs of mortality. Im-
mortal as its most famous exemplar, the infant "best Philosopher"—
"Mighty Prophet! Seer Blest!"—and his big brothers, all the juvenile
rovers through nature that Wordsworth fathered, the interpretive paradigm of Romantic ideology is so much a part of our way of thinking
that it's almost impossible to imagine what children's literature as a critical discipline might look like without it ("Ode: Intimations of Immortality" stanza 8). Thus it's especially important to point out that the
Romantic lens we habitually look through is a culturally conditioned
ideology, a tissue of assumptions, preferences, and perspectives, and
not a transhistorical, universal body of truth about childhood. The Child
doesn't exist; it is always a he or a she, in a particular literary and cultural space. Alan Richardson's essay in this volume demonstrates how
influential Romantic childhood has been—and how male-determined.
Historically, high Romanticism has been a masculine phenomenon can-
onizing poetry as *the* genre. Erasing women's alternative romanticisms,
it paid little attention to the other gender—the only good Romantic heroine is a dead one, like Lucy or Wordsworth's mother—or to genres that
narrativize development socially, that replace the male alone in nature
with children, including females, in community. One sturdy Victorian
lad, for example, recalls detesting Blakean lambs and Wordsworthian
reverie and preferring Edgeworth's juvenile tales for their vigorous action and recognizable world. He also underscores a point implicit in
Richardson's essay: how much Romantic writing is nostalgia *about* childhood rather than stories *for* them (Jones 25–29).[6]

What would accounts of Romantic childhood look like if the feminine gender and prosaic genre now marginalized were written in? To
what extent does women's storying about girls' growth like Edgeworth's, like Austen's, verify the textbook clichés about characters who
are only miniature adults and omniscient tutors, about content that is

leaden fact, all "Geography & Natural History" in Lamb's reductive summary? Because women's cultural status made them specially attentive to domestic interaction, to intergenerational life within doors, adding dialogic female fiction to monovocal male poetic forms offers us insights into child-adult relations. Challenging our preconceptions about what "Romantic" literature is and how its conventions operate, female fictions ask us to learn new ways of reading—and of teaching. Like the period's masculine poetry celebrating asocial, egotistical boys of nature, women's socializing stories resonate with implicit political and cultural meanings that require historical elucidation for fullest effect. Women's fictions not only consider key psychic and political issues; they do so in reformist ways. *Because* they are encoded in "subliterary" genres, they can retain a progressive edge on controversial topics like gender and the relation of the individual to the broader community. These stories, then, raise cultural, political, and maturational issues from a woman's point of view that interrogates the male perspective of high Romanticism. They ask us to think about how men and women address similar issues, why they choose certain literary forms, and how some forms get canonized and others become marginal.

Edgeworth self-consciously used the term *tale* for her fictions not because she is prudish about the novel (the usual explanation) but because she thus signals to contemporary readers the intellectual, argumentative, analytical genre she domesticates, feminizes, and frequently subverts. Romances and novels suggest love and sensibility; for a woman writer who wants to be taken seriously and explore serious issues, who values her youthful protagonists and is interested in more about them than whom they'll marry, the moral tale offers progressive possibilities. It's a matter of form and expectations, not of maxim and adage (the period's wildest romances were thoroughly didactic, as is most contemporary problem fiction and the whole notion of bibliotherapy). Edgeworth's story is a family story, about an adolescent's attempt to maintain her own identity and integrity *and* her bond with her mother and her English surrogate mother, the wealthy Mrs. Somers, the woman who's given these two displaced Frenchwomen a home, but who proves quite impossible to live with. Emilie's consciousness is dignified as normative, though the story isn't trapped there, as are most modern first-person "young adult" narratives, and the two contentious mothers are depicted as bratty children through their wonderfully realistic dialogues. They just cannot live together, and familial intimacy becomes a battleground with Emilie as mediator and victim. Both women have a marriage partner in mind; Emilie prefers to support herself and her mother through her own efforts. The story is about adolescent selfhood and the family matrix, not about the adult novel's typical subject, love and marriage; this is a moral fable about self-worth and the choice of life, a prenuptial plot whose totally ridiculous coincidental

ending underscores the inability of the usual romantic conclusion to re-
solve the child-adult tensions the story has presented. The ending is
delivered as a parodic joke, not a "novelistic" finale. *Emilie,* then, is a
sophisticated variant on the moral tale, in which feminist and intergenerational issues are accorded a formal significance, the child-adult, au-
tonomy-freedom dialectic literally embodied in the dialogic structure,
the satiric characters, and the final send-up of the classic romance paradigm in which hero shows up to save heroine from the competing
mothers who struggle to possess her.

Rather than a full-scale elucidation of this odd and complex tale
what I'm mainly concerned with here is the contrast between Edgeworth's sophisticated fiction and the stodgy ways we have of reading
it—despite the postmodern dispensation in literary analysis, which we
might expect to be having more impact on children's literature studies
than is the case, at least so far as eighteenth-century work is concerned.
Notable exceptions of course exist. Yet it is also surprising how old Romantic ideological verities endure, even when fresh perspectives, like
gender, are brought to bear (Briggs). The past is a foreign country—so
historians like to say. And if history itself is terra incognita where the
natives did things differently and we tourists must encode their mores
and lingo, historical *literary* narratives pose especial problems. History
itself, we moderns agree, is pretty much narrative, words, conventions—somebody's story of what happened. But there are still differences between history as literature and literary history, between the
past as story and stories from the past. It's easier to weigh one record
against another than it is to feel through a past literary form, especially
when it's close enough to us to look superficially familiar.

Eighteenth-century texts participate in distinctive generic traditions, which we may misread as defective forms of what we're familiar
with, rather than as significant inflections of a stylized and conventional
grammar. Edgeworth's delicate variations on established genres—like
the eighteenth-century moral or philosophical tale she inherits from
adult writers such as Voltaire, Johnson, Jean-François Marmontel, and
children's writers like Arnaud Berquin—can be fully appreciated only
when contextualized. The familiar adolescent dilemmas that Emilie
faces, the startlingly lifelike dialogue that is the backbone of Edgeworth's work, the increasing tensions among intimates who continually misread one another that we feel along our nerves—paradoxically,
these "timeless" elements that we can so easily identify with may frus-
trate us the more when the conclusion doesn't seem to fit, when it is
obviously outrageous, parodic, contrived, a coincidence so wild it calls
into question the rational cause and effect we're predisposed to find. A
good case can be made for Edgeworth's psychological and domestic realism as the precursor of later forms of fiction, but there's a lot that
won't be bent into a naturalistic frame, an alternative romanticism of

quotidian domestic life that finishes by serving up a stereotyped fairy tale—and laughing at it too. Paradoxically (again), the parts that *don't* seem to fit our realistic expectations may signal subversive—and recognizably "modern"—variations on customary patterns. To discover the modern, we must decipher the archaic. We need to know our Marmontel before we can appreciate Edgeworth's family utopias and dystopias. Emilie and Edgeworth's other versions of the adolescent heroine's text have to be measured against straightforward stories like Marmontel's "The Good Mother" and "The Bad Mother" before we can appreciate her very "modern" ambivalence toward erring adult authority figures and her flattering presentation of adolescent consciousness and conscience.

"Children's fiction," Jacqueline Rose asserts,

> hangs on an impossibility, one which it rarely ventures to speak. This is the impossible relation between adult and child. Children's fiction is clearly about the relation, but it has the remarkable characteristic of being about something which it hardly ever talks of. (1)

In Rose's formulation, children's literature is the locus of a power struggle, a textual site where cultural issues of authority, power, and control emerge and contend: the seducer story versus the child reader. But Rose's rhetoric enfolds other possibilities also: perhaps the child-adult relation and its varying textualizations over time provide a heuristic to help us answer Perry Nodelman's call for generic identification. Perhaps, also, we might add adult readers and their varying interpretations of childhood to Rose's witch's brew. Readers, writers, critics, child and adult—all have their own notions of children's literature—and if we may never agree on a unitary definition, we need not settle for an overly limited Romantic one that erases so much of our heritage. It's right to look for the ways that children's literature differs from writing for adults, but we also need to look more closely at genres like the moral tale that serve two audiences and at writers, like Edgeworth, who favor developmental plots and juvenile protagonists whether they write for children *or* adults. Despite their having so much in common in period, genre, and attitude, Maria Edgeworth would never have written to a fledgling author as Jane Austen did: "You are but *now* coming to the heart & beauty of your book; till the heroine grows up the fun must be imperfect" (*Letters* 401; 9 Sept. 1814).

Edgeworth felt otherwise, and the continuities and discontinuities between the growing up plots in her moral tales for children and adults suggest that mapping our province of literature requires (1) special attention to the interplay between child and adult and to its varying textualizations over time, and within the *same* period according to gender and genre; (2) precise historical contextualization of genres adapted for children, including the relation between what was being written for children and the period's adult literary forms; (3) a willingness to examine clichés—no more eighteenth-century diminutive adults, no more Wordsworthian infant philosophers, no more naive repetition of Philippe Ariès and Lawrence Stone on the invention of the child and the companionate family, no more fantasy as childhood's natural food, no more instruction *versus* delight—or at least a moratorium until much basic research is done. For example, one might venture to argue that entries like that for the moral tale in the *Oxford Companion*—I choose it not as an egregious example, but precisely because it isn't—substantially need revision (Carpenter and Prichard 358 60). Leaving aside its minor errors and dubious critical judgments, I'd like to suggest an alternative provenance for the moral tale. Instead of positing the familiar moral tale versus fairy tale paradigm based on post-Romantic notions of child and adult, we might more fruitfully consider in what ways the period's moral tales for children differ from those for adults. Just as Edgeworth signs herself feminist by delicate subversions of stylized forms, so child protagonists are empowered within seemingly conventional genres. For most modern critics, eighteenth-century attitudes toward child and adult are summed up by titles like this one published by Elizabeth Newbery around 1789: *Filial Duty, Recommended and Enforced, by a Variety of Instructive and Entertaining Stories, of Children Who Have Been Remarkable for Affection to Their Parents. Also an account of Some Striking Instances of Children, Who Have Behaved in an Undutiful, and Unnatural Manner to Their Parents. The Whole Founded on Historical Facts*—a title under the heading "a new book for the improvement of young gentlemen and ladies" (Bauerle). But historical periods are no more monolithic than our own. Before we can identify children's literature as a separable genre with distinguishing characteristics, we need to see more clearly what it has—and hasn't—been. We need two ways of reading—and more.[7]

University of California, Los Angeles

Notes

[1] Scholes 7; Fleming 4; 104.

[2] To argue that the child-adult relation is central to children's literature as a field or to analyze fully the particular configuration that interplay takes in Georgian writing for young people would require more room than is available here; I am exploring these issues further in a study of Maria Edgeworth. My thinking about child-adult relations, like that of most scholars in historical children's literature, has been informed by U. C. Knoepflmacher's many illuminating articles on Victorian literature.

[3] The contemporary critical rethinking of the origins of the novel as a genre has not yet factored in writing specifically for young people, even when young readers themselves are considered, as in J. Paul Hunter's useful essay. For a start in that direction, see my "Quixotes" essay.

[4] The tendency to read so-called didactic literature didactically—that is, to read it for the bare content and to ignore its literary, generic, and stylistic features—is as commonplace among established scholars (Kramnick) as it is with beginners (Goldstone); so too is an extraordinary amount of factual error, evidenced in these two works, Summerfield's, and many standard historical overviews (see my "Wise Child" and "Missed Opportunities"). Much basic research remains to be done, and no secondary source should be trusted implicitly.

[5] Conversely, one might argue that this duality of readership confers certain aesthetic strengths, as well as an enduring readership; Charlotte Yonge, Juliana Horatia Ewing, and L. M. Montgomery are cases in point.

[6] Though Lamb's tirade is even longer, this is the gist: "Science has succeeded to Poetry no less in the little walks of Children than with Men.—: Is there no possibility of averting this sore evil? Think what you would have been now, if instead of being fed with Tales and old wives fables in childhood, you had been crammed with Geography & Natural History.? *Damn them.* I mean the cursed Barbauld Crew, those *Blights & Blasts* of all that is *Human* in man & child.—" (Marrs 2: 81–82). I have explored the female tradition in "Impeccable Governesses"; Lamb's "Crew," Romantic ideology, and the contours of women's work for younger children are discussed more fully in a forthcoming essay on Anna Laetitia Barbauld. Richardson's essay on the "colonization of the feminine" by male poets and Mary Jacobus's chapter on Wordsworth's erasure of the mother offer relevant insights into gender issues in Romanticism.

[7] I am grateful to the American Council of Learned Societies for the fellowship which enabled me to complete this project.

Works Cited

Ariès, Philippe. *Centuries of Childhood: A Social History of Family Life.* 1960. Trans. Robert Baldick. New York: Vintage-Random, 1962.

Austen, Jane. *Jane Austen's Letters to Her Sister Cassandra and Others.* Ed. R. W. Chapman. 1932. 2nd ed. London: Oxford UP, 1959.

Avery, Gillian, with the assistance of Angela Bull. *Nineteenth-Century Children: Heroes and Heroines in English Children's Stories 1780–1900.* London: Hodder, 1965.

Bauerle, Diane K. "A Checklist of Newbery Family Children's Books at the Lilly Library." *Phaedrus: An International Annual for the History of Children's and Youth Literature* 13 (1988): 15–40.

Briggs, Julia. "Women Writers and Writing for Children: From Sarah Fielding to E. Nesbit." *Children and Their Books: A Celebration of the Work of Iona and Peter Opie.* Ed. Gillian Avery and Julia Briggs. Oxford: Clarendon–Oxford UP, 1989. 221–50.

Carpenter, Humphrey, and Mari Prichard. *The Oxford Companion to Children's Literature.* Oxford: Oxford UP, 1984.

Cross, Nigel. *The Common Writer: Life in Nineteenth-Century Grub Street.* Cambridge: Cambridge UP, 1985.

Darton, F. J. Harvey. *Children's Books in England: Five Centuries of Social Life.* 1932. 3rd ed. Rev. Brian Alderson. Cambridge: Cambridge UP, 1982.

Edgeworth, Maria. *Popular Tales.* 3 vols. London: Johnson, 1804.

———. *Tales of Fashionable Life.* 3 vols. London: Johnson, 1812.

Fleming, Marjory. *The Complete Marjory Fleming: Her Journals, Letters and Verses.* Ed. Frank Sidgwick. London: Sidgwick, 1934.

Goldstone, Bette P. *Lessons to Be Learned: A Study of Eighteenth-Century English Didactic Children's Literature.* American University Studies 14, vol. 7. New York: Lang, 1984.

Hunt, Peter. "Cross-Culturalism and Inter-Generational Communication in Children's Literature." *Cross-Culturalism in Children's Literature: Selected Papers from the 1987 International Conference of the Children's Literature Association.* Ed. Susan R. Gannon and Ruth Anne Thompson. Pace U [1988].

Hunter, J. Paul. " 'The Young, the Ignorant, and the Idle': Some Notes on Readers and the Beginnings of the English Novel." *Anticipations of the Enlightenment in England, France, and Germany.* Ed. Alan Charles Kors and Paul J. Korshin. Philadelphia: U of Pennsylvania P, 1987. 259–82.

Jacobus, Mary. *Romanticism, Writing, and Sexual Difference: Essays on* The Prelude. Oxford: Clarendon–Oxford UP, 1989.

James, Henry. *The American Scene.* 1907. Ed. Leon Edel. London: Hart-Davis, 1968.

——— . "The Schönberg-Cotta Family." *Notes and Reviews.* Cambridge: Dunster, 1921. 77–83.

Jones, L. E. *A Victorian Boyhood.* London: Macmillan, 1955.

Kramnick, Isaac. "Children's Literature and Bourgeois Ideology: Observations on Culture and Industrial Capitalism in the Later Eighteenth Century." *Culture and Politics from Puritanism to the Enlightenment.* Ed. Perez Zagorin. Berkeley: U of California P, 1980. 203–40.

Kuhn, Thomas S. *The Structure of Scientific Revolutions.* 1962. Rev. ed. International Encyclopedia of Unified Science: Foundations of the Unity of Science 2.2. Chicago: U of Chicago P, 1970.

Marmontel, Jean François. *Marmontel's Moral Tales.* Ed. George Saintsbury. London: Allen, 1895.

Marrs, Edwin W., Jr., ed. *The Letters of Charles and Mary Anne Lamb.* 3 vols. Ithaca: Cornell UP, 1975–78.

Myers, Mitzi. "Impeccable Governesses, Rational Dames, and Moral Mothers: Mary Wollstonecraft and the Female Tradition in Georgian Children's Books." *Children's Literature* 14 (1986): 31–59.

——— . "Missed Opportunities and Critical Malpractice: New Historicism and Children's Literature." *Children's Literature Association Quarterly* 13.1 (1988) 41–43.

——— . "Quixotes, Orphans, and Subjectivity: Maria Edgeworth's Georgian Heroinism and the (En)Gendering of Young Adult Fiction." *The Lion and the Unicorn: A Critical Journal of Children's Literature* 13.1 (1989): 21–40.

——— . "Wise Child, Wise Peasant, Wise Guy: Geoffrey Summerfield's Case against the Eighteenth Century." *Children's Literature Association Quarterly* 12.2 (1987): 107–10.

Nodelman, Perry. "*Beyond Genre* and Beyond." *The First Steps: Articles and Columns from the* ChLA Newsletter/Quarterly, *Volume I–VI.* Ed. Patricia Dooley. [West Lafayette]: Children's Literature Assn., 1984. 81–83.

Richardson, Alan. "Romanticism and the Colonization of the Feminine." *Romanticism and Feminism.* Ed. Anne K. Mellor. Bloomington: Indiana UP, 1988. 13–25.

Rose, Jacqueline. *The Case of* Peter Pan: *Or, the Impossibility of Children's Fiction.* London: Macmillan, 1984.

Rousseau, Jean-Jacques. *Emile*. 1762. Trans. Barbara Foxley. Everyman's Library. London: Dent; New York: Dutton, 1911.

Scholes, Robert. *Protocols of Reading*. New Haven: Yale UP, 1989.

Stone, Lawrence. *The Family, Sex, and Marriage in England 1500–1800*. New York: Harper, 1977.

Summerfield, Geoffrey. *Fantasy and Reason: Children's Literature in the Eighteenth Century*. 1984. Athens: U of Georgia P, 1985.

Todd, Janet, ed. *A Dictionary of British and American Women Writers 1600–1800*. Totowa: Rowman, 1985.

Wordsworth, William. *The Poetical Works of Wordsworth*. Ed. Thomas Hutchinson. Rev. ed. by Ernest De Selincourt. London: Oxford UP, 1960.

Part II:
Course Descriptions

Introduction

Pedagogically, as a subject for instruction, literature for children has passed through its adolescence: Alice has managed to grow up Under Ground. Having survived the turbulent years of academic recognition, children's literature is beginning to be accepted in most English departments as a valid part of the undergraduate curriculum. Even before the first Modern Language Association seminar on children's literature was held, in Denver in 1969, courses in the field were being offered, often under disguised titles.

In 1979, at the Modern Language Association convention in New York, children's literature was given a permanent place as an MLA group; in 1980 at Houston, it became an MLA division. There are a number of critical journals in the field. *Children's Literature* (Yale University Press) is the official publication of the division and the Children's Literature Association. The Children's Literature Association, founded in 1973, now has over twelve hundred members.

But in spite of formal academic acceptance, children's literature as a course is generally still segregated, as U. C. Knoepflmacher points out in his introduction to the volume, from mainstream literature courses. Many English departments still do not accept a course in children's literature for credit toward the major, even though, as the survey of course descriptions in parts 2 and 3 of this volume indicates, such courses include widely accepted English and American classics. That such works can—and should be—taught as appealing to a dual child and adult audience has yet to be fully recognized.

A striking feature of children's literature as a course is its interdisciplinary adaptability and creative potential in the classroom. The present MLA survey reflects the eclectic nature of the subject both for instruction and research. The range is very widespread in orientation and in methodology. One finds undergraduate introductory courses, studies of myth and folklore, and historical approaches to the classics, as well as genre courses on fantasy and fairy tales, the picture book, and related studies, such as the linking of children's literature to composition, Third World literature, and feminist criticism. One discovers that, in subject matter and scope, children's literature is world literature.

The course descriptions in this volume demonstrate, furthermore, that children's literature courses can be either broad or specialized. Although literary periods and genres are indicated in most courses, the trend seems to be to disregard such traditional boundaries in favor of courses that emphasize special themes or age-level interests. There is a growing interest in teaching the classics of children's books with special attention to the child-adult voice in such works, an approach that suggests the frequently debated formation of the canon of "children's books." Another topic equally debated is that of stereotypes, especially as they appear in fairy tales, and the use of children's literature as a means of socialization.

For a prospective teacher of children's literature, there are several critical issues to consider.

Defining what "children's literature" *is* as a genre, if in fact it is one, is the first difficulty to overcome. Next, there are discussions regarding the child-adult response to classic children's books, the mythic and archetypal role of the child figure in various literary periods of history, gender and the social function of children's literature.

One of the most difficult tasks for a teacher of children's literature to overcome is the student's frequent sentimental distrust of taking any critical approach at all to the subject. Most undergraduates cherish an affectionate feeling for that special children's book that was read as a child. To introduce a critical discussion of the sexual stereotypes in the fairy tales of Perrault, the Grimms, or Andersen, for example, takes special skill on the part of the instructor. The average undergraduate will still insist on the "innocent child" figure as being essential to an enjoyment of a children's book. Such students often find themselves trying, emotionally, to hold on to their own childhood dreams as they are being asked intellectually to confront issues they would rather not be told exist in *their favorite* children's book. Like Alice before them, such students simply cannot cope with the destruction of the child within.

Perhaps the most critical issue facing those who teach children's literature today is how to cope with the multiculturalism of most undergraduate classes. Ethnic differences must be considered. Teachers can alert students to ethnocentrism, which often leads to stereotyping, by an in-depth consideration of the picture book or the cultural background of folktale adaptations. Another major problem, especially in the field of young adult literature, is how to treat the subject of censorship. Students should be made aware of the various approaches one can take to censorship and how to teach censored books.

As the present survey of workshops, seminars, and graduate programs in part 3 indicates, an ever-increasing number of advanced and graduate programs are offered in the field. Although it has been traditionally tied to educational programs and teacher preparation, there are signs that children's literature is becoming a serious branch of research, one independent of its educational roots. From a literary perspective, more advanced courses pursue the history of children's literature as a genre and its sociocultural implications. Specialized courses on the fairy tale, the picture book, and fantasy fiction are commonly available.

The sections "Selected Bibliography" and "Special Collections of Children's Literature" at the end of this volume present ample evidence that children's literature—as an academic discipline for instruction and serious research—is no longer just for children.

GENERAL UNDERGRADUATE COURSES

Literature for Children

Norma Bagnall
English, Missouri Western State College

Introduction and History   Literature for Children is a theoretical course taught as literature, not a methods course in learning to read. It begins with literary terms as defined by Rebecca Lukens and moves on to the principles espoused by Northrop Frye, as they are outlined by Glenna Davis Sloan. The course concentrates on Frye's theory that all stories are part of one body of stories, that there are discernible dialectical and cyclical patterns, and that literature is the artistic response of people searching to understand and express what it means to be human. Students learn that literature for children is governed by the same principles that guide all literature and that literary criticism is the "study of how imagination works in the creation of art in words" (Sloan 27). The course focuses on the fact that children can study literature in the same way that they study other subjects and can understand basic truths about what literature is. Students are required to look for those elements in children's literature that make a book an artistic achievement and that show how literature is part of a search for meaning in our lives.

Children's literature has been taught in Saint Joseph since 1915, when Saint Joseph Junior College opened. It was originally a two-hour course in education to train teachers; in the early 1940s it was extended into a three-hour course in the same department. In 1963, the course was transferred to the department of English, where it remains.

Structure   The course is structured so that the first five weeks are devoted to picture books, the next seven weeks to the junior novel, and the final four weeks to poetry. Students are undertaking their first study of literature and do not understand that stories have underlying themes and basic structures. They believe stories are just narratives intended to amuse or instruct. During the first five weeks, the class studies basic literary terms and their application to specific works. For beginning students, it is important to establish what point of view, structure, style, and theme are and to use precise terms to discuss literature. The terms students learn with picture books give them the language they need to discuss any literature and to master the theory that all stories are part of a whole governed by cyclical and dialectical patterns.

The study begins with Margaret Wise Brown's *Goodnight Moon* so that students examine, in the simplest way possible (though this is not a simple picture book), point of view, structure, style, and theme. Such an approach shows how writer and illustrator make deliberate choices to elicit a particular response from the reader-listener. Only after students learn that words are skillfully chosen and organized to create an artistic whole do they understand that stories are our attempt to make sense of the human condition. Because of its basic structure (introduction, body, conclusion), distinctive shift in point of view, repetition and rhyme, and readily discovered thematic statement, *Goodnight Moon* is an excellent beginning in theoretical study. It contains literary allusion for the two-year-old (a difficult feat) and humor for the adult audience (the clocks' hands move from 7 to 8:10 p.m. while mama waits for bunny to fall asleep). Students learn that the book could not have been published three years earlier because the green dye used in its production was not available to civilians during World War II. Was the publisher making a statement about war by using this shade of green? That question remains unanswered, as does the question of why the green was unavailable during the war. Through such explorations students become aware of the complexity of a seemingly simple picture book and the importance of close reading and observation.

We move from *Goodnight Moon* to books that are progressively more difficult to comprehend and are intended for older audiences. Maurice Sendak's *Where the Wild Things Are* is of major importance and a good vehicle for the study of how foreshadowing creates unity, how tone establishes mood, and how poetic devices enhance enjoyment. The film *Max Made Mischief*, by Edward A. Mason, shows how techniques used in the college classroom have practical application in teaching schoolchildren, for example, that underneath the surface story there is an underlying theme that speaks to our humanity.

Concepts taught with picture books are repeated and elaborated on in junior novels. *Charlotte's Web*, by E. B. White, is stylistically rich and can be read on several levels of enjoyment and understanding. Students read Sonia Landes's article to learn that the first two chapters serve as frontispiece to reassure the very young that Wilbur, saved from death once, can be saved again. Landes also encourages close attention to Garth Williams's illustrations for the added detail and meaning the pictures give. Concentration on the way language and actions determine character leads to careful study of style and the discovery that each animal in the story is distinctive and remains true to its own nature. To appreciate the importance of word choice and language, we read Janice M. Alberghene's discussion, which focuses on words used in the web, in the education of Wilbur, and eventually in the creation of any well-considered expression.

Katherine Paterson's *Birdge to Terabithia* is outstanding in its presentation of family relationships and friendship and in its straightforward handling of death and grief. Parents and teachers could be perceived as considerably more understanding, for example, were the story not told from a child's point of view. So students learn that choice of point of view is deliberate; they also discover the importance of seeing events from others' perspectives. Foreshadowing occurs from the story's start to alert children that a tragedy will occur; these clues give careful readers the armor they need to accept death near the end. The importance of language to overcome one's otherwise dreary present and to suggest a brighter future is reiterated in Leslie's telling of the story, which opens new worlds to Jess and helps him understand that language can enrich not only his own existence but that of others as well. Several other novels are studied; all contribute to the concept of language used to explore what it means to be human and to see how all stories are one story.

The study of poetry reinforces the concept of the importance of words because of the distilled language and emotional intensity of poetry. While there is room for playfulness with rhyme and figurative speech, students come to realize, the dialectical and cyclical patterns and the search for meaning of the human condition encountered earlier in the course hold true. All elements within the course emphasize that literature is the artistic use of words to explain the human condition and that all of literature fits within established patterns.

Evaluation Testing begins after the study of picture books as students apply the concepts they have learned in class to a picture book in which they have had no instruction. Their success depends on how well they can transfer concepts learned in one work to another. Remaining tests are similar but require increasingly sophisticated response. *All* tests require writing; none are fill-in-the-blank, true-false, or multiple choice.

Weaknesses A weakness of this abstract, in-depth teaching of a few books is that there is little time for nonfiction, such as biography and history. To offset this disadvantage, students are encouraged to use an information book as the basis of their class project and to share their findings with other students.

Texts

Alberghene, Janice M. "Writing in *Charlotte's Web*." *Children's Literature in Education* 1.1 (1985): 32–44.

Brown, Margaret Wise. *Goodnight Moon*. New York: Harper, 1947.

Frye, Northrop. *The Educated Imagination*. Bloomington: Indiana UP, 1964.

Landes, Sonia. "E. B. White's *Charlotte's Web:* Caught in the Web." *Touchstones: Reflections on the Best in Children's Literature*. Ed. Perry Nodelman. Vol. 1. West Lafayette: Children's Literature Assn., 1985. 270–80.

Lukens, Rebecca. *A Critical Handbook of Children's Literature*. 3rd ed. Glenview: Scott, 1986.

Mason, Edward A. *Max Made Mischief* (16 mm film). Cambridge: Harvard University Medical School, 1977.

Paterson, Katherine. *Bridge to Terabithia*. New York: Crowell, 1977.

Sendak, Maurice. *Where the Wild Things Are*. New York: Harper, 1963.

Sloan, Glenna Davis. *The Child as Critic*. 2nd ed. New York: Teachers Coll. P, 1984.

White, E. B. *Charlotte's Web*. New York: Harper, 1952.

Children's Literature
Francelia Butler
English, University of Connecticut

Introduction and History The present advanced undergraduate course was begun in 1965 with an enrollment of 15 and now has over 250 students per semester. The enrollment is voluntary and has remained constant during that period. In addition, there are graduate courses offered, with 12 or 15 enrolled. Discussions in the graduate classes are basically the same but are more demanding and assignments are more involved with literary theory and criticism.

Most literature for children assumes a quality of perception in its audience that literature for adults must create: what T. S. Eliot, in speaking of the metaphysical poets, called "the direct sensuous apprehension of thought" (246). Most adults have lost this capacity, in part, at least, as a result of the enforced segregation of responses that modern education has deemed basic to its process. With this in mind, the following activities are designed to provoke a unified and immediate response to literature. Unorthodox as they may seem, they have all been tried in classes of varying size and makeup and found to be surprisingly successful.

Structure and Method How can one make a course intellectually challenging and at the same time enjoyable and stimulating?

The class might be broken up into workshop groups of four or eight to choose a topic of their own—a childhood experience or whatever—and determine a commencement, a conflict, a climax, and a conclusion. Together they would write a story or narrative poem, imitating the style of some admired writer for children. Students would use similar vocabulary, sentence length, coined words, or other literary devices the author used. If one of the group is talented in art, the booklet could be illustrated as well. If Seuss, for instance, is being imitated, the illustrations might be outrageous animals. Essays by Isaac Bashevis Singer and by P. L. Travers suggest critical theory and techniques for writing literature for children.

One way to make a course stimulating is to take up social issues. A unit on peace, for example, can include a study of such books as Leo

Tolstoy's *Ivan the Fool*, Munro Leaf's *Story of Ferdinand*, Natalie Babbitt's *Search for Delicious*, Seuss's *Butter Battle Book*, and Judy Blume's *Tiger Eyes*, as well as biographies for children of outstanding figures in history, such as Mohandas Gandhi or Martin Luther King, Jr.

Each student can be asked to turn a problem in conflict resolution into a game that tells a story—for example, a board game. In preparation for this activity, students in the Connecticut class act as advisers to middle and high schools in the area. They instruct the children on the preparation of the games. By so doing, the students learn about teaching children and the learning process itself. Recently, a Peace Game Festival, attended by over fifteen hundred children, was held at the University of Connecticut. Awards, as such, were not given, because the event stressed a noncombative approach to war. Instead, certificates were presented to all students who created a game.

In any geographical area, one can utilize the talent at hand and relate it to something in the program the instructor has devised for the class. For instance, if the class is reading *The Secret Garden* and there is an authority on child abuse in the area, he or she might lead a critical class discussion of the psychological significance of the story. Articles on the book such as Gillian Adams's "Secrets and Healing Magic in *The Secret Garden*" could be put on reserve in the library.

Another good subject with critical and social potential is age discrimination in children's literature—a serious and, at the moment, almost unexplored topic. See Catherine Townsend Horner's extensive bibliography *The Aging Adult in Children's Books and Nonprint Media*, in which she indicates that "most of the children's books in the Bibliography dwell morbidly on the depressing aspects of aging, namely death, infirmity, irascibility, and the triple losses of employment, independence, and even dignity" (xxi). An analysis of some of these books appears in the *Lion and Unicorn* 2.1 (1987).

Students might have practice in storytelling through narrating the German folktale "The Bremen Town Musicians" or "The Blanket"—the latter appearing in Clifton Fadiman's *World Treasury of Children's Literature* (vol. 3).

Another unit might be on rhymes for children. Curiously, folk rhymes often have a sophisticated rhythm—far beyond the anapestic tetrameter some teachers attribute to them. Students might study a collection of folk rhymes, such as the Opie *Oxford Dictionary of Nursery Rhymes*, and then write a rhyme of their own on their favorite hang-up and try skipping to it, which provides a good means of learning rhythm in poetry. Such folk rhymes reveal the unification of dance, music, drama, and poetry from earlier cultures that are still beloved by children. Puppetry as a means of telling a story should also not be ignored. Here, music such as Debussy's *Golliwogs' Cakewalk*, Ravel's *Mother Goose Suite*, Prokofiev's *Peter and the Wolf*, Saint-Saëns's *Carnival of the Animals*, or a selection from Glinka's opera *Russlan and Ludmilla* could accompany class presentations.

Guest speakers can often bring unusual insights to class study. A prominent woman broker who has written children's books gave an interesting talk on the way children's fantasies are sometimes the subliminal source for their adult lives as financiers. An astronaut told the students how his childhood reading of Edgar Rice Burroughs's Tarzan books motivated his career. One of the most successful activities was the appearance of a falconer with his live falcon as part of the unit on medieval literature and customs. An imaginative teacher can find other such activities to illustrate the connections between children's literature and history.

Evaluation Besides grades periodically given on day-to-day assignments, two major exams—called "Reflections"—are given each semester. These consist of six essay questions, two each in three categories: fantasy, folktales, drama. The student chooses one question to answer in each category. A typical question might be: "Swallowing is found in a number of children's stories. Discuss swallowing in 'Pinocchio,' 'The Steadfast Tin Soldier,' 'Tom Thumb,' 'Raggedy Ann,' or other children's stories (at least five in all). What in your opinion is the significance of the act in these stories?"

Weaknesses Some teachers complain that the thematic approach is too confining. But because children's literature is such a vast field—not one subject but a whole field—some kind of form beyond genres is helpful. Further, the themes are more inclusive than one might suppose, for they interrelate. Themes give a rationale to what might otherwise be a billy-goat approach of leaping from pinnacle to pinnacle.

For some reason, the ability to recall childhood has not filtered into the consciousness of many teachers in the field. They think that because they have repudiated May Hill Arbuthnot's simplistic approach of the 1960s, and because they teach children's literature as if it were adult literature, they have progressed. They are defensively trying to justify themselves to their department chairs without really studying the literature *as literature*. At least Arbuthnot had a way of trying to recall their own childhood to students, with such subheads in her anthologies as "Let's Fly Away," and she had a lighthearted though somewhat naive approach, which is an improvement over the humorless, dry-as-dust teaching that is often going on now. What we need is more fun in classes, so that students can recall how they felt about books in their own childhood, and at the same time, some sharp criticism. Even something as common as skip-rope jumping can be seen as a form of childhood ritual: "Skip-rope rhymes are fascinating because within the invisible world of the turning rope, children can relieve pain by chanting their need for romance and identity" (Butler 1). The approach could be very much like that of Roger Sale (*Fairy Tales and After*). Writers like Singer, Dr. Seuss, and Maurice Sendak (who often recalls the child's mind because, he says, "I have been a child") affirm that children indeed make the best critics, partly because they are honest. Children are sometimes brought into the classroom and are asked to comment on a story. For in the end, story is still—and perhaps always will be—the heart and soul of children's literature and of teaching it.

Texts

Adams, Gillian. "Secrets and Healing Magic in *The Secret Garden*." *Triumphs of the Spirit in Children's Literature*. Ed. Francelia Butler and Richard Rotert. Hamden: Library Professional, 1986.

Babbitt, Natalie. *Search for Delicious*. New York: Farrar, 1969.

Blume, Judy. *Tiger Eyes*. New York: Bradbury, 1981.

Butler, Francelia, ed. *Skipping around the World: The Ritual Nature of Folk Rhymes*. Hamden: Library Professional–Shoe String, 1989; New York: Ballantine, 1990.

Butler, Francelia, and Richard Rotert, eds. *Reflections on Literature for Children*. Hamden: Library Professional–Shoe String, 1984.

Eliot, T. S. *The Metaphysical Poets: Selected Essays by T. S. Eliot*. New York: Harcourt, 1964.

Fadiman, Clifton, ed. *World Treasury of Children's Literature*. Boston: Little, 1984.

Horner, Catherine Townsend. *The Aging Adult in Children's Books and Nonprint Media*. Metuchen: Scarecrow, 1982.

Leaf, Munro. *The Story of Ferdinand*. Illus. Robert Lawson. New York: Viking, 1936.

Opie, Iona, and Peter Opie, eds. *The Oxford Dictionary of Nursery Rhymes*. New York: Oxford UP, 1951.

Sale, Roger. *Fairy Tales and After: From Snow White to E. B. White*. Cambridge: Harvard UP, 1978.

Seuss, Dr. [Theodor Seuss Geisel]. *The Butter Battle Book*. New York: Random, 1984.

Singer, Isaac Bashevis. "On Writing for Children." Butler and Rotert 51–57.

Tolstoy, Leo. "Ivan the Fool." *Fables and Fairy Tales*. New York: NAL, 1962. 102–37.

Travers, P. L. "On Not Writing for Children." Butler and Rotert 58–65.

SPECIFIC APPROACHES

Myth, Folktale, and Children's Literature
William Moebius
Comparative Literature, University of Massachusetts, Amherst

Introduction and History Children's literature is presented as part of a narrative tradition. The course serves as an introduction to the study of narrative, with a major emphasis on practical criticism and interpretation of texts. Narrative, semiotic, and reader-response theories (Algirdas Greimas, Roland Barthes, Wolfgang Iser) provide fundamental critical methods and terminology; cognitive psychology, cultural anthropology, and folklore studies (Jean Piaget, Claude Lévi-Strauss, Max Luthi) contribute models and analogues.

The course, which was first taught in the fall of 1977, originated in other courses. Since 1967, the instructor had offered Literature and Myth and Artist Novel at the upper undergraduate level, and Theories of Myth and Theories of Literature at the graduate level.

Structure and Methods Myth, Folktale, and Children's Literature is divided into four basic units. In each, students are required to read a selection of folktales and a book for children; for the two critical essays, students must provide interpretation of three picture books and two juvenile novels not discussed in class.

In the first unit, which introduces the class to critical methods, students learn how to read a picture book and become acquainted with components of the reading process as formulated by Barthes and Iser.

The second unit focuses on the representation of ego in traditional tales and in children's stories. We examine the ways in which the main character is presented as becoming more or less "complete" through various actions (including the use of symbols) and the aid of other characters.

In the third unit we consider questions of classification and value in tales and stories. We ask how the world of story, in terms of setting, array of images, and various kinds of narrative discourse (narrative voice, song, animal language) shapes our sympathies and demands our concurrence with certain distinctions and values.

The final unit is devoted to the study of the relationship of character to world, first in the form of contracts (professional, marital, and so on) in traditional tales and then as cultural and political issues raised by contemporary juvenile literature.

Students are given a detailed syllabus at the beginning of the course. It includes a list not only of the required reading for each of the twenty-eight lectures (usually four to six traditional tales or myths per lecture) but also of seven or eight children's books related—in theme, structure, or character—to the required tales. In class, students are given a synopsis (an outline of the lecture) with a list of suggested secondary readings.

For the discussion section, the focus is usually on one tale or children's book. Students are divided into groups of three or four and asked to study a text in the light of a particular concern. In the final fifteen minutes, each group shares its major findings with the other members of the discussion section.

Each week, students are required to fill out an open-ended feedback sheet ("I learned, I liked, I wish"), which is returned the following week with instructor's comments.

Evaluation   Two critical essays (5–7 pages long), a midterm (55 minutes), and a final examination (2 hours) are used as evaluative instruments. A student's contribution to discussion is also taken into account.

For the first paper, the student must write on character development in three picture books, taking into account graphic as well as verbal elements. For the second paper, the student chooses two juvenile novels from a list of eight or ten and writes on the relationship of character to landscape or language, or on the novel's function as social criticism (gender or racial issues, the role of the misfit, for example). For both papers, critical insight, originality, and an ability to formulate a consistent argument are deemed most desirable qualities.

The midterm and final examinations consist of questions requiring short answers as well as essays. The student must draw on a knowledge of specific traditional tales and texts to demonstrate an understanding of form, structure, and pattern and a grasp of the complexity of message imparted in any specific tale.

Weaknesses   The course makes substantial demands on the student's time and intellectual energy. The less motivated student may be initially seduced by the course content but is then sometimes overwhelmed by the amount of reading material and the kind of probing demanded. Students often find it difficult to write on texts that have not been gone over in class. Anticipating the challenge this course represents, especially to lower-level undergraduates, I provide a synopsis of each lecture and require students to fill out feedback sheets (see Structure and Methods). I also meet personally with students.

Texts

Carroll, Lewis. *Alice in Wonderland*. New York: Norton, 1971.

Dahl, Roald. *Charlie and the Chocolate Factory*. New York. Dunlum, 1979.

Dégh, Linda. *Folktales of Hungary*. U of Chicago P, 1965.

Feldman, Susan, ed. *African Myths and Tales*. New York: Dell, 1963. (Out of print; excerpts provided by instructor.)

Grimm, Jacob, and Wilhelm K. Grimm. *German Folk Tales*. Trans. Francis P. Magoun, Jr., and Alexander H. Krappe. Carbondale: Southern Illinois UP, 1969.

Hergé. *Prisoners of the Sun*. Boston: Little, 1975.

Kingston, Maxine Hong. *The Woman Warrier: Memoirs of a Girlhood among Ghosts*. New York: Random, 1978.

Thompson, Stith, ed. *One Hundred Favorite Folktales*. Bloomington: Indiana UP, 1968.

The Tradition of Children's Literature

Hugh T. Keenan
English, Georgia State University

Introduction and History The Tradition of Children's Literature began as a special-topics course in the English department. The course aims to motivate students to rethink the influence of children's literature on their own lives; to become acquainted with the current writers, the books, controversies, and trends in the field; and to learn how to evaluate and select children's literature. The two academic goals were to make students aware of both the scope and history of children's literature on the one hand, and of the special resources available to them in their communities, on the other.

This course uses both university and community resources. Within the university, the interdisciplinary nature of the course is emphasized by having appropriate speakers from the departments of education, art, sociology, psychology, and speech and drama. From outside, writers and illustrators address the class. Also, a private school teacher who has developed a unique program for teaching literature to grades 6–9 talks to the class about exactly what children like in books. There are opportunities for field trips to selected city bookstores and research centers, such as the Center for Puppetry Arts, and the research collection on Joel Chandler Harris at the Woodruff Library of Emory University.

Structure and Methods A major premise is that children's literature is basic to the understanding of self and literary history. For many people, children's literature is the earliest and often the most important literary influence; it shapes the psychic and psychological hidden child figure in the adult. Therefore, it is a natural bridge between the feelings, aspirations, interests, and experiences of children and adults, the author acting as an intermediary to make the connections important for both adult and child.

We begin with a survey of the earlier periods of children's literature, relating the literature to social and cultural forces. In Old English and Middle English literature, for example, we survey what kinds of literature were designed by adults for children and why. The course considers, as well, adaptations of medieval stories for modern children, such as retellings of Malory, *Beowulf*, Chaucer's Nun's Priest's Tale, and a few romances.

From the historical survey, students become aware of the significance of (1) the separation of children's literature into a distinct field mainly since the seventeenth century, (2) fact or fantasy, didacticism or amusement as the alternative magnetic poles of children's literature, and (3) the persistence of certain stories and themes throughout this history.

The class is given mimeographed lists of nineteenth- and twentieth-century authors and titles, a bibliography of how-to books on writing and illustrating, and a bibliography of critical works and reference sources to encourage them to read widely in all of these areas.

The classwork consists of lectures (some by guests), analysis and discussion of readings in the text (see Butler, *Sharing*), and directed individual reading projects.

Students are required to write

1. a skip-rope rhyme, either original or modeled on one they remember;
2. a fable, either original or a reworking of a traditional one;
3. either a brief essay about a children's story and its personal influence or a review of a scholarly book on children's literature;
4. an open assignment—either an original piece of writing or a dramatization of a story, a game, a project, or a second review;
5. either an essay comparing views on a modern children's author such as J. R. R. Tolkien, C. S. Lewis, Maurice Sendak, or Judy Blume or a critique of the children's section in a bookstore;
6. an extended biocritical essay (5 pages) on a late-nineteenth- or twentieth-century children's author.

Evaluation The two examinations, half objective and half essay, count fifty percent of the course grade. The writing assignments and projects constitute the other fifty percent. With the permission of the students, the first two written assignments are duplicated and copies are passed out to the class.

Weaknesses The broad scope of the course and the extent of children's literature could lead to a meandering approach or a mishmash unless the course is tailored each time to the interests of the students. The open assignment has resulted in both the mundane and the creative, such as a stuffed doll of a very modern grandmother with mascara on the eyelashes and hot pants and, most recently, a model of the farm in *Charlotte's Web*.

Texts

Bader, Barbara. *American Picturebooks from Noah's Ark to the Beast Within*. New York: Macmillan, 1976.

Bettelheim, Bruno. *The Uses of Enchantment: The Meaning and Importance of Fairy Tales.* New York: Knopf, 1976.

Butler, Francelia. *Sharing Literature with Children: A Thematic Anthology.* New York: McKay, 1977.

Darton, J. Harvey. *Children's Books in England.* 3rd ed. Ed. and rev. by Brian Alderson. Cambridge: Cambridge UP, 1982.

Dorfman, Ariel. *The Empire's Old Clothes.* New York: Pantheon, 1983.

Egoff, Sheila A. *Thursday's Child: Trends and Patterns in Contemporary Children's Literature.* Chicago: ALA, 1981.

Meigs, Cornelia, et al. *A Critical History of Children's Literature.* Rev. ed. New York: Macmillan, 1969.

An Introduction to the History of Children's Literature

Ronald Reichertz

English, McGill University

Introduction and History   The course began in 1977–78 as a service course for the School of Education. From the outset children's books were discussed in terms of literary features and relationships to literature in general and within a literary-historical context.

The approach used in the course is historical. The course is organized chronologically to demonstrate shifts in the "official" children's literature (literature adults considered appropriate at any given time) that evolved, from the dominance of religious didacticism in the middle of the seventeenth century to the moral and informational didacticism that spanned the end of the eighteenth through the middle of the nineteenth century, to the dominance of imaginative literature at the end of the nineteenth century. Through an examination of a dynamic historical interplay, students come to understand that all the types of children's literature surveyed were present to some degree from the beginning. The official children's literature is compared with the coexisting subordinate types (e.g., "popular" and "adult" literature appropriated by children) during these periods to illustrate the energetic dialectic of the emergence of children's literature.

Several related issues are consistently developed throughout the chronological survey. Representative works are discussed in terms of literary values (genre, narrative technique, theme, characterization, style) and of the way they mirror or alter dominant attitudes toward childhood and literary assumptions. Such discussion necessitates attention to extraliterary issues, including the place of childhood in human development and education theories (John Locke, Jean-Jacques Rousseau, and their disciples).

Structure and Methods   The major chronological units in the course are (1) literature available to children before the self-conscious production of children's literature, (2) religious didacticism from the middle of the sixteenth century to the early eighteenth century, (3) rational moral didacticism from the 1750s into the early nineteenth century, (4) informational didacticism from the early nineteenth century to the 1850s, and (5) imaginative literature (the recovery and consolidation of nursery rhyme and folktale, nonsense, fantasy, domestic fiction, schoolboy fiction, etc.) from the 1840s onward. The focus of the discussions is on the dominant children's literature of the period, the literature considered most appropriate for children. At the same time, as noted, students analyze the relation between the dominant and the popular or suppressed literature, a literature that frequently appealed to children. Religious didacticism in the work of James Janeway, George Wither, Abraham Chear, John Bunyan, and Isaac Watts, for example, is discussed as a dominant type but also as a conscious reaction to available popular literature such as chapbook romances, street songs, and nursery rhymes. Statements of authorial intention by Wither, Watts, and others are used to establish connections between the appropriate literature and that literature (nursery rhymes) Watts called "idle, wanton and profane" (introd.). Wither and Watts both argued that their work was intended as an antidote to the "dangerous" work appropriated by children. A further complication of this period is introduced in books by teachers— for example, William Ronksley's *A Child's Week's Work* (1712)—that were informed by a playful spirit that considered nursery rhymes, riddles, and puns suitable children's reading.

The interplay between dominant types and the coexisting popular works is increasingly important beginning in the nineteenth century. The overwhelming rational, evangelical, and informational didacticism in books by Arnaud Berquin, Mary Wollstonecraft, Anna Barbauld, Hannah More, Maria Edgeworth, William Pinnock, and Peter Parley (Samuel Goodrich) alarmed the early Romantic writers, who developed a concept of childhood at least partially rooted in the popular, unofficial children's literature of folklore, folktale, and nursery rhymes. The importance of childhood and children's literature in Romantic literature helped establish imaginative literature as the predominant mode in the last four decades of the nineteenth century.

Slides are used to support particular ideas, to establish contexts for specific works, and to give an overview of the development of illustration and its functions in children's books. In the first course unit, for example, some fifty slides demonstrate Philippe Ariès's hypothesis concerning the concept of childhood before the production of children's literature. Slides that suggest a context for a specific work include a number of illustrations from eighteenth-century chapbooks and early-nineteenth-century children's books about the "world upside down." These slides of an overturned world are linked to Lewis Carroll's antipodean world of *Alice in Wonderland*. Representative images concerning childhood gathered from a number of nineteenth-century children's magazines are also presented through slides.

Evaluation   The course evaluation is based on a take-home midterm (25%), a ten-page paper (50%), and a final exam (25%). Representative paper topics include "Compare and contrast the theme of the child alone in Watts's *Divine and Moral Songs, Little Goody Two-Shoes, Songs of Innocence, The King of the Golden River,* and *Alice in Wonderland*" and "Using Watts's introduction to *Divine and Moral Songs* as a model, write an introduction to *Songs of Innocence* or *The Princess and Curdie* or *Huckleberry Finn.*

Weaknesses   This kind of historical survey is a broad, encompassing method for studying over two hundred years of children's literature, but it has the limitation of producing a suspect clarity that greater focus on a particular period would disallow.

Texts

Barbauld, Anna. *Hymns in Prose for Children.* London, Baldwin, 1791.

Berquin, Arnaud. *The Looking Glass for the Mind: or, Intellectual Mirror.* . . . London, 1792.

Blake, William. *Songs of Innocence.* New York: Dover, 1971.

Bunyan, John. *A Book for Boys and Girls: Or, Country Rhymes for Children. Being a Facsimile of the Unique First edition. Published in 1686. Deposited in the British Museum.* London, 1899.

Carroll, Lewis. *Alice in Wonderland.* London: Mayflower, 1969.

Chear, Abraham. *A Looking Glass for Children.* Cornhill, 1673.

Clifford, Lucy. "Wooden Tony." *The Anyhow Stories.* London, 1899.

Edgeworth, Maria. "The Purple Jar." *Early Lessons.* London, 1859.

Goodrich, Samuel [Peter Parley]. *Peter Parley's Tales about America.* New York: Dover, 1974. Facsimile of the 1828 edition.

Hughes, Thomas. *Tom Brown's School Days.* Harmondsworth, Eng.: Penguin, 1979.

Janeway, James. *A Token for Children, Being an Exact Account of the Conversion, Holy and Exemplary Lives and Joyful Deaths of Several Young Children.* London, 1821.

Lang, Andrew. *The Blue Fairy Book.* New York: McGraw, 1966.

Lear, Edward. *The Complete Nonsense of Edward Lear.* New York: Dover, 1980.

MacDonald, George. *The Princess and Curdie.* Harmondsworth, Eng.: Penguin, 1980.

More, Hannah. *Cheap Repository Tracts.* London, 1790s–1820s.

Newbery, John. *Little Goody Two-Shoes.* London, 1765.

Pinnock, William. "Catechisms." London, 1820s–1840s.

Ritson, James. *Gammer Gurton's Garland.* London, 1812.

Roscoe, William. *The Butterfly's Ball and the Grasshopper's Feast.* London, 1807.

Ronksley, William. *A Child's Week's Work.* London, 1712.

Ruskin, John. *The King of the Golden River.* Harmondsworth, Eng.: Penguin, 1979.

Sherwood, Mary Martha [Mary Butts]. *The History of the Fairchild Family.* London, n.d.

Sinclair, Catherine. *Holiday House: A Series of Tales.* Edinburgh, 1851.

Taylor, Ann. *Signor Topsy Turvy's Wonderful Magic Lantern: Or, The World Turned Upside Down.* London, 1810.

Trimmer, Sarah. *The Guardian of Education.* London, 1802–06.

Twain, Mark. *Huckleberry Finn.* New York: Norton, 1962.

Watts, Isaac. *Divine and Moral Songs.* London, 1858. N. pag.

Wither, George. "A Rocking Hymn." *Haleluiah: Or, England's Second Remembrancer.* London, 1641.

Wollstonecraft, Mary. *Original Stories from Real Life, with Conversations Calculated to Regulate the Affections, and Form the Mind to Truth and Goodness.* London, 1791.

Children's Literature: Great Books

Mary Elizabeth Meek
English, University of Pittsburgh

Introduction and History The children's literature course at the University of Pittsburgh follows the traditional "great books" format, using individual texts of classic and contemporary children's books in paperback editions that include the illustrations usually associated with the texts. Originally offered for two credits, it became a three-credit course in 1971, to make it acceptable for credit toward the English major. Since 1981, Children's Literature has been one of the three core courses in the interdisciplinary children's literature program designed by the English department and the School of Library and Information Science. A certificate is given to those completing the required eighteen hours, including courses in other areas, such as the social or behavioral sciences.

Structure and Methods The course is divided into six units of varying length: Fairy Tales, Greek Myths and Legends, Picture Books and Illustrators, Fantasy, Fiction, and Poetry. Each unit feeds into the next, with the concepts of plot, characterization, theme, image, symbol, and style introduced in the fairy tale unit being further developed in the next four to explore different patterns and techniques, and with the poetry linked to previous discussions of imagery and language.

The basic methodology in the course is to ask questions about specific scenes or passages that will provoke discussions of the texts. After an introductory lecture on the history of children's literature, we discuss fairy tales, concentrating on the Grimms, Perrault, and Andersen, and ending with Oscar Wilde's "Selfish Giant" and James Thurber's "Many Moons." Students become familiar with the formulaic plotting of the traditional tales; the stereotyped characterization; and the journey, quest, talking beast, and prohibition motifs. We talk about poetic justice and the fact that marrying the prince or princess of one's dreams and living happily ever after simply means finding one's role as a mature member of society. Next we discuss how these elements form the substructure of the literary fairy tales like Andersen's, and how this is modified by the style of individual authors.

In the unit on Greek myths and legends, we explore the similarity of these stories to the myths produced by all cultures. We compare the Greek stories of the "creation of man," the origin of evil, and the Flood with those in Genesis, and then examine the nature myths. Finally we go on to the attributes and domains of the Olympian gods (charts are useful here), emphasizing those who appear in the legends, so that we can discuss, for example, what the friendship of Athena to Odysseus means in terms of his characterization.

In the unit on picture books and illustrators, the students are shown slides and provided with a handout that lists the illustrators and the books from which the slides were made and usually several other books by the same illustrator. Space is left so that students can write down their own impressions either of the slide or the commentary on it—or both.

The slide lectures connect with the fantasy unit, since with the *Alice* books, *The Wizard of Oz*, *The Wind in the Willows*, and *Charlotte's Web* we have the illustrations by Tenniel, Denslow, Shepard, and Williams that have become inseparable from the texts. We can also consider the movie versions of these stories. The main idea to elicit in the fantasy unit is the way the symbolic function of the journey-as-test plot had been psychologized and adapted to what might be called novels of character development or coming of age. Alice, Fern, Wilbur, Mole, and Toad all have adventures in unfamiliar territory and mature. Dorothy is the exception—while she too is in a strange land, she always knows who she is and where she wants to go. Finally, we talk about the varying ways the basic fairy tale plot is arranged in these works: the loosely episodic *Alice in Wonderland* and *Wizard of Oz*, the programmatic *Looking Glass*, the parallel stories of Fern and Wilbur, and the interwoven stories of Mole and Toad.

The examination of various narrative techniques is the major topic of the fiction unit. *Treasure Island* and Mildred Taylor's *Roll of Thunder, Hear My Cry* show how the first-person narrator can be used to bring the historical past to life but also reveal the limitations of the device, particularly when the narrator is a child. In *Tom Sawyer*, the point of view is that of the omniscient author; but Twain's narrator expresses nostalgia for the sort of childhood we all wish we had had, while Ellen Raskin's *Westing Game*'s apparently omniscient author is playing a game with the reader.

The notion of games being played with the reader also applies, however, to *Treasure Island* and *Tom Sawyer*. We observe how improbable it is that Jim sails the *Hispaniola* and yet realize how carefully Stevenson prepares us for the event. His technique is compared with the way Twain plays the same trick on his readers that Tom does on the congregation at his funeral and with Raskin's giving the readers all the clues Turtle has, while diverting them from seeing the significance of the clues.

The idea of the author's leaving clues for the reader also comes up in the poetry unit. Ariel's song "Where the bee sucks" and Emily Dickinson's "I like to see it lap the miles" can be approached as riddles—what kind of creature is being described? But basically the discussion of the poems centers on the questions "What do you see?" "What do you hear?" and "What do you think or feel?" Often we consider what would appeal to a child and what more or less universal childhood experience is being evoked. With a few exceptions, most of the poems we read are by contemporary poets—Eve Merriam, David McCord, Nikki Giovanni.

Evaluation Students are evaluated largely on the basis of their written work. There are three midterm essay-type tests, on the fairy tales, myths, and fantasy, and a two-page paper on a book by one of the illustrators shown in the slide lectures. These together count for three-fifths of the grade, while the two-hour final examination counts for two-fifths. Half of this exam is on the fiction and poetry, and half consists of essays on topics that run through several units in the course, such as the way violence is treated in the fairy tales, *Tom Sawyer,* and *Roll of Thunder.*

Weaknesses The main weakness to this approach is that it does not suggest the scope of children's literature—it does not deal with myths and legends from cultures other than the Greek or with the whole range of nonfiction. Furthermore, depending on what is available in paperback for texts means relying on the whims of publishers, and books often go out of print without notice.

Texts

Baum, L. Frank. *The Wonderful Wizard of Oz.* New York: Dover, 1960.

Carroll, Lewis. Alice's Adventures in Wonderland *and* Through the Looking Glass. Harmondsworth, Eng.: Penguin, 1962.

D'Aulaire, Ingri, and Edgar Parin. *Book of Greek Myths.* Garden City: Doubleday-Zephyr, 1980.

David, Alfred, and Mary Elizabeth Meek, comps. *The Twelve Dancing Princesses and Other Fairy Tales.* Bloomington: Indiana UP, 1974.

Grahame, Kenneth. *The Wind in the Willows.* New York: Macmillan-Aladdin, 1989.

Larrick, Nancy, ed. *Piping down the Valleys Wild.* New York: Dell, 1982.

Children's Fantasy Literature and the Adult Reader

Frank P. Riga
English, Canisius College

Introduction and History   The main purpose of the course, which is premised on adult critical response to literature, is to give upper-level college students a mature experience in the study of fantasy literature for children. In this course students read children's books critically and analytically, as they would the books in any course in literature.

The course began as a result of an NEH seminar and an NEH institute in children's literature (one at Princeton University, 1984, and the other at the University of Connecticut, 1985). Since its first presentation, the course has been a popular English major elective.

Structure and Methods   The course is divided into four units, one dealing with a central theme and three with important genres. The thematic unit treats the concept of transformation. In the units on genre, students focus on the fairy tale, the romance, and the beast fable.

The unit on transformation introduces students to the principal concerns of the course. By reading traditional fairy tales, Carroll's Alice books, and other works, students explore the various meanings of physical transformation, relating them to questions of maturation, moral or social reformation, and the structure of the family and society. These themes and ideas are taken up in later units.

In the unit on the fairy tales, special emphasis is placed on the question of the mixed audience. The reading starts with several tales by the brothers Grimm and includes John Ruskin's *King of the Golden River*, W. M. Thackeray's *Rose and the Ring*, and Carlo Collodi's *Pinocchio*.

Students begin their study of the romance with *Sir Gawain and the Green Knight* and *Sir Orfeo*. The analysis of these medieval works attempts to segregate the characteristics of the genre. George MacDonald's *Princess and the Goblin* is used to demonstrate the problem of defining the genre. Purer examples of children's romance are then introduced. J. R. R. Tolkien's *Hobbit* provides a bridge not only to his own Ring trilogy but to a spate of current adult and children's fantasy books. The unit ends with a concentration on C. S. Lewis's *Chronicles of Narnia*.

The last unit in the course investigates the beast fable, as exemplified by Rudyard Kipling. Students read *The Jungle Books* and selections from *The Panchatantra*, Aesop's *Fables*, and *Uncle Remus*. Kipling's books embrace some of the traditional uses of the form and anticipate recent examples such as George Orwell's *Animal Farm* and Richard Adams's *Watership Down*.

The principal methods of instruction are lecture and discussion, with an emphasis on analysis of texts. Lectures are brief and specific, providing information on history, biography, and major critical methods. Students research some of this material to present to the class. Several films are shown and discussed, and guest speakers are asked to share their knowledge on specified subjects. But the most important classwork occurs in the analytic discussion of the texts. Here, themes and structural properties of individual texts are isolated and then compared with similar points in other texts, whether for children or for adults. Various modes of interpretation are proposed, and questions of genre are considered in detail.

Evaluation   The evaluation of students includes class participation, a midterm and final essay examination, and several brief papers (800–1,000 words each). Students are expected to contribute to class discussion, and each is assigned a specific subject for presentation. These subjects involve the analysis of some theme or formal characteristic of the text for the day. Examinations test students on the common reading list and on the material covered in class. Papers deal with the connection of children's books to the general literary tradition.

Weaknesses   The decision to build the course on children's fantasy fiction omits, by definition, other important genres, such as realistic fiction, poetry, and information books. Goals accomplished through the general survey cannot be attempted here.

Texts

Bettelheim, Bruno. *The Uses of Enchantment: The Meaning and Importance of Fairy Tales*. New York: Knopf, 1976.

Kroeber, Karl. *Romantic Fantasy and Science Fiction*. New Haven: Yale UP, 1988.

Lewis, C. S. *On Stories and other Essays on Literature*. Ed. Walter Hooper. New York: Harcourt, 1982.

MacDonald, George. *A Dish of Orts: Chiefly Papers on the Imagination*. London: Dalton, 1908.

Sale, Roger. *Fairy Tales and After: From Snow White to E. B. White*. Cambridge: Harvard UP, 1978.

Children's Literature: Picture Books, Poetry, and Fiction

Marilyn Apseloff
English, Kent State University

Introduction and History   The approach to the course is literary, with emphasis on art appreciation through picture books as well as the study of books for older readers. The goal of the course is not to teach students how to read a picture book to children but to get them to understand the differences between good and bad books, to learn to appreciate the quality of writing and illustrating.

Children's Literature: Picture Books, Poetry, and Fiction began in 1913 as a course in storytelling. It has been related to courses in reading and effective speaking and in juvenile literature.

Structure and Methods   The course is divided into five major genres: Picture Books and Illustrations; Folktales, Fables and Myth, and Fantasy; Poetry; Realistic Fiction; and Historical Fiction. For the picture books there are examples of surrealism (Anthony Browne), collage (Ezra Jack Keats), plasticine relief (Barbara Reid), inversion (Ann Jonas), photographs (Tana Hoban), and representatives of other art forms to show students the range available. Elements intended for adults (such as the numerous puns in Graham Oakley's *Church Mice* books) are noted as well. Students are told to read to children whenever possible and to keep in mind the child's interests and abilities when choosing books initially for them. Students should develop an awareness of the variety of picture books in their subjects, composition, and intended audience and should feel more secure about choosing good books for children and encouraging children to read.

At the beginning, students are given multiple copies of picture books such as Maurice Sendak's *Where the Wild Things Are*, William Steig's *Sylvester and the Magic Pebble*, Ezra Jack Keats's *Snowy Day* and *Whistle for Willie*. Such books lead to a discussion of characterization, themes, plot structures, and other criteria, and also of reader identification, which adults often overlook, and of problems that arise when adults read into children's books something that is not intended (Garth Williams's *Rabbits' Wedding* is an example). Next, students observe the correlation between text and illustration, noting how, in good books, each reinforces the other, whereas in poor editions the illustrations add nothing to characterization, mood, or an appreciation for detail or line and the use of color and shading for effect. In class the good and the less successful books are frequently contrasted. Classics are compared with their grocery store counterparts for both language and illustrations. Students hear how the rich vocabulary of Beatrix Potter has been reduced to innocuous bare essentials in the inferior version and how Disney has changed characterizations and tone in his assorted versions of *Pinocchio*.

The section on poetry requires a special approach for students, since many of them dislike poetry and do not know how to read it. They learn to assess whether an illustrated version of a poem is a disservice to a child because the illustrations may take the reader away from the poem rather than into it (Frost's *Stopping by Woods on a Snowy Evening* illustrated by Susan Jeffers is one example). Whether the books in the course are for young or older readers, students learn that fresh rather than trite language is necessary, that there should be no talking down to the child, and that the same criteria for judging adult books is applied to those for children, but with a slightly different emphasis.

Evaluation The grade evaluation is in percentages: class participation, quizzes, and outside reading assignments, thirty percent; midterm, thirty-three percent; final examination, thirty-seven percent. Examinations fall into two parts: the first requires an understanding of the text and classroom information; the second consists of essays on the outside readings. In addition, students who bring books when assignments are due and contribute to class discussion receive credit for class participation on a regular basis.

Weaknesses Because of the amount of material that has to be covered in the class, the pace has to be quite rapid. That does not give students with little background in art or literature the opportunity for more extended discussions. Nonfiction can only be touched on because of the lack of time, a deficiency considering the array of good books published in that genre. Lack of an ideal textbook is another problem.

Texts

Grahame, Kenneth. *The Wind in the Willows*. New York: Bantam, 1982.
Sutherland, Zena, and Mary Hill Arbuthnot. *Children and Books*. 6th ed. Glenview: Scott, 1981.

Children's Literature:
An International Perspective
Meena Khorana
Languages, Literature, and Journalism, Coppin State College

Introduction and History This course emphasizes cultural diversity through a study of international children's literature. It enables students to identify with a variety of international characters and settings. This course was originally developed in 1984 for the Internationalizing Teacher Education Project (funded by the Fund for the Improvement of Post-Secondary Education and by Indiana University, Bloomington) to incorporate an international component into selected courses required by elementary education majors. The course has recently been revised for the international studies program being developed at Coppin State College.

Structure and Methods Three genres or units were selected as appropriate vehicles for adding an international dimension to the course: International Biographies, International Fiction, and Folktales. The structure is flexible enough to accommodate any special emphasis that one wants; either all three units may be taught in one semester, or only one may be selected. Each unit is designed to cover four to five weeks of the semester.

International Fiction, which will be discussed in this course description, is approached from two differing standpoints—literary and thematic. In the first part of the unit, students are made aware of the need for establishing special criteria for evaluating fiction with an international setting. Since books by both Western and international authors are examined, we should be sensitive to the differences in perspective and treatment. In the first four class meetings, guidelines for detecting bias and stereotyping in plot, characterization, language, and illustrations are presented through a detailed analysis of three books.

For example, the class considers the question of plot. Though the story should be original and interesting, as in all good fiction, the primary concern is that the book should avoid the common stereotypes associated with a particular nationality, such as political turmoil in Africa, famine and tradition-bound villagers in India, and poverty and corruption in Mexico. A majority of the books written by Western authors dwell on the lack of technological progress and material advancement in Third World countries. *The Road to Agra,* by Aimee Sommerfelt, is discussed as a negative example. Betty Dinneen's *Lion Yellow,* set in newly independent Kenya, in contrast, avoids the implication that developing nations are incapable of solving their own problems.

Students are given similar evaluative guidelines to identify stereotyping in characterization, illustrations, and language. Furthermore, class discussion is generated through an examination of questions: Who takes the leadership role in the book? Do native characters make decisions affecting themselves and their community? Are women always depicted as submissive and downtrodden? Are pejorative and condescending terms used to describe the country and people?

The students are then ready, in the second part of the unit, to discuss whether the cultural values and perspectives of a country are portrayed in an authentic manner. They conduct an in-depth, thematic study of six books and make brief individual presentations to the class. Two weeks before the presentations, the class is divided into six groups and provided with a list of books that represent a variety of cultures and approaches and deal with both modern and traditional issues. From this list each group selects a book it would like to examine.

One student from each group gives a brief plot summary, while the others explore topics that are appropriate to their book. Some of the suggested themes deal with the passage from childhood to adulthood, the position of women and the elderly, the relationship between parents and children, cultural attitudes toward death, and conflict between traditional and Western values. In examining the culture, students determine from whose perspective the customs, holidays and festivals, and religious practices are being presented. Stereotyping and bias occur when only the *exotic* and *quaint* features are highlighted and the complex social, historical, and political issues are either oversimplified or distorted. The ethnic background should not only be treated respectfully but should be depicted as being vital to the characters.

The final class period of this unit is a general discussion and review of International Fiction. Students discuss some of the universal truths about human beings that emerge from this study. They also compare the cultural and environmental influences on the characters with those that might be encountered in works set in the United States.

Evaluation The final grade is based on class participation, short quizzes, a five-to-ten-minute presentation to the class as mentioned above, one examination, and a research paper. For the paper, students are required to read one biography, a collection of folktales, one historical novel, one fictional piece, and one informational book related to any one country and, if possible, to interview someone from that culture.

After reviewing the required material, students write a six-to-eight-page paper focusing on one aspect of life in that country (family life, schooling, festivals, customs, role of children, etc.). They further examine the significance of their topic to individuals, to their society, and to the world community. A one-page summary and bibliography by each student is distributed to the class.

Weaknesses   One problem of this approach is that books written or translated in English by international authors are not readily accessible for classroom use. The problem, however, can be overcome by either purchasing multiple copies of books for the library or by securing them through interlibrary loan and placing them on reserve.

Texts

Bosse, Malcolm J. *Ganesh*. New York: Crowell, 1981.

Carlson, Dale. *The Mountain of Truth*. New York: Atheneum, 1972.

Dinneen, Betty. *Lion Yellow*. New York: Walck, 1975.

Dutta, Arup Kumar. *The Lure of Zangrila*. New Delhi: Children's Book Trust, 1986.

Ekwensi, Cyprian. *The Passport of Mallam Ilia*. London: Cambridge UP, 1960.

Graham, Loren. *I, Momolu*. New York: Crowell, 1966.

Lofting, Hugh. *Doctor Doolittle's Post Office*. New York: Lippincott, 1923.

Seed, Jenny. *The Broken Spear*. London: Hamilton, 1972.

Smith, Rukshana. *Sumitra's Story*. New York: Coward, 1982.

Sommerfelt, Aimee. *The Road to Agra*. New York: Criterion, 1961.

Taylor, Theodore. *Maldonda Miracle*. New York: Doubleday, 1962.

Van Stockum, Hilda. *Mogo's Flute*. New York: Viking, 1966.

Wayne, Kyra Petrovskaya. *The Awakening*. New York: Grosset, 1972.

Wojciechowska, Maria. *Shadow of a Bull*. New York: Atheneum, 1964.

Children's Literature as Social History
Lois Rauch Gibson
Women's Studies Program, Portland State University

Introduction and History Children's Literature as Social History is an upper-division course designed especially for summer session at Portland State University but adaptable for regular terms as well.[1] In this course, participants read some classics, such as *Alice in Wonderland*, *Peter Pan*, and *Little Women*, and some lesser-known British and American books and consider each work's historical context. Students develop their skills at recognizing explicit and implied attitudes toward such areas of experience as sex roles, race, class, religion, and scientific discovery. Students also increase their awareness of the differences in social values from era to era.

This course was originally proposed in 1976, through women's studies, as a supplement to, rather than a replacement for, the more traditional children's literature courses. It has also been listed for credit by the English and education departments and has been offered six times since June 1976. Concerned that most children's literature courses focus mainly or exclusively on literary merit, educational value, and/or the use of books in the classroom, the women's studies program wished to draw attention to the consciously or unconsciously didactic nature of many children's books. By offering the course in the summer, we hoped to reach many teachers and librarians. We particularly hoped to raise the awareness of parents and educators to stereotyping or proselytizing in the books they share with children.

Structure and Methods To enable students to examine social values, we spend the first class period defining and discussing this expression, and we inspect several picture books to discover how both words and illustrations reveal values. Then we review a list of questions to ask when analyzing the social values in children's books. Sample questions include Who are the main characters? What social class, race, religion, sex do the main characters belong to? Which characters are most respected? For what reasons? Are male and female characters respected for the same things? How are old people portrayed?

The first class is also a good time for the instructor to summarize current research. (The Lollipop Power annual bibliography is a good source.)

In some books, social values are clearly and explicitly spelled out. James Janeway, for example, in *A Token for Children* (1671), catalogs the virtues of those good little children who go to heaven, so his little readers may follow suit. Two centuries later, Louisa May Alcott's *Little Women* is equally explicit, arguing for American industriousness: the March girls experiment for a disastrous week with "all play and no work" and conclude that "lounging and larking doesn't pay." Often, however, values and preferred codes of behavior are implied; for example, the beloved Pooh books present the 1920s upper-class British patriarchal values of their author's world, including a kind of xenophobia that leads the animals to fear and resent outsiders, such as Kanga and Roo, when they first appear. The aim of the course is to examine such values as they appear in children's books.

The class examines books from several historical periods, moving chronologically from the 1670s to the present. For each historical period, students are asked to read one or two books assigned to the entire class and at least one additional book of their choice from the same period. For the Victorian period, for example, the whole class reads *Alice in Wonderland* (1865); individual students may select from among books by Julianna Ewing (1860s), Charlotte Yonge (1860s), Thomas Hughes (*Tom Brown's School Days*, 1857), Charles Kingsley (*The Water Babies*, 1863), George MacDonald (*At the Back of the North Wind*, 1871), Dinah Maria Mulock (Craik) (*Adventures of a Brownie*, 1872), and others. Reading these additional books helps students see patterns and conflicting values within a period. Students also read appropriate sections in histories or social histories of children's literature to provide historical context, and they hear "social history reports" on major themes, trends, and events of each era.

Reactions to individual readings are shared either in small groups or with the entire class. The emphasis is on discussion and sharing.

Evaluation   Students keep a written record of their reactions to all the books they read. These comments include bibliographical information and the student's own reactions to the social values expressed in the work.

Students also write a three-to-four-page analytical paper. They may analyze one children's book from a historical period; compare and contrast two books from the same period or two books from different periods; or reread a childhood favorite and analyze their reactions before and after rereading it. Graduate students must in addition prepare an oral and written social history report. Graduate students in the English department must write a research paper.

All students must complete a take-home final exam. Typical final-exam options include (1) establishing criteria for nonsexist literature and providing examples of books that meet these criteria in at least two historical periods or (2) writing a children's book and composing an introduction for adult readers that analyzes the explicit or implied values in the book.

All required work (record of reactions, paper, class participation, final exam, oral and written social history report, and second paper for graduate credit) carries equal weight in determining the final grade.

Weaknesses Because students are learning a new way to read books, there is sometimes too little time for evaluation of literary merit. Although experts on Indian, Chinese, Japanese, or German books occasionally give lectures, the course is primarily limited to British and American works. It might benefit by being expanded to include comparisons with social values in books from other cultures.

Texts

The major texts are children's books from each historical period. The main reference sources include the following texts, which are selected from a much longer bibliography of materials useful for helping students recognize and understand social values:

Bibliography of Materials on Sexism and Sex Role Stereotyping in Children's Books. Comp. Kathleen Gallagher and Alice Peery. Chapel Hill: Lollipop Power (Revised annually.)

Human (and Anti-human) Values in Children's Books. New York: Council on Interracial Books for Children, 1976.

MacCann, Donnarae, and Gloria Woodard. *Cultural Conformity in Books for Children.* Metuchen: Scarecrow, 1977.

Meigs, Cornelia, et al. *A Critical History of Children's Literatures: A Survey of Children's Books in English.* Rev. ed. New York: Macmillan, 1969.

Rudman, Masha. *Children's Literature: An Issues Approach.* 2nd ed. New York: Longman, 1984.

Note

[1] The author currently teaches at Coker College, South Carolina.

Children's Literature and Composition

Alida Allison, Helen Borgens, and Helen Neumeyer
English and Comparative Literature, San Diego State University

Introduction and History Children's Literature, English 501, was first offered at San Diego State in the late 1970s as a three-unit upper-division literature course intended primarily for English majors. Diverse students enrolled, however, and, as the courses grew quickly, so did a concern for writing standards. Thus in the early 1980s the English department, in consultation with the School of Teacher Education, began offering a second six-unit children's literature course combining literature and composition. This class, although open to all students, is designed primarily for those planning to become elementary teachers.

English 306A is a survey course that introduces students to literary terminology, genres, and analysis through children's literature; English 306W is an advanced composition course in which students write essays based on the material they are reading in 306A. Though graded independently and usually taught by different instructors, both three-unit courses must be taken concurrently. To fulfill the university's upper-division writing competency requirement, students must pass 306W with a grade of C or better. The composition sections are limited to enrollments of twenty-five; thus the 306A lecture sections increase in increments of twenty-five. Most 306A sections enroll fifty students, but some sections are as large as two hundred and have eight separate composition sections attached to them. The tandem courses have proved popular; some semesters as many as four hundred students have enrolled.

A graduate seminar in children's literature is taught annually on varying topics—The Illustrated Book, for example. The department's special-topics courses are often devoted to children's literature, covering such subjects as the feral child or Continental children's literature. The course Literature for Adolescents has been approved as well. Faculty members and administrators support further program expansion, once additional funding and staff become available, and university demographics are favorable for such a development.

Structure and Methods San Diego State University's Department of English and Comparative Literature has four full-time specialists in children's literature, and the literature section of the course varies according to the professor. Over several semesters, contents have included animal tales, creation myths, picture books, folk and fairy tales, classic novels, multicultural literature, nursery rhymes, contemporary analytical approaches, fables, and young-adult books. In the composition sections, students read, discuss, and write critical essays on diverse themes, from character analysis and close reading of texts to the application of literary theory. The instructors' aims are to challenge and extend the students' abilities to appreciate and evaluate literature for children and to improve their competencies in writing clearly and substantively. Within the literature and composition framework, the coordination of educational goals and the concentration of student energy has worked well.

Evaluation   Methods of grading vary, but professors in the literature section predominantly test through essay examinations. A typical test includes identification (25%), short answer and paragraph (25%), and essay (50%). Some professors also require short bi-weekly responses to assigned study questions. In the composition components, five or six essays are required, totaling approximately 7,500 words over the semester. Other assignments include prewriting, paragraphs, outlines, rough drafts, revisions, grammar exercises (if necessary), student workshops, individual conferences with the instructor, and additional reading for class discussion.

Children's Literature Certificate   Students who take children's literature courses in the English and Comparative Literature Department, the Drama Department, or the School of Teacher Education may also apply for admission to the children's literature certificate program. This program provides a coherent, multidisciplinary structure for combining upper-division and/or graduate coursework. It stipulates that, in addition to completing the courses required for the bachelor's or master's degree and to earning a minimum grade point average of 3.0, the student has completed eighteen units of advised, articulated, and specialized study in the field of children's literature. The certificate may be earned with an emphasis either in education or in English and comparative literature.

Texts

This sample reading list for English 306A was compiled by Alida Allison and Helen Neumeyer.

Babitt, Natalie. *Tuck Everlasting*. New York: Ballantine, n.d.

Baum, Frank L. *Ozma of Oz.* New York: Ballantine, 1979.

Coerr, Eleanor. *Sadako and the Thousand Paper Cranes.* New York: Dell, 1977.

David, Alfred, and Elizabeth Meeks. *Twelve Dancing Princesses.* Bloomington: U of Indiana P, 1974.

Emecheta, Buchi. *The Moonlight Bride.* New York: Braziller, 1983.

Hoban, Russell. *The Mouse and His Child.* New York: Harper, 1974.

Kennedy, X. J. *Knock at a Star.* New York: Little, 1982.

Lukens, Rebecca. *A Critical Handbook of Children's Literature.* 4th ed. New York: Scott, 1990.

MacLachlan, Patricia. *Sarah, Plain and Tall.* New York: Harper, 1985.

O'Dell, Scott. *Island of the Blue Dolphins.* Boston: Houghton, 1978.

Paterson, Katherine. *The Great Gilly Hopkins.* New York: Macmillan, 1987.

Petersham, Maud, and Miska Petersham. *The Rooster Crows.* New York: Macmillan, 1987.

Potter, Beatrix. *The Tale of Peter Rabbit.* New York: Dover, 1972.

Sendak, Maurice. *Where the Wild Things Are.* New York: Harper, 1984.

Singer, Isaac Bashevis. *Zlateh the Goat.* New York: Harper, 1984.

Stevenson, Robert Louis. *Treasure Island.* New York: Penguin, 1984.

White, E. B. *Charlotte's Web.* New York: Harper, 1986.

Literature for Young Children

Edythe McGovern
English, Los Angeles Valley College

Introduction and History In 1974, students in the regular three-unit children's literature class suggested the need for a course that would concentrate on books for younger children (ages 2–8) exclusively, rather than cover material suitable for students through high school age. The issues involved are not too different from those discussed in the more advanced course. Sexism, for example, is a topic of discussion, since the "pink for girls, blue for boys" syndrome can be found in books written for very young children. There is simply an emphasis on materials, such as well-illustrated picture books, and on the techniques of presenting "good" literature to children who are too young to read independently.

Structure and Methods The course lasts ten weeks, with two one-hour sessions for the morning section and one two-hour session (weekly) for the late afternoon sections. Throughout all units there is demonstration of read-aloud techniques, which students practice as part of evaluation.

Unit 1. The first unit introduces students to the subject of literature for children. Topics include a brief overview of the history of the genre, the benefits of reading to young children, and a discussion of literary elements to be found in all fiction.

Unit 2. The focus here is on differences between fiction and information books, with demonstrations of the way these two forms may merge in books for young children (for example, *The Very Hungry Caterpillar* by Eric Carle). Students explore the wide variations in the use of informational books, such as alphabet books, concept books, and so on, depending on the age groups of the children within the two-to-eight-year-old range.

Unit 3. Students learn to evaluate "good" and "bad" illustration and language level in children's literature. A slide presentation, showing various illustrations of the same books (the Trina Schart Hyman and the Disney versions of *Snow White*, for example), points up the differences in quality very clearly.

Unit 4. This unit examines racism in children's books—overt and implied—and sexism even in books that are otherwise "good." For instance, in William Steig's *Sylvester and the Magic Pebble*, Sylvester's mother is pictured as doing housework while his father sits and reads. Stress is placed on books that eliminate sexism as it works against males. As a counter balance to stereotypical behavior, such books as Charlotte Zolotow's *William's Doll*, Bruce Mack's *Jesse's Dream Skirt*, Nancy Hazen's *Grownups Cry Too*, and Rachel Isadora's *Max* are discussed. All these titles and many others show boys behaving in nonstereotypical ways without compromising their "masculinity."

Unit 5. Here we consider special books for use with children with disabilities, bilingual children, and children who have particular problems—living in a one-parent family, accepting the death of a parent, or dealing with sibling rivalry.

Unit 6. Since humor is an appealing element in children's books, students learn to recognize the various ages at which children appreciate particular types of humor, either in illustration or text (see *The Random House Book of Humor*, comp. Pollack).

Unit 7. The use of puppets or story boards as aids in reading aloud to small children is the focus of this unit. We discuss ways in which the older children in the groups, those who are already in school, can participate in the literature by making pieces for the story board or simple puppets.

Unit 8. The last unit involves a visit from a children's librarian.

Each unit begins with a slide presentation, which is effective because it saves time in the short course. Books are also brought to class by the instructor at each meeting. In unit 8 the librarian introduces many of the newly published books and discusses their use. Students are encouraged to select books for their "read-alouds," one for practice and two additional for grades.

Evaluation   Evaluation sheets are given to all students. Peer evaluation is included as well as the instructor's critique. Students are exposed to approximately one hundred titles during the course. Evaluation includes the read-alouds described above, for about twenty-five percent of the student's grade; two special projects that vary according to the student's interests, for fifty percent of the grade; and a final essay examination, for the remaining twenty-five percent.

Weaknesses   The major weakness in the course is its short length. Students may elect to take the three-unit course in children's literature as well.

Texts

McGovern, Edythe. *They're Never Too Young for Books.* Los Angeles: Mar Vista, 1980.

Pollack, Pamela, comp. *The Random House Book of Humor for Children.* Illus. Paul O. Zelinsky. New York: Random, 1988.

Children's Literature: Children as Audience

Celia Catlett Anderson
English, Eastern Connecticut State University

Introduction and History The course focuses on children as audience and the lively interaction between young people and literature. Geared to those involved with children, the course deals with the theory of good storytelling, reading aloud, and simple puppetry, and gives students a chance to perform in class and to devise a project for sharing literature with children. Storytellers and puppeteers visit the class, and children may attend these performances.

The course grew out of an interest in storytelling and puppetry and a summer (1985) NEH Institute on Children's Literature.

Structure and Methods The course alternates classes devoted to theory and classes devoted to performance. We begin with puppets. The second unit is focused on storytelling techniques, the third on methods of reading aloud effectively. The students choose two out of these three for their performances before the class. During the final sessions of the semester, the students turn in a written record and summary of their experiment in sharing literature with children and give oral reports on what they learned.

Obviously a course of this sort will not come alive if the instructor relies too heavily on straight lectures. We try to draw the class into the action whenever possible. For example, during the opening class, I mention how we all tell stories every day and expand and change our perceptions of our own lives by doing so. Next, I divide the students into four groups as either donkey, dog, cat, or rooster and tell the story "The Bremen Town Musicians" while the class vigorously provides the sound effects. We briefly discuss how narrating a story in our own words, instead of memorizing it, gets the audience involved in the story. Then, after discussing the differences between storytelling and reading aloud, I read a selection from Kipling's *Just So Stories* as a good example of precise and formulaic language that is best left unchanged.

The next class is a puppet-making session. I bring a dozen books on puppets (both histories and how-to manuals) from the library, lecture briefly on the history of puppet theater, demonstrate a few simple techniques, and gather some practical tips from the class. Both the students and instructor should bring materials (like yarn, paste, old socks, and markers) to class.

Evaluation A listening quiz during or after each class helps promote interaction and critical awareness. The students are encouraged to advise the instructor and each other on how to improve puppet handling, storytelling, or reading. The course grade is determined as follows: (1) a major project for sharing stories with children; (2) two performances; (3) a paper on critical theory or storytelling festival; (4) four written essay tests; (5) listening quizzes.

Weaknesses Theory and performance must be balanced so that the students carry away with them something more than happy memories of a class that was fun. The required readings include theories on the practice of puppetry, storytelling, and reading aloud. Readings are supplemented by class discussions and the expertise that guests bring to the course.

The strength of the course is that it involves the students more deeply in literature than does the general survey course.

Texts

Baker, Augusta, and Ellin Greene. *Storytelling: Art and Technique.* New York: Bowker, 1977. (Thorough and sensible; gives background, purposes and value of, and the how-to of storytelling.)

Butler, Francelia. *Sharing Literature with Children: A Thematic Anthology.* New York: Longman, 1977. (An excellent selection of fiction, fantasy, poetry, and critical essays; the "Explorations" sections offer a wealth of ideas on sharing books with children.)

Clarkson, Atelia, and Gilbert Cross. *World Folktales.* New York: Scribner, 1980. (A good resource book for exploring the evolution of folktales; gives a feel for retelling.)

Engler, Larry, and Carol Fijan. *Making Puppets Come Alive: Method of Learning and Teaching Hand Puppetry.* New York: Taplinger, 1973. (Practical and creative ideas.)

Kimmel, Margaret, and Elizabeth Segel. *For Reading Out Loud! A Guide to Sharing Books with Children.* 1983. Rev. and expanded. New York: Delacorte, 1988. (Guidelines for reading to children of elementary and middle school age, with a well-annotated list of 140 books.)

Ross, Ramon Royal. *Storyteller.* Columbus: Merrill, 1972. (A comprehensive approach to reading aloud, puppetry, and "flannel board" stories as well as storytelling.)

SEMINARS AND WORKSHOPS

Graduate Seminar in Children's Literature

Michael Mendelson
English, Iowa State University

Introduction and History Two features mark this seminar as unique: first, it is presented as a two-week course; second, it combines literary history and creative writing. The two-week agenda allows a variety of students to enroll who would not ordinarily be able to take a graduate seminar in English. Foremost among these are teachers, librarians, interested citizens, and graduate students from departments of education and child development. Ultimately, this mix of students contributes to that breadth of interest that seminars depend on to produce lively discussion. The dual focus of the course also involves two independent sessions: a morning seminar in the history of the genre and an afternoon workshop devoted to the creation of an original piece of children's fiction. Together, the two approaches provide for a comprehensive understanding of the themes and methods of the field.[1]

Structure and Methods

The seminar. With only ten sessions, the historical section of the course has to be planned with considerable care. My primary goals are to provide a comprehensive history of the field, to indicate the range of interests included under the rubric of children's literature, and to introduce the classics of the canon. To accomplish these goals, I devised the following schedule:

> Day 1. The Didactic Tradition: John Newbery, excerpt from *Goody Two-Shoes*; Thomas Day, from *Sandford and Merton*; Maria Edgeworth, "A Day of Misfortune," from *Early Lessons*; Anna Laetitia Barbauld, "Order and Disorder: A Fairy Tale," from *Evenings at Home*.
>
> Day 2. Traditional Fairy Tales: selections from Charles Perrault and the Grimms.
>
> Day 3. Original Fairy Tales: Ruskin, "The King of the Golden River"; George MacDonald, "The Golden Key"; Dickens, *A Christmas Carol*.

Day 4. Alice and the New Child: Catherine Sinclair, from *Holiday House;* Lewis Carroll, *Alice in Wonderland.*

Day 5. Women Writers and Realism: Margaret Gatty, "The Unknown Land," from *Parables of Nature;* Louisa May Alcott, *Little Women;* Frances Hodgson Burnett, *The Secret Garden.*

Day 6. Boys' Tales: Mark Twain, *Tom Sawyer;* R. L. Stevenson, *Treasure Island;* Rudyard Kipling, "Mowgli's Brothers," "Kaa's Hunting," and "Red Dog," from *The Jungle Books.*

Day 7. Animal Stories: Kenneth Grahame, *The Wind in the Willows;* Beatrix Potter, from *The Complete Adventures of Peter Rabbit.*

Day 8. The Role of Tragedy: Beatrix Potter, "The Tale of Mr. Tod," and E. B. White, *Charlotte's Web.*

Day 9. The Role of Fantasy: C. S. Lewis, *The Lion, the Witch, and the Wardrobe;* Maurice Sendak, *In the Night Kitchen.*

Day 10. General discussion of enduring themes.

Naturally, the first day involves more lecture than normal because of the need for orientation and the unfamiliarity of the works. I detail the influence of Locke and Rousseau on eighteenth-century and nineteenth-century writers like Newbery and Day, and we discuss the didactic strain that was such a powerful force in early children's literature. Mrs. Barbauld's didactic "fairy tale" sets up an easy transition to the traditional fairy tales of day 2, a session in which we discuss the generic conventions and standard thematic concerns of the traditional tale. I also counterpoint the Grimms' "Aschenputtel" with Perrault's "Cinderella" as a way of clarifying the sociohistorical dimensions of the tales. Finally, tales like "The Brave Little Tailor" and "The Goose Girl" help to establish a contrast between gender roles that will be a useful point of discussion throughout the course. In sum, these first two days serve to establish a dialectic between instruction and entertainment (*utile e dulci*) that we continue to explore during our historical examination of the genre.

Day 3 focuses on the *Kunstmärchen*, and the conventional features of Ruskin's tale make it a reasonable starting point. In contrast, "The Golden Key" illustrates the thematic expansion of the genre into philosophical and metaphysical speculation. *A Christmas Carol* helps to establish the continuity between fairy tales and adult literature. The move to *Alice* on day 4 is a natural one, since Carroll adheres so closely to the standard fairy tale–romance structure of flight, adventure, return. It is also possible to prefigure the revolutionary nature of *Alice* by reference to *Holiday House*, a work that sympathizes with mischief. The examination of Alice, in turn, establishes a context for a careful look at the March girls, in *Little Women,* and for the transformation of Mary Lennox in *The Secret Garden.* The relation of realism to didacticism is also an issue on day 5, as is the distinction between interpretation and criticism, since the sentiment of *Little Women* calls on readers to articulate their own response to melodrama.

The tales of adventure on day 6 involve a considerable amount of reading, and yet the composite examination of the three writers clarifies the major conventions of adventure tales and solidifies the contrast between adventurous boys and heroines like Jo March and Mary Lennox. "Red Dog" also offers an opportunity to initiate a discussion of violence in children's literature, an issue that returns on day 8. On day 7, the bulk of the session is invariably given over to *The Wind in the Willows*. Nonetheless, the inclusion of *Peter Rabbit*, along with a reference to *The Jungle Books*, can stimulate consideration of the social perspective implicit in most beast fables.

While not a tragedy in its resolution, "The Tale of Mr. Tod" (on day 8) has a dark tone that, in conjunction with the elegiac element in *Charlotte's Web*, serves to expand many readers' views of the thematic scope of children's fiction. A general consideration of fantasy, and in particular the theological allegory of Narnia and the sexualized adventure to the Night Kitchen, also helps increase students' perception of the boundaries of the genre (day 9). A host of issues that assert themselves throughout the seminar—including the loss and regaining of identity, the passage from innocence to experience, the conventional gender roles, the interplay of *utile e dulci*, the genre's range of interests, the "classics," and the various subgenres within the field—all provide more than enough material for the summary discussion of day 10.

The workshop.   In contrast to the complexity of the "historical" sessions, the afternoon workshop offers a routine introduction to the procedures and concerns of writing for children. Because most of the students are writing fiction for the first time, it is important to establish an informal atmosphere that emphasizes writing and the sharing of ideas rather than prescriptive guidelines. The agenda is as follows: During the first week students are asked to invoke an audience (day 1), plan out their narrative's progress (day 2), fill out their primary characters and explore point of view (day 3), write a provisional first page (day 4), and share their manuscripts with other members of the class (day 5). By the end of the first week, even the most reluctant author starts to realize that when creative writing is approached as an exercise, the process can be great fun, can stimulate group cohesiveness, and can increase one's awareness of the technical features of fiction.

If the first week of workshops is devoted basically to the challenges of invention, the second week is intended to provide practice in clearing some basic narrative hurdles. These formal problems include providing transitions in time and setting (day 6), dealing with the story's middle (day 7), creating a satisfying close (day 8), and revising the first draft (day 9). The challenges posed by these facets of fiction making are resolved by discussion of the drafts of individual group members and by appeal to the "classic" texts the group has read for the literary sessions.

On the last day, students read excerpts of their manuscripts to one another and generally enjoy a sense of accomplishment that strengthens their involvement with and commitment to children's literature as an area of personal and professional concern.

Evaluation   Since this is a graduate course, evaluation is based solely on two critical papers and the creative project. But because of the compressed nature of the course, all writing is done after the sessions themselves are completed. Papers are mailed to the instructors, who then mail them back to the students with grades and comments.

Special Considerations   The intense, bifocal nature of this course dictates a number of special considerations. In the first place, the course needs to be announced to its unusual audience through mailers. And as soon as a student enrolls, he or she must receive a reading list and begin to read ahead in preparation for the two weeks the course is in session. Once the course begins, the teachers must ensure that the two sessions remain in tandem. This coordination can be achieved if the teachers confer each day in an effort to integrate serendipitous developments into the lesson plans of both seminar and workshop.

It should also be noted that the course in its present form can be given only during the summer and that its unusual mix of students requires some discussion with the registrar. In addition, the course typically involves two professors. There is, however, no reason why the course must run for exactly two weeks or that the two disciplines must be offered together. One can imagine a three- or four-week course in the history of the field that operates along more traditional lines. Nonetheless, this unique combination of literary study and creative writing can produce an unusually comprehensive view of the field, while the intensive schedule creates a sense of involvement that is especially compelling.

Texts

Burnett, Frances Hodgson. *The Secret Garden.* New York: Dell, 1984.

Cott, Jonathan, ed. *Masterworks of Children's Literature.* 8 vols. New York: Stonehill, 1983. (Includes Newbery, Day, Edgeworth, Barbauld, and Sinclair.)

Griffith, John W., and Charles H. Frey, eds. *Classics of Children's Literature.* 2nd ed. New York: Macmillan, 1987. (Includes Perrault, Grimm, Ruskin, Dickens, Carroll, Alcott, Twain, Stevenson, Kipling, Grahame, and Lewis.)

Gatty, Margaret. *Parables from Nature.* London: Bell, 1910.

MacDonald, George. *The Golden Key and Other Fantasy Stories.* Ed. Glenn E. Sadler. Grand Rapids: Eerdmans, 1980.

Potter, Beatrix. *The Complete Adventures of Peter Rabbit*. Harmondsworth, Eng.: Puffin, 1984.

Sendak, Maurice. *In the Night Kitchen*. New York: Harper, 1986.

White, E. B. *Charlotte's Web*. New York: Harper Torchbook, 1986.

Note

[1] This course was first offered in June 1988 and was funded in part by the Iowa Humanities Board and the NEH. The findings and conclusions of this writer do not necessarily represent the views of either the IHB or the NEH.

Writing of Children's Fiction

Kristin Hunter-Lattany
English, University of Pennsylvania

Introduction and History This course makes two fundamental assumptions: that children's fiction can reach the highest levels of the storyteller's art and that college-age adults have a special advantage—fresh memories, along with objectivity—in writing for children.

Though readings and field trips play a part in Writing of Children's Fiction, it is primarily a writing workshop, and guided group discussion of student manuscripts occupies the bulk of class time. The manuscripts provide the basis for discussion of the elements of good children's fiction, which are essentially the same as those of all good fiction except for the special requirements of young readers (subdivided into three age groups: under 7, 8–12, and teens).

Writing of Children's Fiction was first proposed and offered in 1978 and has been an annual offering since 1980. The course was introduced by a professional writer of both adult and juvenile fiction and originated in seven years of regular fiction writing workshops. Over the years, it was observed that many of the best stories coming out of these workshops dealt with childhood. The conclusion that college-age writers had an excellent vantage point for writing about childhood was irresistible. Most of their good stories seemed suitable for young readers, especially since this was the 1970s, the era of liberated children's literature. The fact that many of the taboos that were lifted in the 1970s have since been restored is ignored in the course.

Structure and Methods Student writing assignments commence with the first meeting of class. The initial assignments are to portray an unusual or unlikable child, to present an emotionally significant childhood event, and to describe a child's favorite place or a place in which a child feels uncomfortable. These assignments, which must be written in narrative prose, provide students with the three elements of fiction—character, conflict, and setting—as well as possible starting points for three stories.

Critical discussion of manuscripts is the basic format of the course. Samples of writing submitted the previous semester for admission into the course are used for the first two weeks' discussions of narrative technique. As new narratives are turned in, along with the first of three required book reviews (one picture book, one realistic book, one fantasy), students look for the seeds of stories, and discussions of the elements that make up a good story begin. The genres of children's fiction (fantasy, picture books, etc.) are also explored, with student-reviewed books as examples. Students may write in any genre and for any age level. Authors' names are omitted from manuscripts circulated for discussion, though authors are encouraged to identify themselves at the end of the group discussion and respond to it. Minimum writing requirements are two picture book texts, two short stories, or two chapters of a novel.

In-class writing assignments are most helpful in unblocking imaginations and producing story ideas. Among the exercises used recently have been to present a child's best friend, to portray an unstereotypical grandparent, to depict emotions through physical sensations, to describe a child's choice of a Halloween costume and his or her reasons for selecting it.

The first assignment, to present an unlikable or unusual child, can help dispel any lingering sentimentality about children, as can Matt Groening's book of cartoons *Childhood Is Hell*. The "favorite place" and "Halloween" exercises have been the most successful in leading to stories, notably from students who had been previously stuck for ideas. One semester, the writing exercise resulted in two entirely different stories about tree houses and two interesting variations on a single theme: children overburdened with parental restrictions or adult responsibilities who gained the freedom to behave like children by wearing childish costumes.

A special feature of this course has been excursions off campus, initiated because students must use the collections of the Free Library of Philadelphia to borrow children's books. The most fruitful visit has been to a public school, where two or three students read their stories and got youngsters' reactions.

Rewriting and revision are strongly urged for most manuscripts. Usually, areas of weakness are mutually agreed on in one-to-one conferences, and students find their own ways of shoring them up. Revision is excused only when a piece does not seem worth more work and a new and more promising piece is under way.

In addition to class time (3 hours once a week), the instructor is available for conferences for four hours each week. At least two conferences per student are mandatory.

Every effort is made to encourage freedom of discussion in class, and the result has been lively consideration of topics other than the failure or success of manuscripts. Among them have been the following: Are children ready to handle stories about loss and grief and even death in undisguised form? (the consensus: an emphatic yes). Are frightening stories acceptable for children under twelve? under eight? (the consensus: a qualified yes; stories for readers under eight should end reassuringly). Is ambiguity acceptable in children's fiction? (the consensus: no–this is one of the essential differences between adult and juvenile fiction). Should children's literature promote good ethical values? (consensus, yes, but without preaching). Should gay themes be permitted in children's fiction? (the consensus, after one student wrote a gay fairy tale in which the princes and princesses of two kingdoms married in same-sex pairs and adopted children: why not?). Should satanic themes be permitted? (consensus, after a student produced a satanic fantasy: no).

Evaluation Students are evaluated on the basis of growth—on whether individual manuscript weaknesses improve over the course of the semester. Grades are never written on papers lest they inhibit future writing, but they are available to interested students in private conferences.

Weaknesses Shallowness and a certain moral sleaziness pervaded some manuscripts whose writers had been overly influenced by TV. The group discussion that concluded that children's fiction should have a moral center helped to motivate several authors to strengthen their writing in the area of values.

The class time devoted to child development and to the special requirements of children sometimes takes away more than the instructor would like from the discussion of fictional strategies and writing techniques. But as long as the students write well by semester's end—and they usually do—the course is considered successful.

Texts

Egoff, Sheila, G. T. Stubbs, and L. F. Ashley, eds. *Only Connect: Readings on Children's Literature.* 2nd ed. Toronto: Oxford UP, 1980.

Groening, Matt. *Childhood Is Hell.* New York: Pantheon, 1988.

Strunk, William, Jr., and E. B. White. *The Elements of Style.* 3rd ed. New York: Macmillan, 1979.

Part III:
Selected Advanced Programs

Program in Literature for Children and Adolescents
Illinois State University

Taimi M. Ranta

Introduction and History

Since its founding, in 1857, Illinois State University has offered courses in storytelling and children's literature as part of its teacher preparation program. It was not, however, until 1931, with the reorganization of courses in the English department, that the offerings in literature for children became subject matter rather than methods courses and the term *program* could rightfully be used to describe the cluster of courses. Three graduate-level courses in literature for children and adolescents were developed in the early 1960s and two additional ones in the 1970s. In the mid-1960s a special resource area in children's literature and the language arts was developed for undergraduates who wished to gain expertise in these fields. In the early 1960s the master's program with concentration in literature for children and adolescents became one of the options open to students pursuing graduate work. The doctor of arts in English developed in the 1970s also can include a body of this literature. In June 1991 the conversion of the doctor-of-arts-in-English program to a PhD program in English studies was approved by the Board of Regents.

Program Components

The Total Program in Literature for Children and Adolescents. The program consists of ten continually functioning courses in literature for children and adolescents, plus three others that periodically can focus on some aspect of this literature. Of the ten, five are specifically for undergraduates. These include a basic foundation course in classics, best of the twentieth-century works, folklore and mythology, and wide-reading courses both for young children and for preadolescents. In addition, children's literature faculty members from the English department plan and teach a special course with emphasis on multicultural books for boys and girls in a pluralistic society for elementary education majors and an overview of books suitable for preschoolers for the early childhood majors in the College of Education.

The graduate-level program includes five courses in the history of literature for children and young people, contemporary literature for children and preadolescents, young adult literature, verse for children, and storytelling. The first three can be taken more than once, if the content is different, to provide graduate students with both broad and in-depth coverage of the areas. Periodically, three additional advanced graduate courses are offered in recent research in literature for children and adolescents, concentration on selected American and British figures in literature for children and adolescents, and selected areas of literary study with attention to associated curricular or teaching problems.

Resource Area Program in the English Language Arts for Students in Elementary Education (21 hours). This program provides the opportunity to pursue in some depth the study of English and to become knowledgeable in literature for children and the language arts. The recommended courses include four in literature for children and adolescents, at least one in language arts, and two electives in literature, language, and composition from departmental offerings.

Master's Program with Concentration in Literature for Children and Adolescents (32 hours minimum). This option is designed to meet the academic and professional needs of elementary and advanced teachers, supervisory personnel, elementary and junior high librarians, persons anticipating careers as teachers of literature for children and adolescents and language arts at the university level, prospective writers of literature for children and adolescents, and prospective employees of juvenile departments of publishing houses. The program includes at least three or four courses in literature for children and adolescents, introduction to graduate study, a linguistics class, research in language arts, and four to six selected electives in English, a cognate field, and thesis (if elected).

Doctor of Arts in English (number of hours varies depending on background but usually includes 45 hours of course work and 15 hours for dissertation). This practical degree emphasizes the acquisition of knowledge and skills that lead to excellence especially in undergraduate teaching. It has the six components of a major field in English, English education, higher education, cognate, comprehensive examination, and dissertation. A person can, for example, combine an emphasis on composition theory and practice with children's literature.

Brief Account of the Program

The 1960s and 1970s were the most flourishing years that the program has experienced, in multiple sections of courses in children's literature offered per semester and the total number of undergraduate and graduate students enrolled. For example, a dozen or more sections of the undergraduate foundation course might be offered each semester. The university was growing and preparing large numbers of elementary teachers, all of whom then were required to take at least two courses in children's literature.

As the drop in the national enrollment of elementary education majors was reflected locally and changes took place in the university's teacher education programs, fewer students were able to take as many courses in children's literature as they had earlier. The number of sections of the foundation course stabilized at six per semester in the 1980s, the students enrolled coming from several special-education programs, elementary education, communications, and various departments across the campus. Because the state now requires an eighteen-hour endorsement in a content area, many elementary education majors will be selecting English as a specialization, necessitating additional sections of existing courses and possibly leading to the creation of new offerings.

Currently the graduate students in the 300- and 400-level courses are largely from the special master's option in children's and young adult literature or post-master's programs in English. Most of these students are in-service teachers, librarians, or aspiring authors. Some are working for master's degrees in junior high/middle school education or in reading in the College of Education; occasionally someone who is pursuing a doctorate there elects a cognate in English.

Library Facilities
The university provides about seventy thousand volumes in various campus collections of children's and young adult literature. The Special Collections of the main library has around 3,200 in its juvenile historical collection.

Brief Overview of Advanced Courses
Studies in History of Literature for Young People. This course provides the opportunity to pursue an advanced critical, chronological study of literature for children and young people from the folklore heritage to the beginning of the twentieth century. The focus is primarily on books written in English in the United States and England, but attention is also given to works originally written in other languages. The course traces two parallel paths: literature that has endured and literature now considered mainly out of historical curiosity.

Studies in Contemporary Literature for Young People. In this course, teachers, librarians, and others have the opportunity to update their knowledge of books for children and early adolescents. It involves study in the broader fields of books for these readers; reading in various themes appropriate for elementary school, middle school, and junior high; and work on identified problems of special interest to individuals and groups within the class. Appraisal of books is on the bases of literary quality, principles of child and adolescent growth, curricular uses, and current societal needs. The materials for the course are primarily for kindergarten through grade 8.

Studies in Literature for Adolescents. This course is planned for prospective and experienced teachers and librarians of grades 7 through 12 and others interested in literature for young people. It includes some classics, popular adult books, and significant modern literature appropriated by young people, but the emphasis is on young adult novels, especially ones published after 1970.

Recent Research in the English Language Arts. In some semesters this course is devoted solely to recent research in literature for children and young people. It then provides teachers, prospective teachers, librarians, writers, and others interested in this field with the opportunity to examine significant research (especially dissertations and theses) and to read critical writing that is the outgrowth of research. Time is allocated for each participant to follow individual research interests in the field, including the planning of a study that could develop into a dissertation, thesis, independent study, or article.

Topics in English (Critical Study of Selected Authors). Planned for teachers and librarians in middle school, junior high, and senior high and for others interested in books for young adults, the course is an intensive, critical study of novels by eight to ten representative contemporary writers of young adult fiction. The focus is on student awareness of explicative techniques that grasp the essence of style, structure, characterization, and texture of their works. Students are expected to present analysis of both assigned and self-selected novels

This program shows the commitment of the English Department of Illinois State University to the teaching of literature for children and adolescents. The department has never lost sight of the realization that this literature, which now exists in greater abundance than ever before, must speak in a valid voice to the child or its reason for being becomes nonexistent.

The Children's Literature Program Eastern Michigan University

Alethea K. Helbig and Agnes Perkins

Introduction and History

The children's literature program at Eastern Michigan University is based on the firm conviction that knowledge and appreciation of imaginative literature are among the most valuable assets that those who work with children and young people can have. The program consists of a minor in English with a speciality in children's literature, an interdepartmental major in literature and drama for the young, and a master of arts in English with a concentration in children's literature.

The children's literature program intends, first, to broaden students' knowledge and appreciation of fine literature; second, to acquaint them with the great variety of books published for children and young people; and, third, to prepare them to evaluate books so that they will be able to use the best of the old and the best of the new with discrimination.

The program began to expand in the 1970s. For many years, two courses were offered, one an undergraduate survey of books for children and young people in various genres, the other a graduate course in methods of teaching children's literature.

Program Components

A. The Minor in English with a Specialty in Children's Literature (21 hours)

1. Required six hours: Introduction to Children's Literature; Children's Literature: Criticism and Response
2. Six hours to be chosen from Reading of Literature; Reading of Literature: Fiction; Reading of Literature: Poetry; Reading of Literature: Drama; Bible as Literature; Afro-American Literature; Shakespeare
3. Nine hours to be chosen from American Indian Literature; Shakespeare; Bible as Literature; World Mythology; Ballads and Folktales

In 1968, planning for the undergraduate English minor with a specialty in children's literature took place. Since the bulk of the students are prospective teachers who will be certified through the eighth grade, a selection of the best literature to serve a broad age span was offered. The minor concentrates on courses of basic cultural value and on significant and classic books that can serve as touchstones in judging other works for children.

The arrangements for the children's literature minor parallels those of other minors in the English department, with required classes and electives totaling twenty-one semester hours—that is, seven three-hour classes. Students must take two introductory courses in English literature and a choice of courses that are of general cultural interest. One of the required courses, Introduction to Children's Literature, is a survey course in which students read important books for children in such areas as mythology, folktale, fantasy, historical and realistic fiction, and poetry and examine the work of prominent historical and modern illustrators. The classes are mostly lecture and discussion with occasional group work and films; some critical writing is required. The second of the two required courses focuses on practical criticism that gives further opportunity for evaluating literature for children. Students read eight to ten recent novels and write six to eight papers about them. Some attention is also given to poetry, picture books, and retellings from oral tradition. Discussion is the predominant method of instruction.

B. Interdepartmental Major in Literature and Drama for the Young (36 hours)

1. Six hours from Reading of Literature; Reading of Literature: Fiction; Reading of Literature: Poetry; Reading of Literature: Drama; Bible as Literature; Afro-American Literature; Shakespeare
2. Required twenty to twenty-one hours: Fundamentals of Speech; Introduction to Children's Literature; Children's Literature: Criticism and Response; Drama and Play in Human Experience; Improvising and Role Play; Oral Interpretation of Children's Literature; and either World Mythology or Ballads and Folktales
3. Nine to ten hours from American Indian Literature; Shakespeare; Bible as Literature; World Mythology; Ballads and Folktales; Modern American and British Poetry; Theater for the Young; Plays for the Young; Literature for Young Adults; Storytelling; and selected interpretation and independent studies classes

The interdepartmental major, which began in 1972, provides opportunities for students to pursue interests started in earlier courses in children's literature and dramatic arts and to combine courses from several disciplines. The dramatic arts and education courses build on the English department children's literature courses—for example, Storytelling and Oral Interpretation have as prerequisites Introduction to

Children's Literature, and the Caravan for the Young, the traveling troupe of the department of communication and theater arts, often utilizes old stories introduced in the mythology and folklore classes.

C. Master of Arts in English with Concentration in Children's Literature (30 hours)

1. Twelve hours required: Major Genres in Children's Literature; Teaching of Children's Literature; History of Children's Literature; Seminar in Selected Topics in Children's Literature
2. Twelve hours of graduate-credit English department classes; especially appropriate are Children's Literature: Criticism and Response; Comparative Mythology; Ballads and Folktales; Literature for Early Childhood; Literature for Adolescents; History of Children's Literature: Twentieth Century
3. Six hours of cognates may be chosen from another department

The master of arts in children's literature grew out of the minor and major in children's literature and corresponds in format to other English master's programs. Students must fulfill a major of twelve hours in children's literature, take twelve hours of electives from any English department offerings for which graduate credit is given (which may include more children's literature classes), and may involve a six-hour cognate combination from another department.

The content of History of Children's Literature, one of the required courses, is self-evident. Major Genres is intended not only to acquaint students with the important works in the various areas of children's literature but to build critical awareness and to enable students to pursue special interests. Teaching of Children's Literature emphasizes aesthetics as well as method. Students read a variety of children's novels and books of myths, folktales, and poetry and work individually and in groups. They involve the whole class in the activities they develop and share critical insights about the books themselves and the success of the presentations. Literature for Early Childhood covers the major genres in books for ages preschool to ten, with emphasis on the significance of the combination of illustration and text.

Evaluation of Program

Evaluation has relied primarily on observation. It is significant that faculty members of the College of Education who work in the public schools urge their students to enroll and report that the children's literature offerings have been of great value in preparing students for the classroom. Public school administrators also have given approval and support, and the students themselves have been enthusiastic.

Selected Texts

Clarkson, Atelia, and Gilbert B. Cross. *World Folktales*. New York: Scribner's, 1980.

Griffith, John W., and Charles H. Frey. *Classics of Children's Literature*. New York: Macmillan, 1987.

Hamilton, Edith. *Mythology*. New York: Mentor, 1969.

Helbig, Alethea K. *Nanabozhoo: Giver of Life*. Brighton: Green Oak, 1986.

Hill, Helen, Agnes Perkins, and Alethea Helbig. *Dusk to Dawn: Poems of Night*. New York: Crowell, 1981.

Lukens, Rebecca. *A Critical Handbook of Children's Literature*. 4th ed. Glenview: Scott, 1990.

Perkins, Agnes. *Selective Guide to Children's Literature*. Ann Arbor: Edwards, 1978.

The Worlds of Juvenile Literature
University of North Carolina at Charlotte
M. Sarah Smedman

Introduction and History

In 1985, the University of North Carolina at Charlotte offered an experimental three-credit graduate course, the Worlds of Juvenile Literature, with an optional but integrated one-credit course, Methods of Teaching Literature.[1] Coordinated by the extension program director of the Arts, Humanities, and Education, the course was team-taught off campus by a professor of English and a professor of curriculum and instruction. The class met once a week for three hours in the evening in a public school library. (The university calendar was altered to fit that of the public schools.)

Structure and Methods

Critical theories of reader response, myth and archetypes, and Northrop Frye's cycle of stories provided the frame for the content of the course sessions. The first class focused on myth as the basis for archetypal criticism. For the second session, students read Frye's *Educated Imagination* and Jacob Bronowski's *Origins of Knowledge and Imagination* and in a short paper for an audience of their choice argued the importance of formally educating the imagination in the schools. Through presentation and discussion of the papers in class, Frye's and Bronowski's concepts were clarified—concepts that were adverted to throughout the semester. Forming the basis for the next several sessions was *The Child as Critic*, G. D. Sloan's summary for teachers of Frye's literary theory. To supplement our examination of cyclical and dialectic patterns of imagery in poetry and fiction, the class read selected essays on two major issues: (1) why human beings need stories, for example, James Hillman's "Note on Story," and C. S. Lewis's "On Stories"; and (2) what happens when we read, for example, Barbara Hardy's "Towards a Poetics of Fiction: An Approach through Narrative" and D. W. Harding's "Psychological Processes in the Reading of Fiction" (all articles are in Meek et al., *The Cool Web*). Between the first and second methods segments, five weeks were devoted to study of the patterns of plot, character, setting, atmosphere, and tone typical of the four basic stories. Works discussed included *Dominic, I Am the Cheese, Homesick: My Own Story, A Wizard of Earthsea, Rebels of the Heavenly Kingdom,* and numerous picture books appropriate to various age levels.

The structure of individual class sessions varied to include methods that can be used in teaching literature at the grade levels kindergarten through twelve: namely, lecture-discussion on critical theory and applied criticism; small-group discussion of selected novels, historical fiction, biography, and fantasy, based on questions addressing the unique features of each work as well as the ways each might fit into the cycle of stories and relate to other works read; teacher modeling, followed by student demonstration, of lessons in poetry for children and teenagers; examination, by pairs of students, of a controversial book with collaboration on both a "citizen's request" to have that book censored and an essay expounding an argument for teaching that book or retaining it in the school library.

Evaluation

In addition to the paper deriving from the reading in Frye and Bronowski, to the presentation of a poem, and to the collaborative work on controversial books, the course required a long paper and two exams. Students taking only the literature component had the option of writing a traditional critical-research paper; others developed a unit plan based on a work (or works) of juvenile literature and the critical theory focused on during the semester. For the final examination, students formulated in writing the six or eight most significant criteria for selecting good literature for young people and for evaluating, according to their criteria, several works read during the semester.

Weaknesses

The major problems were lack of library accessibility and lack of time for class discussion. Students seemed to need more guidance than had been expected.

Recommended Texts

Bronowski, Jacob. *The Origins of Knowledge and Imagination.* New Haven: Yale UP, 1978.

Egoff, Sheila, G. T. Stubbs, and L. F. Ashley, eds. *Only Connect: Readings on Children's Literature.* 2nd ed. Toronto: Oxford UP, 1980.

Frye, Northrop. *The Educated Imagination.* Bloomington: Indiana UP, 1970.

Haviland, Virginia, comp. *Children and Literature: Views and Reviews.* Glenview: Scott, 1973.

———, ed. *The Open-hearted Audience.* Washington: Library of Congress, 1980.

Meek, Margaret, Aidan Warlow, and Griselda Barton, eds. *The Cool Web: The Pattern of Children's Reading*. New York: Atheneum, 1978.

Sloan, Glenna Davis. *The Child as Critic*. 2nd ed. New York: Teachers Coll. P, 1984.

Recommended Periodicals

Children's Literature (1969–)
Children's Literature in Education (1969–)
Children's Literature Association Quarterly (1976–)

Note

[1] This was an experimental course that has since been extended to other off-campus sites and modified for an on-campus undergraduate class. The author currently teaches at Moorhead State University.

Center for the Study of Children's Literature Simmons College

Susan P. Bloom and Cathryn M. Mercier

Introduction and History

The underlying premise of the Center for the Study of Children's Literature is that children's books must be submitted to disciplined study in a manner similar to that of literature in general. Children's literature has integrity as art and as literature; it is immense in scope and in definition, encompassing poetry, the picture book, the vast body of mythology and folklore, and fiction for children and young adults. The center at Simmons has two programs—a graduate program leading to a master-of-arts degree in children's literature and a community program that encourages students, faculty members, and staff to serve the community as lecturers, teachers, and advisers and that provides information, materials, and resources. The center was founded in January 1977 with the assistance of the National Endowment for the Humanities. In 1979 a second grant from the endowment made possible the expansion of the community program. With the aid of the Exxon Education Foundation in 1982, the Children's Literature Consortium was established as a prototypical alliance between a graduate program in children's literature and the teachers and librarians in neighboring public school systems. It provides substantive course work to the teachers and librarians.

The master-of-arts degree program provides a year of specialized study to students who are, or intend to be, involved in teaching, library work, editing, publishing, and associated fields; it is a source of inquiry, supports serious creative effort, and stimulates studies in children's literature by other colleges and universities. The center serves as a resource for organizing and synthesizing community literature education; special programs, public lectures, institutes, colloquiums, and teacher workshops constitute a regular part of its activities.

Structure and Methods

The graduate program is not a professional program; it does not certify individuals as librarians or as teachers. It confers an MA in children's literature comparable to an MA in English. Individuals who matriculate without at least an undergraduate minor in English or

American literature must take two of the nine courses required for the graduate degree in English. Students develop a knowledge of children's literature as well as an acquaintance with general literature.

Access to the literature of at least one other language is central to the study of literature for children, and demonstration of a proficiency in a second language is strongly advised for all candidates, particularly those intending to pursue further graduate work, college teaching, and research. A candidate for the degree can elect to write a thesis or a project as part of an independent tutorial during the final semester. The thesis can be a monograph, an essay, or an annotated bibliographical compilation; it must have a scholarly orientation. The project can be in the area of curriculum development, literature education, or creative writing; it should have a practical application in the candidate's professional work and be a model for use by others.

Nine courses, thirty-six credits, are required for the degree, which may be completed in one academic year and one summer of full-time study. The Survey of Children's Literature, an overview including historical and contemporary considerations as well as representative works from major genres, is the only course open to upperclass undergraduates. Grounded in aesthetic concerns, this course introduces the varied body of children's and young adult literature.

The courses required for the MA focus on the history and criticism of literature for the young. For example, in Criticism of Literature for Children, students grapple with issues of definition, function, and derivation as they study the history of criticism and various approaches to criticism, seeking their own critical voices.

In another required course, Victorian Children's Literature, the social and intellectual history of the Victorian period is considered, including important educational, social, and literary movements. With a general adherence to chronology, required readings include selections from such primary sources as Flora Thompson's *Lark Rise to Candleford*, as well as works by Frederick Marryat, John Ruskin, Charles Kingsley, Lewis Carroll, George MacDonald, Hans Christian Andersen, Charlotte Yonge, Juliana Horatia Ewing, Margaret Gatty, and Mary Louisa Molesworth.

A representative recommended course is The Writer's Achievement, in which students examine the complete works of four writers of children's books, seeking to articulate the writer's development, form and content, literary achievement, and stated and unstated ideology.

Institutes and symposiums examine special topics in children's literature and are held in alternate summers. In the 1979 institute, the Child in Literature: Songs of Innocence, Songs of Experience, students considered the dimensions of innocence and experience in selected books for the young. In 1985, students explored the theme of the journey in literature for the young in *Ithaka and Other Journeys*, inspired by

C. P. Cavafy's poem "Ithaka"; Ovid's *Metamorphoses* provided the theme and literary basis for the 1987 one-week institute and three-week symposium. The 1989 institute and symposium addressed the dark side of self and the duality of human nature in children's literature during "Me and My Shadow." In 1991 the institute and symposium "Masquerade" celebrated the provocative implications of disguise.

When the graduate program was developed, the demands of sequence were seriously considered. The cycle of history and criticism courses, including Criticism, the Picture Book, and Victorian Children's Literature, is generally offered during the first semester, and the cycle that includes Fantasy and Realism is usually given during the second semester. Special topics are offered during the summer. In addition, there are a balance of electives; for example, the writing course is intended primarily for those who are interested in writing or in studying the process of writing; the course on the history of childhood is intended primarily for those doing research in the emerging historiography of childhood and its relationship to children's literature.

Instructors vary in teaching styles, but most combine lectures and discussions. Most classes are conducted as seminars, with occasional lectures by the professor; discussions center on research presented by graduate students and on required readings. Team teaching and/or jointly taught courses have also proven successful. Outstanding student papers are published in the Simmons College publication *Essays and Studies*.

Evaluation

Students are asked to complete an evaluation of each course, commenting on course content, the quality of instruction, and the relationship of the course to the total program.

A formal evaluation was administered by TDR Associates, Inc., in 1978 at the end of the crucial and formative second year of the program. Students responded to questions about the program's effect on knowledge of and attitude toward children's literature and addressed, in writing, the program's major strengths and weaknesses. Among the strengths listed were the experience and skill of faculty members, quality of lectures, accessibility of faculty and staff, quality of guest lectures, efforts to establish a community of scholars, substantive nature of institutes and colloquiums, and the degree to which students could become involved in the programs and activities of the center. Major weaknesses were reflected in the requests for more diversity in courses, faculty, and resources.

The Community Program

The community program is closely related to the master-of-arts degree program; its activities are rooted in research and scholarship and provide brief but intensive examinations of topics in children's literature. One-week institutes have been held in cooperation with Vassar College in Poughkeepsie, New York, and with Saint Michael's College in Winooski, Vermont. Colloquiums have included the Perilous Realms of Realism and Fantasy; Motion and Rest: The Art of Illustration; Rememory, on the uses of memory in the writing of children's literature; and This Is My Story, on autobiography in children's literature. Making Connections—Books in the Classroom and Visual Literacy—Emotional Impact were two of a series of in-service workshops for teachers. Courses given in community settings have included Sharing Books with Your Child, designed for visually impaired parents of sighted children, and the Old and the Young, a course for senior citizens and junior high students.

For three years the center published the *Children's Bookletter*, a quarterly newsletter for use by children, parents, and teachers that featured such issues as *Highlighting Humor* (Fall 1979), and *The Sweet Uniqueness of Soul: The African American Experience in Children's Books* (Spring 1981). The center stresses community commitment and represents many groups and agencies. Its resources include collections of current children's books (15,000 plus 1,500 in the historical collection), professional books, journals and reviews, an extensive clipping file, and book exhibits for use by children and adults. The center's facilities and resources are open to the public.

Part IV:
Two Children's
Literature Collections

The UCLA Children's Literature Collection

G. B. Tennyson

The long-lived Dr. Routh (1755–1854), president of Magdalen College, Oxford, for sixty-one years, is remembered chiefly for having said, "Always verify your references, sir." Routh's injunction could well be taken as the motto for all scholarship and the raison d'être of libraries. In the field of children's literature, however, that motto has never been easy to follow, for libraries have not in the main been zealous in gathering and preserving the very sources one needs for verification. One happy exception is the rich assortment of children's literature in the Department of Special Collections of the UCLA Research Library. Here Routh's scholar can verify and indeed discover an abundance of sources in a field that has now come into its own.

The UCLA collection, which now numbers approximately 22,000 items, was acquired mostly since 1946. Five main individual collections acquired between 1946 and 1975 established the emphasis of the total collection, and they contain, as well, many of the showpiece works for which the collection is noted. The gathering has long since overflowed the confines of the Wilbur Jordan Smith room in the department of Special Collections and now occupies stack and other showcase areas. To date, three articles about the collection have appeared, each focusing on one or more of four of the five main collections (Hertel, on the Percival collection; Kerlan, on the Meeks collection; Smith). All three articles contain illustrations from books in the collection.[1]

The five original collections that form the nucleus of the UCLA holdings in children's literature are known by the names of the private collectors who originally assembled them: Olive Percival, Bernard Meeks, Elvah Karshner, d'Alté Welch, and May and George Shiers. Together these five collections constitute about 6,540 books. The remaining 15,000-plus books in the children's collection were acquired through some block purchases and many individual purchases since 1950. In addition, an exceptionally large holding in Special Collections of the works of Maria Edgeworth and Mrs. (Mary Martha) Sherwood, containing among much else many works for children, supplements at many points the volumes in the children's literature collection. Each of the five main collections of children's books, some of the minor gatherings, the Edgeworth and Sherwood collections, and a few individual titles of note are described here.

The oldest of the individual collections is the Percival, containing 540 volumes. Percival was an avid private collector of many items other than children's books, and her personal story has been told in Hertel's 1953 account. The 540 volumes in the Percival group contain 527 individual titles printed between 1707 and 1914, of which seventy-five percent are British imprints. Most of the publications fall between the period 1790 and 1840, "a period," Hertel explains, "in which adult literature changed from the rational and polished exactitude of the 18th century to the emotional, romantic, and imaginative flowering of the early 19th century" (24). Hertel divides the categories of the Percival collection into five main areas: English history, natural history, early textbooks, nursery songs, and manners and morals. There is a good deal of overlap among these categories, since children's books from the period concentrated on by Percival were often rich in moral instruction, even when the ostensible topic was history or spelling or nursery rhymes. In her collection, Percival appears to have been guided by F. J. Harvey Darton's *Children's Books in England* and by his bibliography in the original *CBEL*. There are consequently many Newbery imprints among her volumes. But the most notable fact about the Percival volumes is that they placed the focus of the UCLA collection as a whole on late eighteenth-century and early nineteenth-century British children's books, a focus that has continued to this day.

The next major addition to the UCLA children's book collection was the acquisition, in 1959, of the Bernard Meeks collections. Meeks, a private collector in Arlington, Virginia, sold the library about two thousand volumes as well as some original drawings by such illustrators as Kate Greenaway and Walter Crane. The titles in Meeks range well beyond Percival, dating from 1657 to 1957 and including some of the most celebrated children's books ever printed, among them a very large number of Newbery imprints. There are, for example, an eighteenth-century Perrault *Mother Goose* and an 1805 *Mother Hubbard*. Meeks is especially rich in nineteenth-century titles, including the Lambs' *Tales from Shakespeare*, with William Blake plates, the first edition of Collodi's *Pinocchio*, the first American edition of *Alice in Wonderland*, the first edition of Frances Hodgson Burnett's *Little Lord Fauntleroy*, and many volumes by Greenaway, Crane, and Beatrix Potter. Among twentieth-century first editions are *The Wizard of Oz* and *The Wind in the Willows*. Irvin Kerlan, in his account of the collection, also notes that Meeks's gathering contains such extraliterary bonuses as an unpublished Cruikshank watercolor for *Jack and the Beanstalk* and that in general Meeks added a visual dimension to the UCLA collection as a whole (11).

In 1960, less than a year after the acquisition of Meeks, the library bought the Karshner collection of 2,100 volumes. Like Percival, Karshner was a Los Angeles collector. In describing her books, Wilbur Jordan Smith, former head of Special Collections, noted that the Karshner collection was especially strong in early American volumes, thereby enlarging Percival and Meeks, which were heavily British, and strong in pre-1821 English books, thereby complementing the acquisitions already concentrated in this area. These early American and early British titles constitute about 500 (300 American, 200 British) of the Karshner volumes, the remaining 1,600 being mainly nineteenth-century English and American works. These later titles include such special items as a group of early editions of *Goody Two-Shoes* and the original first appearances (one in periodical, the other in book form) of Sarah Hale's "Mary Had a Little Lamb."

The Karshner collection also contains a group of early children's books known as the Ludford family juveniles. These range in date from 1746 to 1780 and bear armorial bookplates of the Ludford family and Ludford family signatures. In Karshner there are eleven titles in the Ludford group, seven of them apparently unique and all but one in original covers. Nine of the Ludfords are Newbery imprints. Since the acquisition of Karshner, the library has acquired three more Ludford juveniles, for a total of fifteen, a grouping unparalleled in any other collection.

In 1970 the UCLA collection was augmented by the acquisition of an exceptionally rich gathering of early English imprints that had been assembled, from the 1920s on, by d'Alté Welch. Before his death Welch had visited the UCLA collection and photocopied many of the volumes or parts of them and had shown a great interest in the UCLA holdings. Thus, although his will specified a destination—the American Antiquarian Society—for his American imprints but none for the English ones, Welch's heirs made the English titles available to the UCLA library. Of the character of these books, Smith wrote: "It is unlikely that another acquisition of such size and quality and so relatively lacking in duplication will ever be made by UCLA" (152). The 1,000 books are all pre-1821 British titles, 115 of them Newbery and successor imprints. Of these 115, 23 are not known to exist in any other copy. Smith noted that the absence of duplication probably resulted from the fact that Welch advised UCLA on the acquisition of notable children's books as they came to the market and, in so doing, avoided duplicating his own holdings.

An unexpected further benefit of the 1959 Meeks purchase was that Meeks's friends May and George Shiers became aware of the extent of UCLA's holdings. Toward the end of 1975 the Shiers' 840 titles in 904 volumes was added to the children's book collection. These materials, which included more than 100 eighteenth-century publications, were strong in Newbery and John Harris imprints, in early instructional volumes, and in natural history, all areas of particular interest to these Santa Barbara collectors. The Shiers collection, which has not hitherto been reported on, reinforces the traditional emphasis on early children's literature that has been the particular strength of the UCLA holdings.

After the five main collections there are several smaller groupings that deserve notice. A collection of 250 books gathered by a private collector, Raymond Barnett, includes French and German as well as English titles. In addition to the books, the Barnett collection contained what Smith describes as "delicious ephemera"—parlor games, peep-shows, lottery sheets, children's dramas, and many bookmarks (149). Another collection, this of slightly more than 500 volumes, was acquired from Hamill and Barker of Chicago in 1954. It contains 310 French and 200 English imprints, the majority of them pre-1821. "Most of the French books," Smith notes, and "over 40 of the English books were from the famous Gumuchian Collection" (150). Finally, there is a small but uncommon collection of about 150 Soviet picture books from the 1920s to the 1940s.

Other major holdings complementing the children's collection include the Edgeworth, Sherwood, and Broadside ballads collections, and the modern juvenile books presented by Jerome Cushman. Because both Edgeworth and Sherwood wrote many children's books in the formative period of literature for young people—the period especially well covered in the UCLA collection—many of the titles in the Edgeworth and Sherwood groupings are counted as part of the overall holdings in children's literature.

The Edgeworth collection is actually two related groupings, the first consisting of books and manuscripts by Maria Edgeworth herself—probably the finest such collection extant—and the second representing approximately twenty percent of the Edgeworth family library of books in various fields. Among the large number of Edgeworth's children's books, the most notable item is the only known complete set of *Early Lessons* (1801). The Sherwood collection is remarkable not only for its copies of her children's books but for her multivolume manuscript journal, of which only half has ever been printed. The collection of Broadside ballads from the period 1770–1865 totals just under two thousand broadsides and contains many ballads that touch on topics and interests related to children's literature of the pre-1940 period. The Cushman donations, mainly twentieth century, have expanded the collection greatly in the contemporary field, though the particular strength of the UCLA collection overall remains in the period before 1840.

Davis notes that additions to the collection have also proceeded on the basis of individual titles as well as group purchases. Of particular note among recent individual acquisitions, Davis points to several early editions of Mme d'Aulnoy. These include such treasures as a 1708 edition of her *Les contes des fées* and *Nouveaux contes des fées* (first published in 1697—98), which coined the term *fairy tale*. There is also a 1721 English translation of these works, preceding by twenty years the English translations of Perrault. Another recent acquisition of great rarity is the anonymous 1780 *Curious Adventures of a Little White Mouse*, a work not otherwise recorded in any library. It is unusual for its relatively gentle moralizing and even more for the fact that it is illustrated by woodcuts clearly designed for it alone rather than taken from common stock. Such showpieces as the d'Aulnoy editions and *Curious Adventures of a Little White Mouse* rank with the Ludford juveniles and the Edgeworth *Early Lessons* among the jewels of the UCLA collection. But perhaps the most impressive holdings are the size and scope of the Newbery and Harris imprints, which may exceed even those held by the British Library.

Of opportunities for research in children's literature the UCLA collection offers an abundance. Davis stresses the potential of the collection for work on the formative years of children's literature, for the study of publishing practices and publishing houses in the field of children's literature, and for the study of attitudes about children from the eighteenth century to the present. There are also extensive possibilities for research on genres of children's literature, illustrations and illustrators, and changing attitudes on morality and didacticism in writing for children.

Another research aspect of the collection has been under investigation by Mitzi Myers of UCLA. Her work in progress on women writers on the late eighteenth and early nineteenth centuries coincides with the strength of the UCLA children's collection. She notes that in addition to such well-known women writers as Edgeworth, Sherwood, and Hannah More, the collection is strong in such authors as Sarah Trimmer, Anna Laetitia Barbauld, Lady Eleanor Fenn (including a unique copy of the *Friend of the Mothers*), Dorothy and Mary Ann Kilner, and many others of an age of innovation by women writers for children. Myers says that the collection "offers unusual opportunities for those interested in gender and genre of the era when a new world dawned for children" (personal communication 24 Nov. 1986).

In 1975, when Smith described the collection, he estimated that the figure of 6,200 is the likely number of all surviving editions of English children's books published before 1821 (153). At the time of Smith's writing, the UCLA collection held 2,058 of that total. Now, according to James Davis, the number is certainly much greater, but no complete census has been done to establish the total. Nor, indeed, is the collection at present separately indexed or cataloged apart from listings in the main library catalog. A proposal for a complete cross-indexed catalog of the UCLA collection has recently been made. When completed, it would include listings by author, illustrator, publisher, place of publication, subject, chronology, and comparative holdings of English and American titles. Only then will it be possible to grasp the full range of the collection. Still, on the basis of what is now known of the UCLA holdings in children's literature, the collection ranks among the top five in North America and rivals in quality the holdings of the British Library and the Victoria and Albert. Surely here is material aplenty for Dr. Routh's scholar to verify references.

Note

[1] The present survey, the first since 1975, is indebted to those earlier accounts as well as to supplementary information provided by James Davis, rare book librarian in Special Collections. In addition, I have drawn on information in the pamphlet *Department of Special Collections*, distributed by the UCLA Library; the catalog *Early Children's Books, Games and Ephemera*, which was not distributed; the 1985 "Exhibitions in URL," listing titles displayed in an exhibit of items from the children's literature collection; and from a proposal for a developed catalog of children's books at UCLA drawn up by Brian Alderson. I have also profited greatly from discussion with David Zeidberg, head of Special Collections at UCLA.

Specialized studies of the children's book collection are included in the Occasional Papers series published by Special Collections: Alderson, *The Ludford Box and "A Christmass-Box": Their Contribution to Our Knowledge of Eighteenth Century Children's Literature* (on miniature libraries); Andrea Immel, *Revolutionary Reviewing: Sarah Trimmer's "Guardian of Education" and the Cultural Politics of Juvenile Literature* (on the first periodical systematically reviewing children's literature and its cultural implications). These and other specialized historical studies are available directly from Special Collections.

Works Cited

Alderson, Brian. *The Ludford Box and "A Christmass-Box": Their Contribution to Our Knowledge of Eighteenth Century Children's Literature.* Children's Book Collection Occasional Papers 2. Los Angeles: U of California, 1989.

Department of Special Collections. Los Angeles: UCLA Library, 1981.

Early Children's Books, Games and Ephemera. London: Beauchamp Bookshop, 1954.

Exhibitions in URL. Los Angeles: Univ. Research Library, 1985.

Hertel, Robert R. "Remembering Childhood." *Library Journal* 78 (1953): 23–31.

Immel, Andrea. *Revolutionary Reviewing: Sarah Trimmer's "Guardian of Education" and the Cultural Politics of Juvenile Literature.* Intro. Mitzi Myers. Children's Book Collection Occasional Papers 4. Los Angeles: U of California, 1990.

Kerlan, Irvin. "The Bernard Meeks Collection: Three Hundred Years of Children's Books, 1657–1957." *American Book Collector* 10 (1960): 6–11.

Smith, Wilbur Jordan. "UCLA's Trove of Rare Children's Books." *Wilson Library Bulletin* 50 (1975): 149–53. (Published separately as a pamphlet by UCLA Library, 1976.)

The de Grummond Children's Literature Research Collection

Anne Lundin

Lewis Thomas, in his celebrated *Lives of a Cell*, speaks of our human condition as the most social of all social animals. He sees our interconnectedness in this image: "Perhaps we are linked in circuits of the storage, processing, and retrieval of information, since this appears to be the most basic and universal of all human enterprises. It may be our biological function to build a certain kind of Hill" (14).

Special collections of children's literature offer accumulated knowledge, a certain kind of hill. Their particular strength is in the confluence of text and context, embedded in the rich and enormously intricate weave of a nation's social and economic history.

The de Grummond Children's Literature Research Collection at the University of Southern Mississippi is built on this foundation: that children's books need to be studied as an aspect of the culture of a particular time rather than in isolation. The de Grummond Collection's holdings are shaped toward an investigation of the sociohistory of a literary work, from its origins through its subsequent textual adventures.

The de Grummond Collection arose out of the need to build such documentation, to create a scholarly study of the communication between author, publisher, and reader, a necessary jointure of economics and art. Lena de Grummond came to the University of Southern Mississippi in her retirement, after a long career in school libraries in Louisiana. In her former position she had worked with authors and illustrators, visiting schools and viewing the vitality of preliminary sketches, the immediacy of manuscript material. Teaching children's literature from a textbook, she saw how pale the reflection of this process was without the originals at hand.

In 1966 she began writing letters to authors and illustrators, in the great epistolary tradition, asking if they could share the original materials to their works. These materials, often discarded or deteriorating in a warehouse, were to be given a second life. To Lena de Grummond, these prepublication materials were the documents of a golden age in children's book publishing, as vital a part of our cultural heritage as the published books. Her passion was communicated to a growing field of authors and illustrators, who felt enormously buoyed by her interest in the flotsam and jetsam of their work.

The collection evolved from these single contributions of dummies, manuscripts, mechanicals, original artwork, and correspondence. Unlike many other collections, the de Grummond grew from a multiplicity of gifts rather than the largess of one private collector. Twenty-five years later, the de Grummond Collection boasts several thousand contributors and an international community of friends in the children's book world.

Distinguished contributors include Ezra Jack Keats, all of whose original work is now housed in the collection, H. A. Rey and Margret Rey, Marcia Brown, Roger Duvoisin, Richard Peck, James Marshall, Madeline L'Engle, Trina Schart Hyman, Barbara Cooney, Leonard Everett Fisher, Maud Petersham and Miska Petersham, Lois Lenski, Nonny Hogrogian, Edward Ardizzone, Ernest Shepard.

The vision is translated anew to authors and illustrators, who sense the connection between preservation and literacy, an archive of children's literature and the child. The collection's outreach in an annual book festival, a state reading award, and a myriad of exhibits, programs, and publications brings children and books together. The collection's mission is to be a strong research library as well as a resource center and museum of childhood, a delicate balance for an institution as a scholarly and social being.

Manuscripts and artwork speak to the richly textured process of bookmaking, to the book as physical object and signifier. The de Grummond's rare book collection grew out of the manuscript collection, the book as the whole of its parts, reciprocally related. The de Grummond Collection now holds over 32,000 books, representative of five centuries of a literature of childhood. Here you will find fables and fairy tales; courtesy books for young gentlemen and ladies; hornbooks, battledores, primers, and readers; hymns and poems of innocence and experience; Bibles, emblem books, proverbs, street cries, broadsides, chapbooks; riddles, puzzles, picture books. Books are defined generously, encompassing the ephemera of popular culture, periodicals, and the idiosyncratic subliterary formats that reach a child audience.

Some of the collections' specialties are extensive holdings of *Aesop's Fables*, the oldest being a 1530 edition; a significant selection of Hans Christian Andersen's works in Danish and English; original artwork, books, and ephemera by and about Kate Greenaway; page proofs for Randolph Caldecott and woodblocks engraved by Edmund Evans; numerous important editions of works by pioneer publishers like John Newbery, John Marshall, and John Harris; 250 titles of children's periodicals dating from 1788 to the present; and an impressive array of early picture books, fairy tales, and fantasy.

These research materials become primary sources for a study of the cultural, economic, ideological, and social shaping of a text. Notions of text, readers, and society can be examined through a number of disciplines—literary criticism, education, philosophy, sociology, cultural studies. A special collection like the de Grummond becomes a literary witness to the universe of knowledge. Critics become historians, coming to special collections for comparative literature and social history, in primary and secondary forms.

Their scholarship reveals how special collections are spacious landscapes for humanistic research. Special collections of children's literature are strategically poised to accommodate interdisciplinary pursuits of texts as reflections or re-visions of a social order. R. Gordon Kelly, in his study of American children's periodicals, draws on a wide range of materials—autobiographies, conduct books, editorial statements. Of particular interest is an author's correspondence with editors and publishers, in order to know as much as possible about the processes that generate the documents to which the historian turns. Mitzi Myers demonstrates in her work on Maria Edgeworth and the Georgian period how children's texts can be restored to their political and literary contexts, their ideological and historical juncture, emboldened as literature. Indeed, feminist criticism has helped to open up the canon to popular culture, works by women, and nonfictional discourse—the advice books, diaries, tract society reports, the factual formats that often complement the fictional worldview. Like Mitzi Myers, Jane Tompkins is interested in communicating neglected texts as "cultural work," to understand their impact in their original setting. In *Sensational Designs*, Tompkins looks to the cultural work of American fiction, 1790–1860, its continuities rather than ruptures, the strands that connect one discrete text to another. Literature becomes a web of intertextuality, a commerce that words have with each other.

Discovering texts and their context of production and interpretation is the business of special collections like the de Grummond. Researchers come with a particularity of need, which becomes enlarged within a gossamer of continuity, disentangling ties of textual and graphic transmission. As Brian Alderson notes, investigating an 1807 John Harris imprint of the *Arabian Nights* raises questions about what is and is not a children's book and other critical issues related to the translation, abridgment, and adaptation of texts. The longevity of one text is a piece of the puzzle, the mysterious relationship between aesthetic value and a text's historical existence, the survival patterns of childhood's books as cultural work.

Curators in special collections work on these collaborative possibilities. Collection building, cataloging, processing, and bibliographic instruction make visible the tenuous connections of text and context. Chronological and provincial imprint files expedite the research into a period or publisher. Inclusion into national databases makes public the private holdings of the institution and democratizes access through a

network of electronic information highways. The old and the new con-
join as a museum without walls.

Special collections of children's literature are small hills in the
mountains of academia, a stimulus to the further exploration of the hin-
terlands. In the books, manuscripts, and artwork encompassing five
centuries of literature read by children, the de Grummond Collection
shapes a topography of knowledge, a delicate interdependence in a
larger universe of scholars and scholarship. Like the performance of
reader and poem, a special collection converses as text and context,
word and image, child and adult, dwelling in possibilities.

Works Cited

Alderson, Brian. "Collecting Children's Books." *Children and Their Books: A Celebration of the Work of Iona and Peter Opie.* Ed. Gillian Avery and Julia Briggs.
Oxford: Clarendon–Oxford UP, 1989. 7–17.

Kelly, R. Gordon. "Social Factors Shaping Some Late Nineteenth-Century Children's Periodical Fiction." *Society and Children's Literature.* Ed. James H.
Fraser. New York: Godine, 1978.

Myers, Mitzi. "Socializing Rosamond: Educational Ideology and Fictional
Form." *Children's Literature Association Quarterly* 14 (1989): 52–58.

Thomas, Lewis. *The Lives of a Cell: Notes of a Biology Watcher.* New York: Viking,
1974.

Tompkins, Jane. *Sensational Designs: The Cultural Work of American Fiction, 1789–
1860.* New York: Oxford UP, 1985.

Part V:
Readings and Resources

Rachel Fordyce and Mary Beth Dunhouse

Selected Bibliography

Reference Works

Blanck, Jacob N. *Peter Parley to Penrod: A Bibliographical Description of the Best-Loved American Juvenile Books.* 1938. Waltham: Mark, 1974, vi, 153 pp.

Briggs, Katharine M. *A Dictionary of British Folk-tales in the English Language.* Bloomington: Indiana UP, 1970–.

Carlson, Ruth Kearney, ed. and comp. *Folklore and Folktales around the World.* Newark: International Reading Assn., 1972, x, 172 pp.

Carpenter, Charles. *History of American School-Books.* Philadelphia: U of Pennsylvania P, 1963, 322 pp.

Cech, John, ed. *American Writers for Children, 1900–1960.* Vol. 22 of *Dictionary of Literary Biography.* Detroit: Gale, 1983, xiii, 412 pp.

Chambers, Aidan. *Introducing Books to Children.* 2nd ed. Rev. and expanded. Boston: Horn, 1983, vii, 223 pp.

Children's Book Council. *Children's Books: Awards and Prizes.* New York: Children's Book Council, 1981, ix, 215 pp.

"Collections of Rare Children's Books: A Symposium, Parts 1–6." *Library Journal* 63 (1938): 20–21, 105–07, 192–93, 360–62, 452–53, 535–37.

Commire, Anne, ed. *Something about the Author: Facts and Pictures about Contemporary Authors and Illustrators of Books for Young People.* Detroit: Gale, 1971–.

—————, ed. *Yesterday's Authors of Books for Children.* 2 vols. Detroit: Gale, 1977–.

De Montreville, Doris, and Elizabeth D. Crawford, eds. *Fourth Book of Junior Authors and Illustrators.* New York: Wilson, 1978, 370 pp.

De Montreville, Doris, and Donna Hill, eds. *Third Book of Junior Authors.* 1972. New York: Wilson, 1988, 325 pp.

Dill, Barbara E., ed. *Children's Catalog.* 13th ed. New York: Wilson, 1976, xii, 1,408 pp.

Field, Carolyn W., ed. *Special Collections in Children's Literature.* Chicago: ALA, 1982, xiii, 257 pp.

———, ed. *Subject Collections in Children's Literature*. New York: Bowker, 1969, 142 pp.

Fisher, Margery. *Who's Who in Children's Books: A Treasury of the Familiar Characters of Childhood*. New York: Holt, 1975, 399 pp.

Fordyce, Rachel. "Dissertations of Note." *Children's Literature*, 1975–.

Fraser, James H. *Children's Authors and Illustrators: A Guide to Manuscript Collections in United States Research Libraries*. New York: Saur, 1980, xi, 119 pp.

Fuller, Muriel, ed. *More Junior Authors*. New York. Wilson, 1963, vi, 235 pp.

Halsey, Rosalie V. *Forgotten Books of the American Nursery: A History of the Development of the American Story-Book*. 1911. Detroit: Gale, 1984, viii, 244 pp.

Haviland, Virginia. *Children's Literature: A Guide to Reference Sources*. Washington: Library of Congress, 1966, 341 pp. 1st supp., 1972, vii, 316 pp.; 2nd supp., 1977, ix, 413 pp.

———. "Serving Those Who Serve Children: A National Reference Library of Children's Books." *Quarterly Journal of the Library of Congress* 22 (1965): 301–16.

Hendrickson, Linnea. *Children's Literature: A Guide to the Criticism*. Boston: Hall, 1987, xxvi, 664 pp.

Holtze, Sally Holmes, ed. *Fifth Book of Junior Authors and Illustrators*. New York: Wilson, 1983, vii, 357 pp.

Hunt, Mary Alice, ed. *A Multimedia Approach to Children's Literature: A Selective List of Films, Filmstrips, and Recordings Based on Children's Books*. Foreword Ellin Greene. 3rd ed. Chicago: ALA, 1983, xxix, 182 pp.

Kellman, Amy. *Guide to Children's Libraries and Literature outside the United States*. Chicago: ALA, 1982, vi, 32 pp.

Kelly, R. Gordon, ed. *Children's Periodicals of the United States*. Westport: Greenwood, 1984, xxix, 591 pp.

Kingman, Lee, Joanna Foster, and Ruth Giles Lontoft, comps. *Ilustrators of Children's Books: 1957–1966*. Boston: Horn, 1968, xvii, 295 pp.

Kingman, Lee, Grace Allen Hogarth, and Harriet Quimby, comps. *Illustrators of Children's Books: 1967–1976*. Boston: Horn, 1978, xiv, 290 pp.

Kirkpatrick, D. L., ed. *Twentieth-Century Children's Writers*. 3rd ed. Chicago: St. James, 1989, xxi, 1288 pp.

Kunitz, Stanley J., and Howard Haycraft, eds. *The Junior Book of Authors*. 2nd ed., 1978. New York: Wilson, 1985, vii, 309 pp.

Leif, Irving P. *Children's Literature: A Historical and Contemporary Bibliography.* Troy: Whitston, 1977, xvii, 338 pp.

Library Literature, 1921–1932: A Supplement to Cannons' Bibliography of Library Economy, 1876–1920. Comp. Junior Members Round Table of the ALA, under editorship of Lucile M. Morsch. 1934. New York: Wilson, 1970, x, 430 pp.

Lukenbill, W. Bernard. *A Working Bibliography of American Doctoral Dissertations in Children's and Adolescents' Literature, 1930–1971.* Occasional Papers, no. 103. Champaign: U of Illinois Graduate School of Library Science, 1972, 56 pp.

MacDonald, Ruth. "Proceedings: An Index to the First Five Years." *Children's Literature Association Quarterly* 8. 4 (1983): 46–48.

Meacham, Mary. *Information Sources in Children's Literature: A Practical Reference Guide for Children's Librarians, Elementary School Teachers, and Students of Children's Literature.* Westport: Greenwood, 1978, xvii, 256 pp.

Miller, Bertha E. Mahony, Louise Payson Latimer, and Beulah Folmsbee, comps. *Illustrators of Children's Books, 1744–1945.* Boston: Horn, 1970, xvi, 527 pp.

Monson, Dianne L., and Bette Peltola, comps. *Research in Children's Literature: An Annotated Bibliography.* Newark: International Reading Assn., 1976, 96 pp.

Nakamura, Joyce, ed. *Children's Authors and Illustrators: An Index to Biographical Dictionaries.* 4th ed. Detroit: Gale, 1987, lxvi, 799 pp.

Quimby, Harriet B., and Margaret Mary Kimmel. *Building a Children's Literature Collection: A Suggested Basic Reference Collection for Academic Libraries and a Suggested Basic Collection of Children's Books.* 3rd ed. Middletown: Choice, 1983, iv, 48 pp.

Rahn, Suzanne. *Children's Literature: An Annotated Bibliography of the History and Criticism.* New York: Garland, 1981, xxviii, 451 pp.

Richardson, Selma K. *Magazines for Children: A Guide for Parents, Teachers, and Librarians.* 2nd ed. Chicago: ALA, 1991, xxxv, 139 pp.

——— . *Magazines for Young Adults: Selections for School and Public Libraries.* Chicago: ALA, 1984, xxix, 329 pp.

Roginski, Jim, comp. *Newbery and Caldecott Medalists and Honor Book Winners: Bibliographies and Resource Material through 1977.* Littleton: Libraries Unlimited, 1982, 339 pp.

Rose, Jacqueline. *The Case of Peter Pan; or, The Impossibility of Children's Fiction.* London: Macmillan, 1984, viii, 181 pp.

Rosenblatt, Louise M. *Literature as Exploration.* 4th ed. New York: MLA, 1983, xiv, 304 pp.

Salway, Lance. *A Peculiar Gift: Nineteenth Century Writings on Books for Children*. Harmondsworth, Eng.: Kestrel, 1976, 573 pp.

Shannon, George W. B. *Folk Literature and Children: An Annotated Bibliography of Secondary Materials*. Westport: Greenwood, 1981, xvi, 124 pp.

Sloan, Glenna Davis. *The Child as Critic: Teaching Literature in Elementary and Middle Schools*. 2nd ed. New York: Teachers Coll. P, 1984, xxi, 168 pp.

Viguers, Ruth Hill, Marcia Dalphin, and Bertha Mahony Miller, comps. *Illustrators of Children's Books, 1946–1956*. Boston: Horn, 1972, xvii, 299 pp.

Whitaker, Muriel A., ed. *Children's Literature: A Guide to Criticism*. Edmonton: Athabascan, 1976, 64 pp.

White, Virginia L., and Emerita S. Schulte, comps. *Books about Children's Books: An Annotated Bibliography*. Newark: International Reading Assn., 1979, 48 pp.

Zipes, Jack David. *Breaking the Magic Spell: Radical Theories of Folk and Fairy Tales*. Austin: U of Texas P, 1979, xix, 201 pp.

——— , ed. *Don't Bet on the Prince: Contemporary Feminist Fairy Tales in North America and England*. Aldershot, Eng.: Gower; New York: Methuen, 1986, xiv, 270 pp.

——— . *Fairy Tales and the Art of Subversion: The Classical Genre for Children and the Process of Civilization*. New York. Methuen, 1983, 214 pp.

——— . *Victorian Fairy Tales: The Revolt of the Fairies and Elves*. New York: Routledge, 1989, xxix, 381 pp.

Texts and Anthologies

Butler, Francelia. *Sharing Literature with Children: A Thematic Anthology*. New York: McKay, 1977, 492 pp.

Butler, Francelia, Anne Devereaux Jordan, and Richard Rotert, eds. *The Wide World All Around: An Anthology of Children's Literature*. New York: Longman, 1987, 398 pp.

Carpenter, Humphrey, and Mari Prichard. *The Oxford Companion to Children's Literature*. New York: Oxford UP, 1984, x, 586 pp.

Cott, Jonathan, ed. *Masterworks of Children's Literature*. 8 vols. in 9. New York: Stonehill, 1983–86.

Demers, Patricia, ed. *A Garland from the Golden Age: An Anthology of Children's Literature from 1850 to 1900*. Toronto: Oxford UP, 1983, xiv, 508 pp.

Demers, Patricia, and Gordon Moyles, eds. *From Instruction to Delight: An Anthology of Children's Literature to 1850.* Oxford: Oxford UP, 1982, xii, 310 pp.

Fiction, Folklore, Fantasy, and Poetry for Children, 1876–1985. 2 vols. New York: Bowker, 1986.

Ford, Boris, ed. *Young Writers, Young Readers: An Anthology of Children's Reading and Writing.* Rev. ed. London: Hutchinson, 1963, ix, 173 pp.

Glazer, Joan I., and Gurney Williams. *Introduction to Children's Literature.* New York: McGraw, 1979, xiii, 737 pp.

Griffith, John W., and Charles H. Frey. *Classics of Children's Literature.* 2nd ed. New York: Macmillan, 1987, xx, 1,305 pp.

Haviland, Virginia, and Margaret N. Coughlan. *Yankee Doodle's Literary Sampler of Prose, Poetry, and Pictures: Being an Anthology of Diverse Works Published for the Edification and/or Entertainment of Young Readers in America before 1900.* New York: Crowell, 1974, 466 pp.

Hearn, Michael Patrick, ed. *The Victorian Fairy Tale Book.* New York: Pantheon, 1988, xxvii, 385 pp.

Huck, Charlotte S., Susan Hepler, and Janet Hickman. *Children's Literature in the Elementary School.* 4th ed. New York: Holt, 1987, xii, 753 pp.

Moss, Anita, and Jon C. Stott, eds. *The Family of Stories: An Anthology of Children's Literature.* New York: Holt, 1986, 698 pp.

Norton, Donna E. *Through the Eyes of a Child: An Introduction to Children's Literature.* 3rd ed. New York: Macmillan, 1991, xxiii, 754 pp.

Sadler, Glenn E., ed. *The Gifts of the Child Christ: Fairy Tales and Stories for the Childlike.* By George MacDonald. 2 vols. Grand Rapids: Eerdmans, 1973.

Saltman, Judith. *The Riverside Anthology of Children's Literature.* 6th ed. Boston: Houghton, 1985, xxix, 1,373 pp.

Schwartz, Sheila. *Teaching Adolescent Literature: A Humanistic Approach.* Rochelle Park: Hayden, 1979, 216 pp.

Sutherland, Zena, May Hill Arbuthnot, and Dianne L. Monson. *Children and Books.* 8th ed. New York: HarperCollins, 1991, xv, 768 pp.

Tiedt, Iris M. *Exploring Books with Children.* Boston: Houghton, 1979, xv, 560 pp.

Varlejs, Jana, ed. *Young Adult Literature in the Seventies: A Selection of Readings.* Metuchen: Scarecrow, 1978, ix, 452 pp.

Works of History and Criticism

Adamson, Lynda G. *A Reference Guide to Historical Fiction for Children and Young Adults.* Westport: Greenwood, 1987, xix, 401 pp.

Andrews, Siri, ed. *The Hewins Lectures 1947–1962*. Boston: Horn, 1963, xii, 375 pp.

Antczak, Janice. *Science Fiction: The Mythos of a New Romance*. New York: Neal-Schuman, 1985, xxiii, 233 pp.

Assn. for Library Service to Children, comp. *Arbuthnot Lectures: 1970–79*. Chicago: ALA, 1980, x, 203 pp.

Bader, Barbara. *American Picturebooks from Noah's Ark to the Beast Within*. New York: Macmillan, 1976, 615 pp.

Bamberger, Richard, comp. *Reading and Children's Books· Essays and Papers. A Collection of Reprints*. Vienna: International Inst. for Children's, Juvenile, and Popular Literature, 1971, 108 pp.

Barron, Neil, ed. *Anatomy of Wonder: A Critical Guide to Science Fiction*. 3rd ed. New York: Bowker, 1987, xii, 874 pp.

Barron, Pamela Petrick, and Jennifer Q. Burley, eds. *Jump over the Moon: Selected Professional Readings*. New York: Holt, 1984, xiii, 512 pp.

Bator, Robert. *Signposts to Criticism of Children's Literature*. Chicago: ALA, 1983, xiv, 346 pp.

Behn, Harry. *Chrysalis: Concerning Children and Poetry*. New York: Harcourt, 1968, 92 pp.

Beilke, Patricia F., and Frank J. Sciara. *Selecting Materials for and about Hispanic and East Asian Children and Young People*. Hamden: Library Professional, 1986, xiii, 178 pp.

Bettelheim, Bruno. *The Uses of Enchantment: The Meaning and Importance of Fairy Tales*. New York: Vintage-Random, 1989, 328 pp.

Bingham, Jane, and Grayce Scholt. *Fifteen Centuries of Children's Literature: An Annotated Chronology of British and American Works in Historical Context*. Westport: Greenwood, 1980, l, 540 pp.

Blishen, Edward, ed. *The Thorny Paradise: Writers on Writing for Children*. New York: Horn, 1976, 175 pp.

Blout, Margaret. *Animal Land: The Creatures of Children's Fiction*. New York: Hutchinson, 1974, 336 pp.

Bratton, J. S. *The Impact of Victorian Children's Fiction*. London: Croom Helm; Totowa: Barnes, 1981, 230 pp.

Broderick, Dorothy M. *Images of the Black in Children's Fiction*. New York: Bowker, 1973, viii, 219 pp.

Butler, Francelia, ed. *Skipping around the World: The Ritual Nature of Folk Rhymes*. Foreword Sir Stephen Spender. New York: Ballantine, 1990, xiv, 203 pp.

Butler, Francelia, and Richard Rotert, eds. *Reflections on Literature for Children*. Foreword Leland B. Jacobs. Hamden: Library Professional, 1984, xiv, 281 pp.

Butts, Dennis, ed. *Good Writers for Young Readers.* St. Albans, Eng.: Hart-Davis, 1977, 144 pp.

Cadogan, Mary, and Patricia Craig. *You're a Brick, Angela! The Girls' Story, 1839 to 1985.* London: Gollancz, 1986, 405 pp.

Cameron, Eleanor. *The Green and Burning Tree: On the Writing and Enjoyment of Children's Books.* 2nd ed. Boston: Little, 1985, xiv, 377 pp.

Carlson, Ruth Kearney. *Emerging Humanity: Multiethnic Literature for Children and Adolescents.* Dubuque: Brown, 1972, ix, 246 pp.

Carpenter, Humphrey. *Secret Gardens: A Study of the Golden Age of Children's Literature.* 1985. London: Unwin, 1987, xi, 235 pp.

Carr, Jo, comp. *Beyond Fact: Nonfiction for Children and Young People.* Chicago: ALA, 1982, xi, 224 pp.

Chambers, Nancy, ed. *The Signal Approach to Children's Books.* Harmondsworth, Eng.: Kestrel; Metuchen: Scarecrow, 1980, 352 pp.

Cianciolo, Patricia J. *Picture Books for Children.* 3rd ed. Chicago: ALA, 1990, xiii, 230 pp.

Cook, Elizabeth. *The Ordinary and the Fabulous: An Introduction to Myths, Legends, and Fairy Tales.* 2nd ed. Cambridge: Cambridge UP, 1978, xx, 182 pp.

Cott, Jonathan. *Pipers at the Gates of Dawn: The Wisdom of Children's Literature.* New York: McGraw, 1983, xiii, 327 pp.

Crouch, Marcus. *The Nesbit Tradition: The Children's Novel in England 1945–1970.* London: Benn, 1972, 239 pp.

Culpan, Norman, and Clifford Waite, eds. *Variety Is King: Aspects of Fiction for Children.* Oxford: School Library Assn., 1977, vii, 173 pp.

Darton, F. J. Harvey. *Children's Books in England: Five Centuries of Social Life.* Rev. Brian Alderson. 3rd ed. Cambridge: Cambridge UP, 1982, xviii, 398 pp.

Dixon, Bob. *Catching Them Young: Sex, Race, and Class in Children's Fiction.* 2 vols. London: Pluto, 1977.

Donelson, Kenneth, and Alleen Pace Nilsen. *Literature for Today's Young Adults.* 3rd ed. Glenview: Scott, 1989, 620 pp.

Dooley, Patricia, ed. and comp. *The First Steps: Articles and Columns from the ChLA Newsletter/Quarterly, Volume I–VI.* Lafayette: Children's Literature Assn., 1984, 148 pp.

Egoff, Sheila, ed. *One Ocean Touching: Papers from the First Pacific Rim Conference on Literature.* Metuchen: Scarecrow, 1979, viii, 252 pp.

———. *The Republic of Childhood: A Critical Guide to Canadian Children's Literature in English.* 2nd ed. Toronto: Oxford UP, 1975, vii, 335 pp.

———. *Thursday's Child: Trends and Patterns in Contemporary Children's Literature.* Chicago: ALA, 1981, xv, 323 pp.

Egoff, Sheila, G. T. Stubbs, and L. F. Ashley, eds. *Only Connect: Readings on Children's Literature.* 2nd ed. Toronto: Oxford UP, 1980, xix, 457 pp.

Escarpit, Denise, ed. *The Portrayal of the Child in Children's Literature: Proceedings of the Sixth Conference of the International Research Society for Children's Literature.* University of Gascony, Bordeaux, France, Sept. 1983. New York: Saur, 1985, xii, 392 pp.

Esmonde, Margaret P., and Priscilla Ord, eds. *Proceedings of the Fifth Annual conference of the ChLA.* Villanova: Villanova UP, 1979, 122 pp.

Favat, F. André. *Child and Tale: The Origin of Interest.* Urbana: NCTE, 1977, x, 102 pp.

Feaver, William. *When We Were Young: Two Centuries of Children's Book Illustration.* New York: Holt, 1977, 96 pp.

Feminists on Children's Media. *Little Miss Muffet Fights Back.* Rev. ed. Flushing: Feminist Book, 1974, 62 pp.

Fenwick, Sara Innis, ed. *A Critical Approach to Children's Literature: The Thirty-First Annual Conference of the Graduate Library School, August 1–3, 1966.* Chicago: U of Chicago P, 1967, v, 129 pp. Rpt. in *Library Quarterly* 37 (1967): 1–130.

Field, Carolyn W., and Jaqueline Shachter Weiss. *Values in Selected Children's Books of Fiction and Fantasy.* Hamden: Library Professional, 1987, ix, 298 pp.

Fisher, Margery Turner. *Matters of Fact: Aspects of Non-fiction for Children.* New York: Crowell, 1972, 488 pp.

Fox, Geoff, et al., eds. *Writers, Critics, and Children: Articles from Children's Literature in Education.* New York: Agathon; London: Heinemann, 1976, ix, 245 pp.

Fox, Geoff, and Graham Hammond, eds. *Responses to Children's Literature: Proceedings of the Fourth Symposium of the International Research Society for Children's Literature.* New York: Saur, 1983, vii, 141 pp.

Fryatt, Norma R., ed. *A Horn Book Sampler: On Children's Books and Readings, Selected from Twenty-five Years of the* Horn Book *Magazine, 1924–1948.* Boston: Horn, 1959, 261 pp.

Gerhardt, Lillian, ed. *Issues in Children's Book Selection.* New York: Bowker, 1973, x, 216 pp.

Gersoni-Edelman, Diane, ed. *Sexism and Youth.* New York: Bowker, 1974, xxviii, 468 pp.

Grambs, Jean D., et al., eds. *Black Image: Education Copes with Color.* Dubuque: Brown, 1972, x, 196 pp.

Haviland, Virginia, comp. *Children and Literature: Views and Reviews.* London: Bodley; Glenview: Scott, 1974, 468 pp.

Hazard, Paul. *Books, Children, and Men.* Trans. Marguerite Mitchell. 5th ed. Boston: Horn, 1983, xi, 196 pp.

Hearne, Betsy, and Marilyn Kaye, eds. *Celebrating Children's Books: Essays on Children's Literature in Honor of Zena Sutherland.* New York: Lothrop, 1981, 244 pp.

Heins, Paul, ed. *Crosscurrents of Criticism:* Horn Book *Essays, 1968–1977.* Boston: Horn, 1977, xiii, 359 pp.

Higgins, James E. *Beyond Words: Mystical Fancy in Children's Literature.* New York: Teachers Coll. P, 1970, 112 pp.

Hoffman, Miriam, and Eva Samuels, comps. *Authors and Illustrators of Children's Books: Writings on Their Lives and Works.* New York: Bowker, 1972, xi, 471 pp.

Hunt, Peter, ed. *Further Approaches to Research in Children's Literature: Proceedings of the Second British Research Seminar in Children's Literature, Cardiff, September, 1981.* Cardiff: U of Wales, Inst. of Science and Technology, Dept. of English, 1982, 129 pp.

Hunter, Mollie. *Talent Is Not Enough: Mollie Hunter on Writing for Children.* Introd. Paul Heins. New York: Harper, 1975, 126 pp.

Hürlimann, Bettina. *Three Centuries of Children's Books in Europe.* Trans. and ed. Brian Alderson. Cleveland: World, 1968, xviii, 297 pp.

Inglis, Fred. *The Promise of Happiness: Value and Meaning in Children's Fiction.* Cambridge: Cambridge UP, 1981, xiv, 333 pp.

Jan, Isabelle. *On Children's Literature.* Trans. and ed. Catherine Storr. Pref. Anne Pellowski. New York: Schocken, 1974, 189 pp.

Jones, Cornelia, and Oliver R. Way. *British Children's Authors: Interviews at Home.* Chicago: ALA, 1976, viii, 176 pp.

Kingston, Carolyn T. *The Tragic Mode in Children's Literature.* New York: Teachers Coll. P, 1974, vi, 177 pp.

Koefoed, Ingerlise, ed. *Children's Literature and the Child: Lectures and Debates.* International Course on Children's Literature, Loughborough Summer School 1972, Hindsgavl, Denmark. Copenhagen: Danish Library Assn.–Scandinavian Library Center, 1975, 70 pp.

Lanes, Selma G. *Down the Rabbit Hole: Adventures and Misadventures in the Realm of Children's Literature.* New York: Atheneum, 1976, xiii, 241 pp.

Lenz, Millicent, and Ramona M. Mahood, comps. *Young Adult Literature: Background and Criticism.* Chicago: ALA, 1980, viii, 516 pp.

Lukens, Rebecca J. *A Critical Handbook of Children's Literature.* 4th ed. Glenview: Scott, 1990, 309 pp.

Lüthi, Max. *Once upon a Time: On the Nature of Fairy Tales.* Trans. Lee Chadeayne and Paul Gottwald. Rev. ed. Bloomington: Indiana UP, 1976, 179 pp.

MacCann, Donnarae, and Olga Richard. *The Child's First Books: A Critical Study of Pictures and Texts.* New York: Wilson, 1973, 135 pp.

MacCann, Donnarae, and Gloria Woodard, eds. *The Black American in Books for Children: Readings in Racism.* 2nd ed. Metuchen: Scarecrow, 1985, ix, 298 pp.

MacLeod, Anne S., ed. *Children's Literature: Selected Essays and Bibliographies.* Student Contribution Series 9. College Park: U of Maryland, Coll. of Library and Information Services, 1977, iii, 153 pp.

McVitty, Walter. *Innocence and Experience: Essays on Contemporary Australian Children's Writers.* Melbourne: Nelson, 1981, 277 pp.

Mason, Bobbie Ann. *The Girl Sleuth: A Feminist Guide.* Old Westbury: Feminist, 1975, xi, 144 pp.

May, Jill P., ed. *Children and Their Literature: A Readings Book.* West Lafayette: Children's Literature Assn., 1983, 179 pp.

Meek, Margaret, Aidan Warlow, and Griselda Barton, eds. *The Cool Web: The Pattern of Children's Reading.* New York: Atheneum, 1978, 427 pp.

Meigs, Cornelia, et al. *A Critical History of Children's Literature: A Survey of Children's Books in English.* Rev. ed. New York: Macmillan, 1969, xxviii, 708 pp.

Muir, Percy. *English Children's Books, 1600 to 1900.* 1954. London: Batsford, 1985, ix, 263 pp.

Nodelman, Perry, and Jill P. May, eds. *Festschrift: A Ten-Year Retrospective.* West Lafayette. Children's Literature Assn., 1983, 79 pp.

Norton, Eloise S., ed. *Folk Literature of the British Isles: Readings for Librarians, Teachers, and Those Who Work with Children and Young Adults.* Metuchen: Scarecrow, 1978, 263 pp.

Pellowski, Anne. *Made to Measure: Children's Books in Developing Countries.* Paris: UNESCO, 1980, 129 pp.

——— . *The World of Children's Literature.* New York: Bowker, 1968, x, 538 pp.

——— . *The World of Storytelling.* Rev. ed. New York: Wilson, 1990, xxi, 311 pp.

Prager, Arthur. *Rascals at Large; or, The Clue in the Old Nostalgia.* Garden City: Doubleday, 1971, 334 pp.

Rees, David. *Marble in the Water: Essays on Contemporary Writers of Fiction for Children and Young Adults.* Boston: Horn, 1980, xi, 211 pp.

Robinson, Evelyn R., ed. *Readings about Children's Literature.* New York: McKay, 1966, xiii, 431 pp.

Robinson, Moira, ed. *Readings in Children's Literature: Proceedings of the National Seminar on Children's Literature.* Frankston, Victoria, Austral.: Frankston State Coll., 1977, 291 pp.

Rudman, Masha K. *Children's Literature: An Issues Approach.* 2nd ed. Lexington: Wilson, 1984, xvi, 476 pp.

Sale, Roger. *Fairy Tales and After: From Snow White to E. B. White*. Cambridge: Harvard UP, 1978, 280 pp.

Sayers, Frances Clarke. *Summoned by Books: Essays and Speeches*. Comp. Marjeanne Jensen Blinn. Foreword Lawrence Clark Powell. New York: Viking, 1965, 173 pp.

Schmidt, Nancy J. *Children's Fiction about Africa in English*. New York: Conch, 1981, iv, 248 pp.

Schwarcz, Joseph H. *Ways of the Illustrator: Visual Communication in Children's Literature*. Chicago: ALA, 1982, x, 202 pp.

Smith, Elva S. *Elva S. Smith's "The History of Children's Literature: A Syllabus with Selected Bibliographies."* Rev. and enl. by Margaret Hodges and Susan Steinfirst. Chicago: ALA, 1980, xiii, 290 pp.

Smith, James S. *A Critical Approach to Children's Literature*. New York: McGraw, 1967, ix, 442 pp.

Smith, Lillian H. *The Unreluctant Years: A Critical Approach to Children's Literature*. New York: Penguin, 1976, 193 pp.

Thwaite, Mary F. *From Primer to Pleasure in Reading: An Introduction to the History of Children's Books in England from the Invention of Printing to 1914, with an Outline of Some Developments in Other Countries*. Boston: Horn, 1972, x, 340 pp.

Townsend, John Rowe. *A Sense of Story: Essays on Contemporary Writers for Children*. London: Longman, 1971, 216 pp.

—————. *Written for Children: An Outline of English-Language Children's Literature*. 3rd rev. ed. New York: Lippincott, 1987, xii, 364 pp.

Tucker, Nicholas. *The Child and the Book: A Psychological and Literary Exploration*. New York: Cambridge UP, 1990, ix, 259 pp.

—————, ed. *Suitable for Children? Controversies in Children's Literature*. Berkeley: U of California P, 1976, 224 pp.

Vandergrift, Kay E. *Child and Story: The Literary Connection*. 1980. New York: Neal-Schuman, 1986, xix, 340 pp.

Vries, Leonard de, ed. *Flowers of Delight: An Agreeable Garland of Prose and Poetry for the Instruction and Amusement of Little Masters and Misses and Their Distinguished Parents*. New York: Pantheon, 1965, 232 pp.

Whalley, Joyce I. *Cobwebs to Catch Flies: Illustrated Books for the Nursery and Schoolroom, 1700–1900*. Berkeley: U of California P, 1975, 163 pp.

White, Mary Lou, ed. *Children's Literature: Criticism and Response*. Columbus: Merrill, 1976, xi, 252 pp.

Wintle, Justin, and Emma Fisher. *The Pied Pipers: Interviews with the Influential Creators of Children's Literature*. New York: Paddington, 1975, 320 pp.

Yolen, Jane. *Touch Magic: Fantasy, Faerie, and Folklore in the Literature of Childhood*. New York: Philomel, 1981, 96 pp.

Periodicals and Annuals

Advocate, 1981–.

ALAN Review, 1973–.

Bookbird: Literature for Children and Young People, Problems of Juvenile Reading, Best Books from All over the World, 1963–.

Booklist, 1905–.

Bulletin of the Center for Children's Books, 1947–.

Canadian Children's Literature/Littérature canadienne pour la jeunesse, 1975–.

Children's Books in Print, 1969–.

Children's Literature, 1972–.

Children's Literature Abstracts, 1973–.

Children's Literature Assembly of NCTE Bulletin, 1975–.

Children's Literature Association Quarterly, 1976–.

Children's Literature in Education, 1969–.

Children's Literature Review: Excerpts from Reviews, Criticism, and Commentary on Books for Children and Young People, 1976–.

English in Education, 1966–.

English Journal, 1912–.

Horn Book, 1924–.

International Review of Children's Literature and Librarianship, 1986–.

Interracial Books for Children Bulletin, 1966–.

Journal of Popular Culture, 1967–.

Journal of Youth Services in Libraries [formerly *Top of the News*], 1987–.

Junior Bookshelf, 1936–.

Kirkus Review, 1933–.

Language Arts, 1924–.

Library Literature, 1933–.

Lion and the Unicorn, 1977–.

London Review of Books, 1979–.

New York Times Book Review, 1896–.

Orana: Journal for School and Children's Librarianship, 1976–.

Paedrus: An International Annual of Children's Literature Research, 1973–, 1988.

Publisher's Weekly, 1872–.
Reading Teacher, 1947–.
School Librarian, 1937–.
School Library Journal, 1954–.
Signal: Approaches to Children's Books, 1970–.
Subject Guide to Children's Books in Print, 1969–.
Top of the News, 1942–87.
Touchstones: Reflections on the Best in Children's Literature, 1985–.
Use of English, 1951–.
Voice of Youth Advocates, 1978–.
Wilson Library Bulletin, 1914–.

Special Collections

Entries are in alphabetical order by state or province.

Bancroft Library
Univ. of California at Berkeley
Berkeley, CA 94720

Department of Special
    Collections
Univ. Research Library
Univ. of California at Los
    Angeles
Los Angeles, CA 90024

Dorothy Daniels Collection
Riverside City and County
    Public Library
Civic Center
San Francisco, CA 94102

Henry E. Huntington Library
1151 Oxford Rd.
San Marino, CA 91108

Los Angeles Public Library
630 W. Fifth St.
Los Angeles, CA 90071

Mary Schofield Collection
Cecil H. Green Library
Stanford Univ.
Stanford, CA 94305

Carolyn Sherwin Bailey
    Historical Collection
    of Children's Books
Buley Library
Southern Connecticut State Univ.
501 Crescent St.
New Haven, CT 06515

Library of Congress
First and Independence, S.E.
Washington, DC 20540

Balwin Collection
Balwin Library
Univ. of Florida
210 Library W.
Gainesville, FL 32611

John M. Shaw Collection
Robert Manning Strozier Library
Florida State Univ.
Tallahassee, FL 32306

Idaho State Library
325 W. State St.
Boise, ID 83702

Center for Research Libraries
6050 S. Kenwood Ave.
Chicago, IL 60637

Regenstein Library
Univ. of Chicago
1100 E. 57th St.
Chicago, IL 60637

Lilly Library
Indiana Univ.
Seventh St.
Bloomington, IN 47401

May Massee Collection
William Allen White Library
Emporia State Univ.
Emporia, KS 66801

Enoch Pratt Free Library
400 Cathedral St.
Baltimore, MD 21201

Alice M. Jordan Collection
Research Library
Boston Public Library
Copley Square
Boston, MA 02117

American Antiquarian Society
185 Salisbury St.
Worcester, MA 01609

Boston Athenaeum
10 1/2 Beacon Street
Boston, MA 02108

Essex Institute
132 Essex St.
Salem, MA 01970

Houghton Library
Harvard Univ.
Cambridge, MA 02138

Knapp Collection
Simmons College
300 The Fenway
Boston, MA 02115

Detroit Public Library
5201 Woodward Ave.
Detroit, MI 48202

Kerlan Collection
Walter Library
Univ. of Minnesota Libraries
Minneapolis, MN 55455

De Grummond Collection
William David McCain
    Graduate Library
Univ. of Southern Mississippi
Southern Stat., Box 5148
Hattiesburg, MS 39406

University Art Gallery
Rutgers Univ.
205 Voorhees Hall
Hamilton St.
New Brunswick, NJ 08903

Brooklyn Public Library
Grand Army Plaza
Brooklyn, NY 11238

Donnell Library Center
New York Public Library
20 W. 53rd St.
New York, NY 10019

Harvey Darton Collection
Columbia Univ. Libraries
Columbia Univ.
New York, NY 10027

New York State Historical
    Association Library
Lake Road, POB 800
Cooperstown, NY 13326

Pierpont Morgan Library
29 E. 36th Street
New York, NY 10016

Walter Clinton Jackson Library
Univ. of North Carolina
Greensboro, NC 27412

Edgar W. and Faith King
    Juvenile Collection
King Library
Miami Univ.
Oxford, OH 45056

Kent State University
    Libraries
Kent, OH 44242

Treasure Room Collection of
    Early Children's Books
Cleveland Public Library
325 Superior Ave.
Cleveland, OH 44114

University of Oregon
Library
Eugene, OR 97403

Elizabeth Nesbitt Room
School of Library and
Information Sciences
Univ. of Pittsburgh
Pittsburgh, PA 15260

Rosenbach Collection
Free Library of Philadelphia
Logan Square
Philadelphia, PA 19103

Sendak Collection
Rosenback Museum and Library
2010 Delancey Pl.
Philadelphia, PA 19103

Edith Wemore Collection of
Children's Books
Providence Public Library
150 Empire St.
Providence, RI 02903

Dallas Public Library
1515 Young St.
Dallas, TX 75201

Humanities Research Center
Univ. of Texas at Austin
Harry Ransom Center 2114
Austin, TX 78713

Historical Children's Literature
Collection
Suzzallo Library
Univ. of Washington
Seattle, WA 98195

Cooperative Children's Book
Center
600 North Park St.
Madison, WI 53706

Canada

Rose and Stanley Arkley
Collection of Early and
Historical Children's Books
Univ. of British Columbia
2075 Wesbrook Pl.
Vancouver, BC V6T 1W5

Osborne Collection
Boys and Girls House
Toronto Public Library
40 Saint George St.
Toronto, ON M5S 2E4

United Kingdom

Bodleian Library
Oxford Univ.
Oxford OX1 3BG

Organizations Sponsoring Children's Literature

Associations for Library Service
    to Children
American Library Assn.
50 E. Huron St.
Chicago, IL 60611

Children's Literature
    Association
210 Education Dept.
Purdue Univ.
West Lafayette, IN 47907

Council on Interracial Books for
    Children
1841 Broadway, Rm 500
New York, NY 10023

International Reading
    Association
800 Barksdale Rd.
Box 8139
Newark, DE 19714

Modern Language Association
10 Astor Pl.
New York, NY 10003

National Council of Teachers of
    English
1111 Kenyon Rd.
Urbana, IL 61801

Teachers of Children's Literature
    Discussion Group
Assn. for Library Service to
    Children
American Library Assn.
50 E. Huron St.
Chicago, IL 60611

AFTERWORD

A Conversation with Maurice Sendak and Dr. Seuss

Glenn Edward Sadler

> *If a child doesn't like a book, throw it away. Children don't give a damn about awards; why should they? We should let children choose their own books. What they don't like, they will toss aside. What disturbs them too much, they will not look at; and if they look at the wrong book, it isn't going to do them that much damage. We treat children in a very peculiar way, I think; we don't treat them like the strong creatures they really are.*
> *—Maurice Sendak*

> *Children are tough critics. You can't kid kids. They have a relentless sense of logic. If you create a character who is supposed to be stingy, say, and you suddenly make him do something that indicates some other dominant characteristic, jealousy perhaps, or a violent temper, the kids know instantly that you're violating the law of simplicity and consistency. They also know if you begin to condescend or write down to them. That's been the trouble with children's books and elementary textbooks for years—this "now my little man" approach. The kids don't like it; why should they? The old tellers of fantastic fairy tales, Grimm and Andersen, never talked down to their audience.*
> *—Dr. Seuss*

Maurice Sendak and Dr. Seuss share a respect for the integrity of the child and the child reader. Of all the comments made at the public interview at the San Diego Museum of Art in Balboa Park, in 1982, this was the most significant fact that repeatedly emerged. Although differing in style, Sendak and Geisel share more than talent. Each believes in the intelligence of children, that one cannot talk down to an audience. "Children are tough critics. You can't kid kids," Geisel affirms.

To hear these "two lions" (as one reviewer designated them) of children's literature together in a public interview is something I had long dreamed of happening. It all began with a visit to Sendak's art studio in New York City in 1970 (the year *In the Night Kitchen* was published). I recall dashing down with him to a local deli to get a sandwich as we exchanged quips on what some librarians would think when they saw the nudity of Mickey, whose name came from Mickey Mouse. I had come to talk with him about George MacDonald (the subject of my doctoral dissertation) and was fully prepared to flood him with questions: Why had MacDonald's stories had such an influence on him? And what was the connection between his great admiration for Mickey Mouse and MacDonald (a question to which I would still like to get an answer)? Through the years our friendship grew as we talked of the condescending attitude some academics and critics have toward writers for children.

It was while teaching at the University of California, San Diego, that I decided to try to get Sendak and Seuss together. I had suggested the meeting to Sendak, and he agreed. Getting to see Ted Geisel was another matter. For years he had remained a recluse in his La Jolla tower-parapet home overlooking the Pacific Ocean. The day I visited him he was doing a possible sequel to *The Cat in the Hat*, the publication of which, in 1957, was a turning point in his career as "Dr. Seuss." We talked about the neighbors who were building a structure that would obscure his view and how he was wishing for its demise. On a subsequent visit, after the interview took place, we talked of my plans possibly to leave San Diego and take a position in Bloomsburg. Geisel recalled visiting Wilkes-Barre many years ago, and we discussed how the town, whose name amused him, was founded. It was on my first visit, in 1981, however, that I approached Geisel with the idea of meeting Sendak in a public question-answer interview. To my delight and surprise, he agreed.

There were, of course, all the arrangements that followed: getting adequate funding and space for the interview and deciding when and how the event should take place. It was decided between the San Diego Museum of Art and the Programs for Extended Studies at the University of California, San Diego, that it should be a jointly sponsored event. The university would offer one unit credit and charge a fee, and the museum would have an exhibit of Sendak's art; Seuss's work would be on display in the library at the university.

It is difficult now to recall all the problems that kept jumping out of the hat, but I do remember the tremendous excitement and anticipation that mounted as the date for the event neared. Calls came from all the major newspapers, which gave the event front page coverage, and there was an endless stream of fans, all wanting a personal interview and their books autographed. (I did manage to arrange a private lunch for Sendak and Seuss).

Finally, the evening of Wednesday, 8 December 1982, arrived.

There was a sellout crowd of over five hundred at the Copley Auditorium of the San Diego Museum of Art. Sendak and Seuss, wired for sound, sat on the brightly lit stage: My decades-old dream of seeing these two men sitting together in a public exchange was to become a reality.

From the beginning, the interview was lighthearted, filled with laughter and repartees. The audience wrote questions that were given to two question-readers at either side of the auditorium. As coordinator, I repeated the questions asked alternately by the monitors. There were thirty-five selected questions in all.

Although the edited (by Sendak and Seuss) selection of questions here printed is representative, it is not inclusive. Many amusing comments are missing. One I recall—here omitted—was made by Sendak as he told of an autographing experience. Commenting on the parents' egocentricity in wanting to have their child's book autographed, Sendak noted that it is the parents' "presumption that children *like* to have their books autographed." Turning to Geisel, Sendak continued: "How many times has this happened to you, when you get a whole line of fatigued children who have been waiting for what? To come and see this nasty old man—what has he got to do with the pleasure they get out of books? The one extraordinary circumstance (I recall) was a little boy who had waited a very long time, was enraged, and here is his mother carrying on about this being the man that wrote your *favorite book*. He couldn't care less. He couldn't even make the association. The boy loved the book, but who was I? And then the book was handed to me. I began to autograph it. Suddenly the boy grabs the book, pulls it back, and screams: 'Don't crap up my book!' He probably had been taught at home never to write in a book, and here he is publicly taken to a place by his mother where a total stranger is trying to write in *his* book."

Dr. Seuss recalled, "The greatest autographing experience I ever had was in Detroit, in one of the Northlands, were one afternoon, two thousand mothers dragged two thousand children in for autographing. I got pretty conceited by the end of the day: I thought, look at all the people I'm dragging in. The next day I went to Boston, and only one child showed up, and he was looking for the toilet."

It was indeed an evening of jovial exchange. The audience applauded heartily as these men relived events from their own childhood and adolescence, which are celebrated in their books. Candidly, the unspoken laws of writing for children and young adults were expressed.

Law number 1: Try to find some way to outwit the adults in the story. For example, Max (*Where the Wild Things Are*) must go to bed without his supper and accept his punishment. But this does not mean that he cannot dream himself away from Adultland to the place where the Wild Things live: he can and does escape adult authority. Or take, for example, the young hero in Seuss's *I Am Not Going to Get Up Today!* who defies all the pleasurable incitements of the child and the adult world and who proves conclusively in the end that the child can win ("I guess he really means it").

Law number 2: Always keep the child reader guessing as to the outcome of the story. Finding the "hook" (Seuss's word) at the end of each page is, he claims, the secret. "Keep the child turning the pages," he insists. In discussing his famous beginner book *The Cat in the Hat*, Seuss explains, "The story has to develop clearly and logically with a valid problem and a valid solution. The characters, no matter how weird, have to be vivid and believable and consistent."

Law number 3: Never explain away the fantastic parts of the story. Perhaps Sendak's and Seuss's greatest legacy in literature for children— as indicated by the comments made during the interview—is their honest approach to what it means to be a child or an adolescent. One does not find in their stories and illustrations the modern trend toward "glitzy" (Sendak's word) illustrations that merely decorate the page. The fantastic in their stories remains the driving force that penetrates commonplace experiences. Commenting on his seventy-eighth Christmas, Dr. Seuss notes, with a chortle, "I hope Dick and Jane have a very sparse Christmas, and the Grinch steals all their toys." Seuss is proudest of the fact "that I had something to do with getting rid of Dick and Jane."

Of all the statements made during the interview, I think the most significant was Sendak's insistence on the influence of his own childhood on his work and, in contrast, Seuss's claim that his adolescence, not his childhood, affected him most. It is a difference of viewpoint that an adult senses when reading both writers' books. There is, especially in Sendak's illustrations, the subconscious feeling that the author is exploring, perhaps even at times exploiting, the dark fears and frustrations of childhood (the fear of the dark and nighttime is one of Sendak's favorites). As he often has remarked, Sendak *knows* what it is like to be a child because he has been one and has never forgotten the feelings of his own childhood. As in the work of Hans Christian Andersen, such an awareness of the dark side of childhood emotions is at the heart of Sendak's genius.

In sharp contrast is Ted Geisel's rejuvenating understanding of the adolescent mind. It is as if, in a Dr. Seuss story, the young adult or the child reader has just met a secret buddy with whom he or she can play. More than wacky characters, convoluted logic, or even silly vocabulary, for the teen reader there is the refuge of words in Seuss's books. One discovers the teenage game of developing an in-language that leaves the adults totally out of the picture. Such comradeship between reader and author through the security of words is Dr. Seuss's greatest achievement.

There probably never again will be two geniuses like Maurice Sendak and Dr. Seuss. Coming from different worlds and points in time (Sendak is now 63 and Seuss is 81), they nevertheless share a high regard for readers of all ages, although their modes of writing are quite different. "None of my books," says Maurice Sendak, "come about through ideas or by thinking of a particular subject and claiming, 'Gee, that's terrific. I'll just put it down.' They never happen quite that way. They well up just as dreams come to us at night; feelings come to me; so I build a kind of house around them, the story; and the painting of the house is the picture making. Essentially, however, it's a dream or fantasy."

For Ted Geisel, creating a story is quite a different matter. "Now some writers, I am told," replies Seuss, "really do dream their stories. They just crawl into bed, they say, and along about four o'clock in the morning, a story idea comes floating into their heads. Then all they have to do when they wake up is write it down, but I never had any luck with my dreams."

Whether or not writing a children's story is a process of creative dreaming, Sendak and Seuss would agree that to enter the dream world of the child or young adult reader is essential. I recall vividly Sendak pointing this out to me after the interview, as we walked along the midnight crashing surf of Point Loma, San Diego, while the fairytale-like lights of La Jolla peninsula twinkled in the distance. We talked of many things. But I will never forget Sendak saying that writing or illustrating a children's book (or any book) is like giving the reader the present of, in Hans Christian Andersen's words, "the whole world—and a pair of skates." Maurice Sendak and Dr. Seuss have done just that.

Interviewer: How do you get your ideas for books?

Seuss: This is the most asked question of any successful author. Most authors will not disclose their source for fear that other, less successful authors will chisel in on their territory. However, I am willing to take a chance. I get all my ideas in Switzerland near the Forka Pass. There is a little town called Gletch, and two thousand feet up above Gletch there is a smaller hamlet called Uber Gletch. I go there on the fourth of August every summer to get my cuckoo clock repaired. While the cuckoo is in the hospital, I wander around and talk to the people in the streets. They are very strange people, and I get my ideas from them.

Interviewer: Mr. Sendak, I know a four-year-old who is afraid of your books. Should she be encouraged to work through those feelings and read the books aloud with us?

Sendak: I think you should leave her alone. I mean there's absolutely no reason why, if the child is frightened, that you would frighten the child still further by trying to make her read the book. Obviously this is a child with a problem. But taking that into consideration, I would not torment the child.

Interviewer: Mr. Sendak, were you Pierre as a child?

Sendak: No, I was never Pierre at any point in my life. Perhaps I harbored his thoughts, but I would not have dared speak to my parents in such a way. That's why I wrote the book.

Interviewer: Dr. Seuss, how do you handle the nonsense words in translation?

Seuss: The books have been translated into about fifteen foreign languages. I have no idea how they handled it in the Japanese. Oddly enough, the Germanic and Nordic languages—German, Norwegian, Swedish, Danish—are much more successful for translating the nonsense words than the Romance languages are. Why that is, I don't know. The Germans will take a name like Bartholomew Cubbins and turn it into Bartel Lugepros, which I think is a very beautiful approximation.

Interviewer: Mr. Sendak, when you illustrate books for other authors, do you become closely involved with them? Whom do you admire most, and how have they influenced your work?

Sendak: Well, I've worked with many, many writers. A good many of them don't want to be involved in the illustration process. They have written the book; the illustrator gets it; and that's the end of the relationship. That is, of course, the least interesting way to work. But I've had some half dozen or so writers—such as Randall Jarrell, Ruth Krauss, and Isaac Singer—who were intensely involved with the business of illustrating the book. The work is much better for that involvement. There's the joy of collaboration. One would assume that the writer would want to be involved because, after all, it is primarily his book. I'm just there to adorn and decorate.

Interviewer: How would you motivate the child who does not like to read?

Seuss: That is the job of the mother, I think. The motivation of the child is not Maurice's or my responsibility. It falls to the school and the parents. All we can do is create books and hope that someone steers them into children's hands.

Sendak: I think Ted is right. We're often confused with being sociologists and psychologists and teachers and parents. We're not. Primarily we are artists. We cannot urge children to read books. I don't know how one goes about doing that.

Interviewer: Mr. Sendak, do you ever draw for your own diversions? What do you like to draw?

Sendak: Occasionally portraits of friends, which I never show except to the people who posed. Mostly I draw to music as an imagination exercise. I put some favorite piece on the record player. I start with my hand at the top of the paper, and the whole point of the exercise is to finish that page by the end of the first movement. Needless to say, you get very few good drawings. It is a kind of pleasure drawing I do for myself for the most part.

Interviewer: Have the responses of critics made it easier or more difficult for you to accomplish the task of achieving your goals?

Sendak: It's made no difference whatsoever, alas. It just causes irritation and migraine. If one could learn something from criticism, it would be a marvelous thing. Reading criticism has been a grave disappointment in terms of what one doesn't learn. The process is hurtful for the most part, and in a sense the good reviews are no better than the bad because they don't tell you anything.

Seuss: I think about the only positive thing is that a good review sells more books than a bad review.

Sendak: It makes you more cheerful that morning.

Seuss: It wakes you up.

Sendak: Your friends, who are waiting for you to get the bad review, don't call you up to commiserate with you.

Seuss: And you always agree with the good reviews.

Sendak: You always agree with them. That person has hope for a long life.

Interviewer: Do you think there will still be a place for the traditional fairy tale in twenty years?

Seuss: I would like to see it come back, but I don't think the average child is going to fall for it. No, I miss it, don't you?

Sendak: Well, there's almost not a place right now for the old-fashioned fairy tale or fantasy. It's hard to imagine where children's literature is going; it's gotten so slippery and glitzy at this point. One almost feels that children's books are going to slide off the face of the earth. The old-fashioned fairy tale at this point, I think, has already slid off. It is not considered seriously. It's already out of date, and most fairy tales, when they are done, are watered down considerably. So we are not getting the real thing.

Interviewer: Do your characters live with you all the time?

Sendak: Well, I hope not. I think we would all be in the madhouse at this point. Is that true for you?

Seuss: Yes, that's so.

Sendak: We rid ourselves of these characters by writing them out of our lives.

Seuss: Yes, we expunge them.

Sendak: Then new horrors keep springing up all the time. If I ran into these people in my social life, I would flee. I think we are always being chased by these people, and we keep creating books to get rid of them.

Seuss: If I were invited to a dinner party with my characters, I wouldn't show up.

Interviewer: Would you comment on the effect of the media on children today?

Sendak: Well, it always aggravates me when people get colossally worked up about certain things in my books that supposedly will upset children or upset librarians or parents or teachers. But there seem to be no restrictions on what children can watch on television. Children see massacres continuously on the news—how do you control that? Books are quite controllable. The media is totally uncontrollable and vastly disgusting for the most part, and children are watching it all the time. I wonder how anybody's going to solve that problem. To make a great fuss over an odd word in a Dr. Seuss book or a naked child in a Sendak book seems so fatuously simple-minded in relation to television, where children are being poisoned.

Interviewer: Mr. Sendak, do you have a preference for writing or illustrating?

Sendak: I have a preference for writing. Writing is very difficult and gives me a great deal of pleasure, partly because it is so difficult. Illustrating is very automatic. I have a Polaroid kind of brain. I have to stem the tide of pictures. I don't get those writing images quickly; I have to struggle for them. So naturally I like writing better. When I do achieve something, it feels more victorious. I know I'm going to get illustrations if I just hang in long enough, and that's less challenging at this point in my life.

Interviewer: Dr. Seuss, was your first book, *And to Think That I Saw It on Mulberry Street*, rejected by many publishers before it was accepted?

Seuss: Twenty-seven or twenty-nine, I forget which. The excuse I got for all those rejections was that there was nothing on the market quite like it, so they didn't know whether it would sell.

Sendak: Publishers are always nervous about original work. They are worried about financial aspects, which corrupt their consideration of a new work. When *Wild Things* came out, there was a concern about the effect of this book on the public. It was a natural nervousness about publishing an odd book.

Interviewer: Would each of you comment on how much your own early childhood has influenced your work?

Seuss: Not to a very great extent. I think my aberrations started when I got out of early childhood. My father, however, in my early childhood, did, among other things, run a zoo, and I used to play with the baby lions and the antelope and a few other things of that sort. Generally speaking, I don't think my childhood influenced my work. But I know Maurice's did.

Sendak: I have profited mightily from my early childhood.

Seuss: I think I skipped my childhood.

Sendak: I skipped my adolescence. Total amnesia.

Seuss: Well, I used my adolescence.

Sendak: Isn't that interesting, because you get your inspiration from young manhood, and I go all the way back to the crib days for mine.

Interviewer: Mr. Sendak, how did your parents feel when you told them you wanted to be a book illustrator?

Sendak: They were relieved. They had no idea that I could do anything. I did so badly in school. I had a very brilliant sister who skipped grades. I hated her. I had a brother who was dutiful and serious, so I hated him, too. But I could draw, which seemed to be my salvation. In fact, when I could earn a living from that, my father was tearfully content.

Interviewer: Do your ideas for books spring forth from free drawing you might be doing, and do you have a direction for your books?

Sendak: There is a vague sense of a direction; there is no formulated plot. There are certain elements I want to get into the book, and I just dive off and don't know if there's any water in the pond. I find a kind of pleasure in that process. With perseverance I will gradually evolve a book. Creating is a kind of groping-in-the-dark procedure. Yet, when the book is finished, it should have all those elements that satisfy some part of me.

Seuss: Mine always start as a doodle. I may doodle a couple of animals. If they bite each other, it's going to be a good book. If you doodle enough, the characters begin to take over themselves—after a year and a half or so.

Sendak: Sometimes that happens quite accidentally. In 1969, I was doing a Mother Goose book, and I found that I was picking out poems that had to do with food, like bread and milk. It seemed a peculiar obsessive interest: "Little Jumping Joan, / She ate so much, / She went bananas." I finally decided that under the guise of preparing a Mother Goose, my own book was being written. It ended up being called *In the Night Kitchen*, and I even stole one of the verses. "I see the moon, and the moon sees me" became "I'm not the milk and the milk's not me." So my homage to the original project was in that book. But I had no knowledge that my book was sneaking in.

Seuss: Sometimes you have luck when you are doodling. I did one day when I was drawing some trees. Then I began drawing elephants. I had a window that was open, and the wind blew the elephant on top of a tree. I looked at it and said, "What do you suppose that elephant is doing there?" The answer was: "He is hatching an egg." Then all I had to do was write a book about it. I have left that window open ever since, but it's never happened again.

Interviewer: Dr. Seuss, I understand that much of your work contains actual figures from history and some political commentary. Could you identify these figures?

Seuss: Not in their actual form. Yertle the Turtle is Adolf Hitler. In

Yertle, the turtle Mack was on the bottom of the pile until he solved the problem by burping. It makes me realize how much children's book publishing has changed to recall that they had a meeting at Random House to see whether I could use the word *burp,* and that was in the late 1950s. The other historical characters, I don't know about.

Interviewer: How do you shut out the reality of the world when you're creating your books? Do nuclear weapons, cancer, unemployment, and pollution affect you?

Sendak: Well, there is no way you can shut out those facts unless you're insane. Perhaps they permeate the work and color it in some particular way, but there is no magic way you can shut the door on all these things. We don't work in "airy fairy land" when we're doing books for children. We are dealing with real life, even though we're using forms that are nonsensical or funny or bizarre. In fact, real life should be in the book. It has to permeate the work. I live in this world.

Seuss: They're all there, but we look at them through the wrong end of the telescope. We change them in that way.

Interviewer: I encountered several discourses concerned with the underlying psychological meanings of your books, Mr. Sendak. How do you feel about that? It doesn't sound like you had those things in mind when you were writing your books.

Sendak: Well, I didn't. Of course, it's always fun to read about them. There are so many variations, some of them may be quite accurate; I don't know. As an artist you cannot consciously construct a book psychologically because it would not be a work of art. But such interpretations are fun to read.

Interviewer: As a closing note, I'd like to leave you with a little quote, something to take with you:

> Ninety-nine zillion,
> Nine trillion and two
> Creatures are sleeping!
> So . . .
> How about you?

Ted Geisel died 24 September 1991.

Index

Prepared by Alex Hartmann